A NIGHT IN THE PECH VALLEY

By Grant McGarry

Second Platoon, Charlie Company, 1st Ranger Battalion,
75th Ranger Regiment

February 14, 2007 – January 9, 2011

LTRC Publishing
www.LTRC-Ops.com

For information contact Live The Ranger Creed LLC in Roswell, GA

McGarry, Grant
A Night in the Pech Valley
Second Platoon, Charlie Company, 1st Ranger Battalion,
75th Ranger Regiment
February 14, 2007 – January 9, 2011

ISBN 978-0-9970414-0-8
Library of Congress Control Number: 2015919686

First Edition
Printed in the United States of America

Cover by Matt Frederick
Typesetting by Matt Frederick and Canopy Web Design LLC

DEDICATION

Specialist Christopher Shane Wright

Died August 19, 2010
Operation Enduring Freedom

One for the Airborne Ranger in the Sky!

Greater love hath no man than this,
that a man lay down his life for his friends.

-John 15:13

ii

TABLE OF CONTENTS

PROLOGUE

When I returned home from my fifth and final deployment in October 2010, I didn't sleep much, in fact, I went a straight week without sleep. I spent most of my days and especially nights drowning in survivor's guilt. When I finally did start getting some sleep the dreams were so vivid and real that I almost didn't want to fall asleep. The survivor's guilt got worse. It almost crushed me. In December 2010, as I was preparing to get out of the Army the following month, I went to my parent's house for the holidays. For Christmas my mom got me a journal. She knew I was going through hard times and thought it would be good for me to put my nightmares into words and onto paper. Turns out it was exactly what I needed to do.

Throughout 2011, while I was working at the US Embassy in Baghdad as a personal security specialist, I wrote in that journal about anything and everything that happened while I was in the Army. I wrote about what compelled me to join the military in 2006 and everything that happened up to January 9, 2011– my last day as a Ranger in 2nd Platoon, Charlie Company, 1st Ranger Battalion, 75th Ranger Regiment.   I never planned to do anything with the stories, because after all I was a quiet professional. So when I got back stateside from Iraq for Christmas in 2011, I tucked the journal away in my nightstand.

Then in January of 2013 I felt compelled to tell my story and transferred everything from my journal over to a Microsoft Word document. As soon as I finished the transfer of about twenty thousand words I mailed it to Jim and Michele Cochran, Chris Wright's parents, and asked for their approval to tell of their son's last day. With their approval, I decided to write this book.

My personality is more of a doer than a teller, so I knew this was not going to be an easy journey for me but was determined to give it my all. I spent countless hours writing and editing. One day I listened to six hours of Beethoven's greatest hits and wrote six thousand words. I was compelled to tell my story and it eventually took over my life. As with any firsthand account, this book is from my point of view, but I made sure to account for all points of view to best articulate exactly what happened. Anyone who has been in combat knows that everyone involved in a firefight remembers certain incidents with no recollection of details from someone else's account. Even though each person involved might have a few differences because of their vantage points, all accounts tell the same story. I have spoken with everyone involved and spent hours going through each incident to describe in detail exactly what happened.

Because of the attention to detail, I was advised of and followed all guidelines set out by the Army's Office of the Chief of Public Affairs during the writing, editing and publishing of this work. I have changed many individual's names to not reveal their identity. All call signs, missions, objectives, and operations have been changed to keep from releasing classified information.

I strived for perfection and accuracy, but these stories should not be read as official AARs (after action reports). The Ranger Regiment Public Affairs Officer reviewed this book, but neither the 75th Ranger Regiment, the U.S. Army, nor the Department of Defense officially endorse its content. This book is a living, breathing extension of me. I am proud of not only me and my brothers and how hard we fought, but also the ones that are still fighting; they have my utmost respect. To each person that reads this book, I hope you are able to learn from it and I ask that you not forget that these are real people and the sweat, tears, bloodshed, and lives lost are real too.

RLTW!

Grant McGarry

viii

INTRODUCTION

It is not the critic who counts; not the man who points out how the strong man stumbles, or where the doer of deeds could have done them better. The credit belongs to the man who is actually in the arena, whose face is marred by dust and sweat and blood; who strives valiantly; who errs, and comes short again and again, because there is no effort without error and shortcoming; but who does actually strive to do the deeds; who knows the great enthusiasms, the great devotions; who spends himself in a worthy cause; who at the best knows in the end the triumph of high achievement, and who at the worst, if he fails, at least fails while daring greatly, so that his place shall never be with those cold and timid souls who know neither victory nor defeat.

-Theodore Roosevelt, 26th President of the United States of America

After four years and twenty weeks of service to my country, my time was up, and I decided to close the warrior chapter of my life; I was honorably discharged from the United States Army on January 9, 2011. During my four years in second platoon, Charlie Company, 1st Ranger Battalion, 75th Ranger Regiment, I met some of the finest men in the United States of America. When it was all said and done, my time as an Army Ranger in Charlie Company (Two Charlie) was the proudest period of my life and can be summed up in four words: It was an honor.

To close this chapter in my life, my platoon had a "going away" formation behind the Company Operating Facility (COF) and presented me with a plaque that included a picture of Two Charlie standing on a ridge in Afghanistan. After I was presented this plaque, a friend spoke on my behalf; his few words made me more proud than any accomplishment I have ever achieved or any award I have ever received. Sergeant Cousins, as he stood in front of the platoon of about twenty Rangers, said that I was "one of the top five Rangers he had ever served with." This speech, coming from the person that gave me my in-processing counseling when I was first assigned to Two Charlie and one of—if not the—most respected Ranger in the platoon, had a profound impact on me. As I began to reflect on everything and anything that had happened over the past four years, I thought about the day I had arrived to Two Charlie and how much I had changed since then. I thought about when I showed up that day thinking I was a man, but little did I know, I was far from it. I snapped out of my momentary daydream to speak. As I stood in front of such an amazing group of men, I couldn't help but feel ashamed. I felt ashamed that I was leaving the fight and asking my brothers to go on and continue to fight without me. I had spent every waking moment with these Rangers and had laid it all on the line with them, shedding blood, sweat, and tears. Some I had known longer than others, but regardless, they were all my brothers and I was sad to leave.

Before I even finished what I had to say to the men of Two Charlie, I was bum-rushed by a mob of privates, stripped out of my new cowboy boots, and carried off to the showers to receive my "going away" plunge. It is a ritual to throw a deserving Ranger into the showers or the pond out back when he leaves his platoon and company. Although I was not upset about this, I was not about to go down without putting up a fight. I put up a decent fight for a few seconds until I was pinned to the ground. Even after being pinned, I continued to yell at the privates just because they were privates and continued to try and punch and kick them wherever possible. It was not the best fight I had ever put up, but looking back on it, I sure did enjoy the moment.

After being tossed into the cold Charlie Company locker room showers, I dried off and shook a few of the privates' hands and said my goodbye. I then got into my truck and drove off of Hunter Army Airfield in Georgia for the last time. I couldn't help but shed a tear as the gate disappeared in my rearview mirror.

The years that have followed have been an interesting ride, and in a selfish way, I have written this book to rid what I have bottled up inside. Even more important than my own inner ambitions and goals, I have written this book to tell the story of the warrior class that makes up Two Charlie so that our

sacrifices will not be forgotten. For those that have not fought
for America, I hope this book enlightens you on the warrior
experience; for those who say we should not have fought wars
in Iraq or Afghanistan, I hope this book provides you a greater
understanding of the purpose of these wars. It is only the chosen
few that dare travel the road that leads down a warrior's path and
we warriors must continue to hold ourselves up high. To stand
for something and to not let anyone take it from you is your
God given right, and I was not scared to pick up a rifle and say,
"Send me!" I feel pity for people who have no backbone to fight
for what they stand for and feel even sorrier for those who are
not willing to die for what they believe in. What it boils down
to is that most people in today's society just do not have the
courage or intestinal fortitude to sacrifice their freedom so that
others can enjoy the fruits of their blood, sweat, and tears. Of
course nobody wants to die, but once you mentally grip that you
are fighting for a cause greater than your life and are willing to
die for the brother standing to your right and left, life becomes
that much sweeter. Yes, I was afraid at times and think that at
some moment throughout each warrior's path we are all afraid
of what the outcome could be, but that does not stop a warrior
from lacing up his boots and throwing a rifle over his shoulder
to take the fight to the enemy without knowing his destiny.
We never knew what was waiting for us in a cave hidden in a
mountain or behind a closed door and that is what made us
courageous. We did not ask for anything and we did not want
handouts. We earned the right to call ourselves Army Rangers,
we earned the respect of our brothers, and we earned honor
through integrity and sacrifice. I remember coming home from

deployments and walking off the C-17, smelling America the beautiful, and thinking how amazing it was to see the scenery of Savannah, Georgia. These are the little things in life that the ones who have not fought for it take for granted and only the one percent that volunteered to defend it can appreciate.

BACK IN THE SADDLE

"Lick 'em tomorrow."

- Ulysses S. Grant, 18th President of the United States of America and Commanding General of the Union Army

Beginning on the night after the memorial, our squad trained every night behind our hooch in an open gravel field. We went over react to contact drills, fire commands, close quarters combat tactics and many other drills with Blaise and Sesh. We thought it best to keep our minds right by training and after losing two tried and tested brothers we wanted to make sure Blaise and Sesh were good to go for what was coming their way. Blaise and Sesh were the newest guys in the squad and the platoon and each day they stepped up to the plate without missing a beat. They impressed their chain of command all the way to the top. Blaise and Sesh bettered themselves because they knew that they soon would have their opportunity.

It was a different feeling to not have Wright and Gronbeck hanging out around the hooch–a very quiet an ominous feeling. It was so off-putting that we rearranged the room to give it a new appearance. In addition to Wright, Wyatt, Plagge, and Gronbeck's absences, Staff Sergeant Cousins also had to go home to be with his wife, who was expecting a baby any day. To add fuel to the fire Staff Sergeant Cousins's alpha team leader was sick with malaria. In a matter of a few days we went from having years and years of experience to being very slim with experience. We were running thin.

A few days had passed since Wright's memorial and things seemed to be slow, but just as I thought there was nothing going on we got word of a mission. Objective Blackbeard was a single target building and word was there was the potential for a firefight. This was music to our ears, because we wanted nothing short of a firefight. Rooster, Escobar, and I were looking for more than revenge; we were blood thirsty.

I was excited about the new mission, but when I started to get all of my mission-essential gear ready, I had an onset rush of nervous and anxious energy. I tried to brush off the response, but as I went through what was expected of me tonight to try and take my mind off of the nervous feeling, I couldn't help but notice how real the reaction was. The feeling was like a punch in the gut and the sensation was almost visceral. It was the feeling of no longer feeling invincible.

Preparing for this mission was a lot different than all the previous missions I had been on. There was a more sobering feeling in the air. There was not as much small talk–no joking around amongst us buddies–and there was definitely no laughing. As I finished connecting my battery to my MBITR (multiband internal team radio), I began to put it back into my radio pouch on my kit and noticed how Escobar was taking the time to make sure Blaise   was good to go. Escobar was a great leader and he truly took the time to take care of the boys. Our squad had a great working relationship that complemented all of our personalities.

After Escobar finished helping Blaise I mentioned in passing to Escobar that I was feeling nervous and anxious. I am not sure if I was the only one having the feeling of no longer being invincible, but I can almost guarantee that he had his own thoughts that he was dealing with prior to this mission. More and more guys were coming into the ready room and the volume of noise from conversation started to rise and slowly the unsettled vibe in the room began to vanish. I finished checking all my gear and batteries and sprayed some CLP into the bolt carrying group of my M4 and charged it a few times. After making sure my M4 was good to go, I closed the dust cover and hung it back up in my locker and headed to the TOC to link up with Rooster. He had a look on his face that can be best defined as stoic and confident. We had a small conversation in which he divulged as much as he knew about tonight's mission, and then we headed over to the SEALs' AO for the mission brief.

The intel for the mission set the tone. Objective Blackbeard was a lone house with a few surrounding homes. This target was in the farmlands of Afghanistan … basically out in the middle of nowhere. There was reported movement throughout the day with armed men in and around the house. Weapons had been positively identified via ISR (intelligence, surveillance, and reconnaissance) footage. Following a quick brief from the SEAL platoon sergeant, we headed out to the flight line once again like we had done so many times prior. After the short bus ride out to the airfield, we had to pause for a moment, take a knee, and let the crew chief and the Chinook personnel finish the aircraft PMCS (preventive maintenance checks and services). As we waited Rooster and I chatted on the tarmac about how loading up on a helicopter in the middle of the night with a ton of ammo and explosives and seeing your brothers to your right and left was our favorite part of the job. Nothing was cooler than this in my mind.

Once the crew was done servicing the Chinook, he waved us on board. The small talk stopped and we flipped that switch put our night vision goggles down and went to work. After about a thirty minute ride, we were dropped off and the normal routine of taking a quick piss before we stepped off commenced as usual. As I took a knee, I could see tracer rounds behind a mountain range popping off and streaking through the air as if they were shooting stars. I finished my business and checked out my wrist Garmin to make sure the satellites were linking up so that the infil route would load. At about the time my route loaded in my Garmin the joint assault force started the movement to the objective building. The movement was at a good pace, and as we came to the ridgeline that looked down on the target, weapons squad positioned themselves up on the ridge in a support by fire line providing over watch of the target rooftop and the surrounding areas.

Weapons squad had open bolt, fully automatic machine guns nestled into a fortified fighting position and the gunners were like carnivores ready to chew up flesh. As the assault force took a half moon approach into the valley where the target building sat nestled into the side of the mountain, I peered down on the target area to get a good frame of reference to features of and around the target. We walked down a rocky mountainous cliff as quietly as possible, making sure to carefully and precisely place each step as we descended.

Once we navigated through the ravine and were down on the valley floor, we started to spread out and cover more area with the intent to get more muzzles aimed toward the target building. There were a few trees between us and the target building, which was about a hundred meters away, so we didn't have a clear view of the target building yet. As we picked up the pace and

headed straight towards the "X," I thought I saw a something
run between the shadows of the trees. I quickly fixed my infared
laser in the direction of travel the potential person would appear.
Before I could locate anyone or anything, I heard pop shots from
what sounded like an AK-47. It was definitely not an open bolt
weapon and it was not suppressed so it had to be an insurgent.

Weapons squad was taking fire and what was a brisk walking
pace turned into an all-out fifty-yard dash toward the target
building at full speed. Rooster and I were running as fast as
we could, jumping from one farm field down to the other and
hurdling over small tributaries of water and sink mud. As we
were sprinting the AK-47 fire was picking up and it sounded like
there were multiple combatants engaging with AKs. Specialist
Dave Wilkie, one of the gunners on the ridgeline, remembers
hearing his squad leader say, "We are taking fire," as rounds were
popping over their heads and all around them. Wilkie began to
scan the rooftop and then saw an armed insurgent running on
the rooftop. Wilkie quickly acquired the insurgent and opened
up on him at a cyclic rate of fire, stopping him dead in his
tracks.

The sound of the open bolt weapon and the sight of the tracer
rounds rip through the sky and leave a trail of green fire until
burning out was like watching a Fourth of July firework display
… except better. Rooster and I were off to the races, closing
the gap, spreading out, and creating a wall searching for armed
insurgents. As we were sprinting, hurdling, and jumping at
speeds that would rival an NFL running back on Sunday
afternoon, we spotted insurgents maneuvering around the target

building and one was running away from the target building. Rooster and I–at a full sprint–started engaging an insurgent and the SEAL team to our left began engaging the other insurgent. I could hear Rooster's M4 release round after round and I am sure they were passing only a few feet from the back of my head. He was only a few feet behind me and offset to my right. Then all of a sudden, as I had my laser aimed in on an insurgent preparing to take a shot, I went head over tea kettle into a muddy mess. The twenty-five foot flat farm patty ended and I fell about a foot straight into the wet and muddy ravine. My left shoulder and my face went straight into the wet soil. I quickly tried to brush my gear off and regain my composure, getting up as if nothing happened. Rule number one: Always look cool.

I could hear Rooster laughing as he jumped down and landed onto his two feet. I was determined to beat him to the kill and started sprinting back into the fight. I was no longer leading the way on this charge, but once I caught back up with Rooster we took a knee at the end of the farm field that we were currently on, turned on our lasers, and started engaging the combatant. We dropped him in his tracks with precision fired shots. Despite knowing that he was dead, which was obvious due to how he crumbled to the ground, we continued to engage. Escobar and Blaise showed up; they didn't hesitate to join the party. We would later positively identify one round went straight through the back of the insurgent's head splitting the top portion of his skull in half, revealing bloody brain matter, and leaving what skin was left flap over his face. Parts of the skin left with hair was covering parts of his head as if it were some kind of comb-over hairstyle. The second gun shot was straight through his chest.

We quickly separated and Rooster and I moved toward the
left side of the field while Escobar and Blaise covered the right
sector. The four of us had interlocking sectors of fire, and we
were scanning for targets. We were getting radio calls from ISR
that there were movers still in the wood line that the armed
insurgent we killed had been making a run for. A fire mission
was being prepped. ISR flexed over and starting shining down
pulsating infrared flashes twenty-five feet in front of us in a
patch of trees and brush. Immediately following there was an
infrared sparkle about fifty meters off to our eleven o'clock in the
tall grass that stood about four feet tall. Radio traffic confirmed
that the ISR platform had eyes on two armed insurgents marked
by the pulsating infrared beam streaming directly in front of
Rooster and me from the aircraft. Rooster and I didn't hesitate
and dumped the rest of the ammo in our mag, inserted a new
one, and continued to engage into the small wooded area being
marked by the pulsating sparkle.

While we were engaging these two combatants, a Ranger from
another squad sent a 40-mm HEDP (high-explosive, dual-
purpose) round that landed and exploded directly on the ISR
beam illuminating the armed insurgent taking cover in the
tall grass. After complete domination of this target and the
immediate surrounding areas, we pulled back and the four of us
laid down in a dried up portion of the ravine that I had fallen in
earlier and took cover. The fast movers were in route and they
were dropping a thousand pound JDAM (Joint Direct Action
Munition). With a precision guided munition set to impact
directly into the insurgents in the wood line approximately one
hundred meters away, we quickly laid down on our bellies and

waited for the grand finale of the firework show. We started to joke and small talk. The feeling of being invincible was back and we were having a blast. Then, I could feel the ground beneath me rumble and I was moved by the force created by the bomb, which left behind a fifteen-foot deep and twenty-foot wide crater and one destroyed wood line that looked like a tornado ripped through destroying everything.

HOSTAGE RESCUE

"Treat your men as you would your own beloved sons. And they will follow you into the deepest valley."

- Sun Tzu, "The Art of War"

All missions ceased when a woman named Linda Norgrove was captured on September 26, 2010. Immediately following news of her capture by Taliban insurgents, all assets were utilized in an effort to rescue her from the insurgents holding her captive. Intel reports stated that Linda Norgrove was a British aid worker working for other government agencies, and while driving on a main highway in the Kunar province from Jalalabad to Asadabad in the Dewagal Valley in two unarmored, unmarked vehicles, Norgrove, along with three Afghanistan colleagues, were ambushed. In an attempt to rescue Norgrove, a company from the 101st Airborne Division, assisted by elements from the Afghan Army and Afghan Police, began a house-to- house search. The joint element also set up roadblocks posted at the Dewagal Valley entrance to prevent Norgrove's captors from being able to take her eastward into Pakistan. The rugged and mountainous terrain made the search difficult. However, the task force contained the Taliban insurgents and Linda Norgrove.

Immediately following the containment, we were given the order through the ranks to rescue Norgrove starting all the way at the top. British Prime Minister Cameron and William Hague gave the initial green light, which was funneled all the way down to our task force in Jalalabad; it was go time. The SEALs were the main effort and Two Charlie brought to the fight two line squads to provide security via blocking positions.

The intent of the blocking positions for this operation was to keep insurgents from coming or going into the target area, allowing the SEALs to focus on making a successful rescue. This mission was a time sensitive target so we had a hasty/quick brief and GRGs (ground reference graphic) were passed out as usual so that we could all have a reference of the target area and its surroundings. I quickly glanced at my GRG and checked out the location where we would be setting up our blocking position, the target building, and the terrain in relation to where we were and where the target building was located. With the urgency to rescue Linda Norgrove compounded by the rugged terrain, a fifteen to twenty foot fast rope right into the middle of the small village was the best method of infiltration. Conveniently, second squad's blocking position was only twenty feet from where the Chinook was planned to insert us. This would make for an easy sprint to get where we needed to be once our boots hit the ground. Our method of infiltration for the task force out of the Jalalabad Airfield was two Chinook helicopters. The Rangers selected to secure the blocking position with second squad included me, Staff Sergeant Rooster, our platoon sergeant, Escobar, Smitty, and Blaise. After the brief we all loaded up on our respective buses and were driven out to the flight line.

It is always a quiet ride when on the drive out to the flight line. Each warrior went over last minute checks on their weapons, radios, and gear. On this specific mission Escobar was not only going over his own equipment, but was also triple checking Blaise to make sure he was good to go. Blaise was the newest and youngest Ranger going out on the mission and Escobar was looking after him.

I always had a certain sequence of events that took place prior to loading up on the helicopter, and once my routine was completed, an internal switch flipped inside me making me

feel invincible. After the short ride I stepped off the bus and
was accompanied by a joint task force of American Jedis and
we walked like the giants we were. As I flipped down my night
vision goggles and entered a world seen in a green tint, I charged
a round into the chamber of my M4, gave a quick slap to the
forward assist with the palm of my hand to make sure my round
was properly seated, and then closed my dust cover. I then drew
my Beretta M9 and charged a round into the chamber of my
secondary weapon. I gently pulled the slide back and shined a
white light to see the brass of a 9-mm casing glisten in the light,
confirming I had a round in the chamber. I quickly holstered my
sidearm and turned around from the cement barrier I had my
muzzle pointed at while loading my weapons and then headed
for my chalk, which was lining up to board the Chinook. I took
a deep breath of JP8 exhaust coming out of the massive Chinook
that was taking us into battle. Smelling the jet fuel and hearing
the loud noise of the spinning above and watching the Chinook
vibrate on the tarmac got my blood flowing every time; I started
to come alive. After the chalk leader waved us forward, we
started to walk onto the aircraft and load up. Blaise sat in front
of me and Escobar, Smitty, and Rooster were in front leading
the way, which is customary for team cohesiveness. As we all got
situated and comfortable, the Chinook started to pull off the
ground and we quickly ascended, banking toward the objective.
The Jalalabad Airfield lights disappear into the night.

As we were en route I looked around at the guys and noticed
everyone was doing the same thing; we were all going over the
plan. After going over the plan one last time, I then reminded
myself to focus on the task at hand and everything else will

work itself out. Over the radio our platoon sergeant said, "One minute."

I immediately looked at Blaise and raised my right index finger letting him know ropes were dropping in one minute. He made eye-to-eye contact with me letting me know he was good to go. Then the rope master motioned a thirty second call to the entire chalk. No one had to say anything. We all placed our hands on our safety line (a piece of bungee cord connected to our riggers belt via a metal clasp) snap link that had us hooked into the bird.

Immediately following the thirty second call the crew chief/rope master looked at the chalk and said, "Ropes! Ropes! Ropes!" He then did an about face (turned around) and released the fast ropes by pulling the pin that secured the coiled rope dangling in the air at the aft of the Chinook. It didn't take more than a few seconds for him to confirm the rope was successfully deployed by looking down at the ground through his night vision.

As guys started exiting the aircraft, I followed suit and traced the skin of the aircraft with my left hand. Through my night vision I could start to see the top of the rope hanging as I got closer to the tail of the aircraft. I walked forward, watching one guy after another slide down the rope. After Blaise slid down the rope like a firefighter it was finally my turn. I reached out and grabbed the rope with my right hand and then pulled my left hand from the skin of the aircraft, gripped the rope, and in sequence brought my feet out, turned, and slid down at a controlled descent, all the while looking down at Blaise a few feet beneath me through my night vision. As I slid down the rope I felt the

notches of the rope vibrate as they passed through the leather
of the gloves protecting my hands from burning. Although the
gloves protected my hands, I could feel the heat as the leather
began to soften from the friction. It was very apparent that there
was a little separation starting in the seam of my left pinkie
finger, because one spot was particularly hot where the glove was
starting to tear. That didn't matter though because the ground
was approaching fast and as soon as I hit the ground I let go of
the rope, grabbed my M-4 from my side, and took off sprinting
to our blocking position.

The updraft and wind from the two twin rotors made running
a little interesting but I did not have any issues. Running
underneath such a massive aircraft made you light on your feet.
As I continued to sprint I noticed the tall grass ripping in the
wind from the twin rotor blades, and as I got further away the
noise from the rotors started to die down. Being that I was one
of the last off of the Chinnook, the crew chief then unhooked
the ropes and let them fall to the ground. Our war bus flew away
and the noise left with its disappearance into the night sky.

Once everyone linked up at the blocking position, Rooster
disseminated a hasty plan. He, Escobar, and Blaise had the area
to the west of the target building/village locked down and told
me to take Smitty with the SAW and lock down the north side.
There wasn't a lot of conversation, just a quick, "Roger that,"
and we were off like a prom dress. As Smitty and I scouted out a
good spot for us, we slowly crept about twenty meters to inquire
about a light that was turned on outside of a home. We were
now about thirty meters from Rooster and his blocking element.

Smitty and I nestled in and took cover and concealment behind a few trees in a small wood line.

I immediately noticed very suspicious activity happening in the house. There were males dressed in dishdashes conversing outside. It seemed odd that there were fighting-aged males fully dressed and awake in the middle of the night. I couldn't get an exact count but I thought I saw around five males huddled up having a conversation. They then all separated and went their own way. Looking through my night vision, I raised my M4 and put my infrared laser right on the chest of one of the males, but because of the light I could not see the infrared dot from my optic. This was very frustrating. I made a quick radio call to Rooster letting him know of the nefarious activity.

I knew through muscle memory that I was zeroed in on the chest of the fighting-aged male, but I could not confirm it. At about that same time the SEALs were approaching the target compound. Then a fire fight opened up on the target compound and I could hear M4 and AK-47 fire being exchanged at the target building. This changed the rules of engagement immediately. I then looked over at Smitty and said, "If these guys turn their lights off and start maneuvering towards us I'm shooting them." I then made a radio call and informed Rooster and the PSG that we still had two roaming guards at a house twenty-five meters to our twelve o'clock. After that I told Smitty to "Keep scanning the wood line for the others." He responded with a quick, "Roger." I had worked with Smitty for a long time; he was in my team on our last rotation in Afghanistan, and he and I were on the vehicle crew in Baghdad as well.

Right after the radio call the other males started to walk back toward the house, including the guy I had my laser on. This same fighting-aged male then turned off the light and bent over at the waist to pick something up that was leaning on the house. He then maneuvered toward our position. This guy was now armed with an AK-47. What he didn't know was that we had the drop on him. As he continued to walk straight toward me, I could hear the continued fire fight still going on at the target compound.

As the armed fighting-aged male continued to move closer, I braced the rail of my M4 and rested it onto the trunk of the tree to my right. I took a deep breath, confirmed my laser on his chest, and then slowly exhaled as I squeezed the trigger and fired two rounds into his chest. He dropped instantly and as the metallic smell from my weapon filled my nostrils, I shifted my position on the tree and started to scan with my M4 for more targets. The rest of the guys must all be lying down now because neither Smitty nor I could find any of them. They were using the rocks, shrubs, and trees for cover just like we were.

I made a quick radio call to my squad leader, but he was already sprinting to our position. Rooster arrived in a matter of a few seconds and took a knee next to me, putting his hand on my shoulder and asking what was going on. I was so jacked up from the adrenaline that I didn't make much sense but told him, "I shot a guy and there are more out there and they are moving toward us." Rooster understood what I was saying but couldn't find them either, so we pulled back and used a dirt wall as cover. Once behind cover Rooster made a quick radio call to the PL letting him know what was going on and the PL contacted the FSO who in sequence directed the CAS (close air support) gunship to our location to check out the situation. The gunship overhead and ISR identified seven moving packs headed toward our direction.

Quickly there was a call for fire mission prepped, and we pulled back to a minimum safe distance and took cover as the CAS gunship flew overhead. Once we were in a safe place that provided cover, Rooster let the PL know. The seven insurgents maneuvering toward our blocking position had no idea what was coming next. It was like music in the air to hear the overpressure thud of rounds fired from a CAS gunship and even more amazing to hear the detonation thirty to fifty meters away. The CAS gunship finished off the gun fight in the village and at about the same time the SEALs were back from the target building and we were getting radio calls to start prepping for exfil. As we were getting ready to exfil, we started taking fire from a house across the valley. A SEAL in the chalk between second squad and where the fires were coming from loaded a 40-mm HEDP grenade into his hand held 203 (grenade launcher) and sent it toward the house. I never saw it detonate as I was running to board the Chinook as fast as possible. It didn't take long to board and we soon we were flying out of the village and back to the Jalalabad Airfield. The mission was a dry hole. Linda Norgrove was not there.

A RANGER CHILDHOOD

*"I only regret that I have but one life
to give for my country."*

- Nathan Hale

When I was twelve years old my family packed up everything we
owned and piled into the family Chevy Suburban. My father,
Andy McGarry, was tired of the rat race in Fort Lauderdale,
Florida, and wanted to start over. So, he sold everything he
owned in Fort Lauderdale, including the business that he and
my mother, Lynn, started with $100. My father used the profits
to take his wife and three boys to McDonough, Georgia—
an hour south of Atlanta— where he planned to start a new
business venture. As a kid I was just excited to go somewhere
new, and so my two younger brothers, Conor and Kurt, and I
did like any son would and watched our old home disappear in
the distance. Once we finally arrived in McDonough, Conor and
I ran for the woods and explored for hours on end that day while
the movers helped my parents move us into our new home.
Kurt, my youngest brother, would also join Conor and me from
time to time. We were so excited to have a backyard with endless
acres of woods—something we hadn't been able to experience in
south Florida. All the animals, creeks, and red Georgia clay were
new to us and we didn't want to waste any time. In a matter of
a few days I fell in love with the outdoors. Conor and I built a
fort out of lumber scraps that we gathered from construction
sites and used hatchets my Dad got us to cut down trees. We
also used the back of our hatchets to drive in the nails we found
at construction sites. After chopping down numerous pine trees
and hanging plywood, we eventually had the framework for
our massive fortified fort. After we got our fort up, we would go
out on hunts to stalk white-tailed deer. We knew exactly where
they were every morning and night and would low crawl for
what seemed like hundreds of feet to see how close we could get

before being spotted.

Dad noticed our passion for the outdoors and bought us BB and pellet guns to hunt squirrels, birds, and anything that moved. I hunted and shot anything that walked—including my brother. We got so into hunting that after we killed dozens of birds and squirrels, we decided to hunt each other in what we called BB-gun wars. Being three years older than Conor, I had an unfair advantage and took complete advantage of this. In what was our first and final one-on-one BB-gun war, I shot Conor right in the forehead from twenty-five meters. It stunned him so bad that he dropped his BB gun and stood up cursing at the top of his lungs at me. After that Conor refused to play against me so I had to start recruiting guys in the neighborhood. It did not take long to get someone to join us, but his tenure was also short lived. During our first match I shot him in the back of the head from about twenty meters as he tried to run away. I literally saw the BB leave my barrel, and to my surprise, it hit right where I was aiming. He didn't even stop to turn around; he ran all the way home crying and screaming. Conor and I never saw him again and I couldn't tell you his name now if a gun was pointed at my head. When Conor and I decided that we had had enough of playing BB-gun wars (due to a lack of volunteers) we got back into hunting animals, particularly copperhead snakes.

My weapon of choice for our snake hunts was a six-foot long, one- by-two inch piece of wood from the lumber yard that had three nails, each an inch apart in a triangle pattern. It became known as the "snake killer." My plan was to creep up from behind the snake and whack it over the head, piercing the snake with all three nails. One afternoon Conor found a four-foot Copperhead sunbathing in the woods right below our fort, which was nestled by a tree about six feet above the intruder. Just like I had planned, I crept up from behind the snake but was doing so from an elevated position on the patio of our fort. When I got to the edge of the fort patio, I jumped off and as soon as I landed on my two feet, I simultaneously struck the copperhead from behind, nailing it in the head with all three nails. The snake was dead before it knew what had happened. I held the snake up in the air and watched it squirm back and forth. I turned around and held it over my head screaming at Conor, who was staring at me wide-eyed from the fort above. We were both so happy that we got on our bikes and headed home to show mom.

After a year in McDonough, my family packed up the same green Suburban for another adventure. This time we moved to Roswell, Georgia. On my first day of seventh grade, I met a kid named Carper Davis. He and I were fast friends. Carper also enjoyed the woods and we soon ran into a group of older kids led by Brett Schroeder. These older kids were playing war games, acting as if they were a team of Navy SEALs, and were taking it fairly serious for a young group of kids. It looked like fun to us so Carper and I quickly jumped in and started to build lean-to huts and forts throughout the neighborhood woods with these guys. We used the huts and forts we built to sleep in at night on the weekends, and we would conduct planned assaults on a lone, abandoned house in the woods. We each used nicknames when we went out on our missions, and we each had a specific duty/job that we performed in the team, such as walking point or rear security. After conducting a few planned assaults without doing anything but shoot out a couple of lights, we wanted more action. We talked about having a BB-gun war and everyone liked the idea, so we started to plan the inaugural war. We had enough guys to have three-on-three teams, and we even went as far as to designate a war field that was bordered by the Chattahoochee River. Just before a BB-gun war we would camouflage our faces with army green colored paint sticks. Even if we didn't camo up, we all wore our boonie hats (which I never went in the woods without). Once we went through all of our pre BB-gun war rituals and last minute checks, we would flip a coin to see which side of the field each team would start on. Once this was decided, the mood and tone changed and we walked off into the playing grounds and went silent, watching every step we made and trying not to make a noise, with a mission to shoot anyone and everyone on the other team. There were two rules: (1) one shot anywhere on the body and you are out; (2) there was a two-pump limit on your BB gun. With that said, no one ever obeyed the two-pump limit, and to this day I have a scar on my left chest muscle from a friend going over the limit by about ten pumps on his air-compressed pump BB gun.

One day while playing a BB-gun war, I was hiding out behind a log by the Chattahoochee River waiting to ambush anyone that walked by. At that moment—at thirteen years old—I made a promise to myself that no matter what I will serve my country when I am of age. It was a calling that I recognized at a young age and was anxious to have the opportunity to fulfill this dream. To build my imagination, I bought a diary written by Navy Seal Gary Smith, called Death in the Jungle. I read it

in a few days. I was fascinated with his stories about Vietnam
and this catapulted my desire to join the military to a whole new
level. I had also always been fascinated with my Uncle Mike's
service as a Naval Aviator in Vietnam and my Grandpa John
McGarry's military service. My Uncle Mike Nuechterlein joined
the Navy after college and graduated Aviation Officer Candidate
School with the "Snowflake Award" for being the top in his
class in all three categories: leadership, fitness, and scholastics.
He would then go to flight school and serve in Vietnam as Air
Operations Officer for the Seventh Fleet air services in Da Nang
Vietnam. My Grandpa John Francis McGarry (nicknamed Jack)
enlisted to be an infantryman soldier in World War II before the
draft while he was attending the University of Mount Union
in Ohio. Grandpa started out there on the football team and
was doing great in school, but he decided he wanted to serve
his country in the military like his father had done. Before my
grandpa was shipped off to fight in the trenches in the horn
of Africa, the military tested his entire unit and took three
candidates with the highest test score to send to medical school
to fill the needs of the army as a doctor. One of these candidates,
with the highest test score out of thousands tested, happened to
be my grandpa and the army sent him to medical school at the
Ohio State University. My grandpa had a photographic memory,
and on one of the specific portions of the test candidates had
to view a picture of the brain on a projector screen for a short
period of time. When the proctors turned the projector off,
the test-takers had to write the name for each specific part
of the brain that was shown; my Grandpa Jack remembered
everything and scored a perfect score on this section. Later in

his military career, my grandpa was reunited with a friend, who he had not seen since he left his infantry unit, in the hospital he was working at. His friend was missing a leg and having major complications with staph infections and pain. His friend told him that most everyone my grandpa knew and remembered from his old unit was wounded or killed in action. Grandpa saw a lot of battle-wounded veterans but took this specific instance as a sign of how lucky he was to have not gone to Africa to fight. When he told me this story he emphasized the importance of education and how in this specific instance it could have been the difference between life and death. Jack McGarry ended up serving his country as a military doctor all over the world and later in the reserves until he retired as a colonel. When NASA asked my grandpa to be the first doctor to support astronauts he responded, "We aren't going to the moon," and declined the job offer.

Taking this lesson learned from my grandpa about the importance of education was starting to pay off. After three years of maintaining a good GPA, I was asked to join the National Honor Society my junior year. Not only was I doing well in my classes, but I was also the starting free safety on the varsity football team. In my senior year—2001—I began looking at college opportunities and where I wanted to go to college. On September 11 of that year, I walked into my criminal justice class and sat down next to Ben Miller. The world as I knew it was about to change. I said hello and Ben didn't even blink an eye or respond. He was staring at the TV in the front of the room, and I wanted to know what the big deal was, then I noticed the lone tower standing without its twin. As I gazed at the television, I listened to the news broadcaster talk about two planes colliding into the twin towers, and as he was explaining this, I saw the second plane fly into one of the towers on a re-play. Like everyone else old enough to remember, I watched the second tower fall and crumble to the ground. As my classmates and I watched in confusion, my teacher turned to the class and asked, "Are any of you eighteen years old?" I raised my hand and he looked at me and said, "We are at war!" I remember the impact that those words had on me, and I can still hear them echo in my mind as if my teacher had said it five minutes ago.

Later that week I saw a Marine recruiter in the high school cafeteria and approached him about enlisting. Being that I was still in high school, I did not understand what the process was, but he explained to me that I could enlist under the delayed entry program and then ship out the day after I graduate. At first I thought it was a great idea, but I eventually talked myself out of it. The Marine didn't let up on me and called my house during dinner to talk to me about options in the Marine Corps for most of my senior year. With his continuous efforts I went back and forth with the thought of enlisting. It all changed though when I got my acceptance letter from the University of Alabama and from there it was easy to tell the Marine recruiter thanks, but no thanks. It was a clear decision and an easy road to take to move forward to further my education, but I was more excited about the freedom of getting out from under the house than anything. It just wasn't my time to join the military. Before heading off to school, my mom asked me to do her one favor. She said, "Please go to college. Earn your degree and after you graduate, you can do whatever you want. The military is not going anywhere, so after college if you still want to join, then you can do so then."

COLLEGE AND THE CRIMSON TIDE

*"If you believe in yourself and have
dedication and pride – and never quit –
you'll be a winner. The price of victory is
high but so are the rewards."*

- Paul "Bear" Bryant

As a freshman at the University of Alabama, I took some classes in the ROTC program with the long-term goal of becoming an army infantry officer. After completing the first year prerequisite classes in ROTC, I went back home for summer break to make some money. When I went back to school, I became more involved in my major and the demands of the business school and decided that ROTC was not my "cup of tea." So to focus more on my classes, I did not pursue the ROTC program. After spending the next two years in the library and going to frat parties and bars till the early morning hours, I was in my senior year of college and had taken a fast interest in the ex-NFL star Pat Tillman. I couldn't believe that someone could turn down millions of dollars to play in the NFL with the Arizona Cardinals to join the military, specifically the Army Rangers. I was in complete amazement that someone would sacrifice his freedom and a chance to have a great NFL career to serve his country. Pat Tillman was an American Patriot—a hero to me— and it was stories like his that made me really feel like I hadn't done anything for my country. Which also made me ask myself, "Why not me? Why am I so damn important that I don't have the time to serve my country?" I also asked myself why more young men aren't serving their country during a time of war. It was not until a few years later that I was able to answer these questions. I now know that it is a certain breed of people cut from a different cloth that would dare to volunteer to serve his or her country, especially to be an Army Ranger, which requires you to volunteer not once but three times. At about the same time I read the story on Army Ranger Pat Tillman, the 2006 Best Ranger Competition aired on ESPN, and I was completely mesmerized by the mental toughness of the Rangers in the competition. The next day I talked to a friend I had made at Alabama who had recently gotten out of the army and asked him what it was that he did in the army. I had heard rumors he was a Ranger but was not sure and wanted to learn more about it. Turned out that my Alabama buddy enlisted right out of high school and served in the 3rd Ranger Battalion, 75th Ranger Regiment. This decorated Ranger Battalion is known for its valorous actions in the 1993 battle in Mogadishu, Somalia, and was described and depicted in the book-turned-movie Black Hawk Down. Come to find out, not only was this Alabama student a combat veteran, but he was also on both of the initial invasion combat jumps conducted by the 75th Ranger Regiment into Afghanistan and Iraq that spearheaded the Global War on Terrorism. As he and I became better friends, I went over to his apartment one night and he showed me his army dress uniform and pointed at the two mustard stains on his jump wings, explaining to me what these meant: a signifier of his two combat jumps. I was in awe and honored to be in the presence of a warrior, and as I took it all in, I realized that I wanted to be a part of this brotherhood. With the culmination of these events, I was thinking very hard on what I wanted to do with my future and was seriously considering joining the military. I had already run into an army recruiter on the University of Alabama campus a few weeks ago but did not do anything except ask for his business card.

I continued to digest everything and organize my thoughts over the next few weeks. One morning on my way to class I stopped in a coffee shop called Bad Ass Coffee off of University

Boulevard. I was on my way to take a finance test that I had been studying for till the early hours of the morning and needed a pick-up to get through the test. After ordering my coffee I took a seat at a table and watched the news. As I waited for my coffee, I watched the headlines on the bottom of the screen flash, announcing "WAR in IRAQ" and accompanied by news clips of gunfire and bombs going off in the distance. At that exact moment I said to myself, "I am doing it; I am joining the army today!" It was as simple as that. There was not ever a moment that I looked back and second guessed my decision. I still had the army recruiter's information at my apartment, and after my test I ran back to my apartment and e-mailed the recruiter to set an appointment. He responded in literally five minutes with one sentence: "Come on down whenever." I immediately ran out of my apartment and hopped into my 1995 red Chevrolet Z71 and laid rubber out of the parking lot of my apartment and headed over to the recruiting station. When I pulled up I had a moment of apprehension and then said, "Screw it. I am doing this." So I got out of my truck, flung open the door of the recruiting station, and with my chest out and head high, I said—even before introducing myself, "What's the hardest thing you got?" The recruiter looked at me wide eyed, half grinning, and said I have an Army Ranger contract and a Special Forces contract. I asked what the difference was, and he replied, "If you want to kill people and be hard core then be a Ranger." Before he could even explain the SF contract I said, "Great! Sign me up!" He immediately followed up and asked, "Right now?" I said, "Yes, before I change my mind." I signed up with a student loan repayment plan to pay off all of my student loans, which amounted to more than $50,000, and a $10,000 signing bonus. To date that was the best and easiest business decision I have ever made! After I did the initial paperwork and pissed in a cup, I walked out of the recruiting station with a four-year, twenty-week contract (called an Option 40 contract) in my hand to be a Special Operations Army Ranger in the 75th Ranger Regiment.

On the way home from the recruiting station, I stopped in the Barnes and Noble book store off of 15th Street in Tuscaloosa and bought a book called *To Be A U.S. Army Ranger*, by Russ Bryant. That night I went home and read it front to back. I didn't sleep a wink that night. Something in me changed for the better and I have been different since that day. The next morning I put all of my books in my backpack and ran to class with about thirty pounds on my back. From that day forward, while I was still in college, I ran to every class wearing a black t-shirt that my recruiter got for me with a black and gold Army Ranger Tab on the front. I worked out in it, slept in it, and studied in it. I was determined. I was no longer a regular at the local watering holes in downtown Tuscaloosa where I used to join in drinking with my friends. Instead, I was a regular at the gym, working out to the point of complete exhaustion and seeing a whole new side of the world that happened before nine o'clock in the morning. The friends that I had made at the Pike Fraternity house where I spent the better half of my college years were not the least bit surprised that I volunteered to be an Army Ranger, though some were skeptical and made comments that I just brushed off. One said to me, "Why would you join the army after going to college? Are you trying to be a hero?" At the time I didn't know what to say, but looking back now I would say, "You just don't

get it." There were other comments made, and I am not sure
if my friends made these comments out of jealousy or if they
were serious, but I didn't care and I wasn't about to waste my
time thinking about it either. I wanted to be an Army Ranger;
I wanted to go to war and I didn't care what anyone else had
to say or what they thought about it. It was a calling and it was
a promise that I made to myself ten years ago; it was time to
act on that promise. This was the first decision I ever made by
myself without the influence of anyone else, and my mind was
crystal clear on what I was going to do. I had blinders on and I
was not about to let anyone get in the way of me accomplishing
my goal to be an Army Ranger. If someone tried I just removed
them from my life or bulldozed right through them.

A week later I went home to Roswell, Georgia, for Easter to
inform my parents of my decision to join the military. My
parents always knew that I usually took the road less travelled,
but they were not expecting this. So to make it as easy as
possible for them to adjust to the idea, as soon as I walked in
the door from Tuscaloosa I said, "Mom, I joined the army." She
immediately responded with a firm "No, none of my boys are
joining the military." I said, "I already did." My mom was in
utter disbelief and shock for about fifteen minutes, and when she
came too after the initial shock, she never stopped supporting
my decision. She was proud from minute sixteen on and is
still to this day very proud of my service. My dad was also very
proud and excited, but after the dust settled, he realized that I
had enlisted to be an Army Ranger, "the hardest thing the army
has to offer." Still to this day my dad does not understand why
I would enlist after graduating from the University of Alabama.

My dad had always been my biggest fan and supported anything I ever did, but I do not think he ever completely bought into this decision. Even though he did not understand my decision, it did not take away from how proud he was of me. Before I left to go back to Tuscaloosa, I gave dad the book I bought, *To Be A U.S. Army Ranger.* My mom later told me that my dad would sit in his chair and read that book every night while I was going through the Army Ranger selection pipeline. He would read what phase of training I was in to have a better understanding of what I was going through and so that he could imagine what it was like. When I was in basic training, he read about infantry school. When I was in Airborne School, he read about jumping out of airplanes. When I was in the Ranger Indoctrination Program (RIP), he read about RIP. And lastly when I was in Ranger School, he read about each phase that made up Ranger School (Darby phase, mountain phase, and Florida phase). He did this so that he could feel as though he were walking with me. Dad was fascinated with the military and loved the history of the Rangers. He eventually would pin my airborne wings on my chest and my Ranger Tab on my left shoulder.

When I was in high school I enjoyed working out and was a competitive wrestler and football player. As a free safety and the captain of the Centennial Knights football team, I led my team in tackles and to the second round of the state playoffs. I was never the best athlete or the biggest, but my father instilled a hard work ethic in me as a young kid that has been what all of my successes in life can be credited to. My dad never asked at dinner how many passes I caught in football practice; instead, he asked how many passes I dropped. He would always remind me that your coach will not call on you in the big game if he remembers you as the guy dropping balls in practice. He taught me to be mentally focused at all times, and when a pass was thrown, I would say the three phrases he taught me: see the ball, catch the ball, and tuck the ball. With these three phrases and mental preparation, I never dropped a single pass in a varsity football game. My plan was to use these transferable skills that I had learned on the high school football team and use them to set myself up for success in the army while I finished my finance degree.

August 12, 2006, finally came around and I graduated from Alabama with a finance degree and did so with a 3.3 GPA at twenty-three years old. It was a proud day for me and my family. Everyone in my family, including my mom's parents, came to Tuscaloosa and watched me walk across the stage and receive my diploma. It was my mom's dream for her son to graduate college, and after walking across the stage, I remembered what my mom said: "When you get your degree, you can do whatever you want." As I sat down and watched the rest of the graduating class receive their degrees, I soaked it all in and knew that my life was about to change. To help kick off this upcoming chapter in my life, my family, along my friend Charlie Barry, who also graduated that day, and his family went out to lunch. We were all enjoying a few cocktails and celebrating. While I was sitting at the table, all I could think about was August 23, my report date to the U.S. Army. It was kind of the white elephant in the room that my parents did not want to talk about. Truth be told, I believe that my parents would have much rather seen me coming home or going to law school to continue my education like Charlie, but to be brutally honest, I didn't care. After lunch Charlie's dad told me a story about his father who was awarded a Bronze Star for heroic actions in World War II. He told me that Charlie's grandpa was awarded a Bronze Star for killing twenty-two Japanese soldiers before they had breakfast, and he said he still had the swords his dad took from the dead Japanese soldiers after the battle. I was in awe as I listened to this war story and thought maybe one day that I may have a story like that to tell to my son.

I too had a warrior in my family. My Great Grandpa Jon McGarry was shot in the head in World War I, and because of the trajectory of the bullet, it traveled between the skin of his forehead and skull wrapping around the side of his head until it exited out the back of his head, never penetrating his skull. The blunt force knocked him unconscious immediately, and he was thought to be dead, so his body was left on the battlefield. When he finally came to, he crawled and stumbled until he was able to find help and treatment from a German family. He was in and out of consciousness for six to eight months with no way to contact his family. The United States Army even sent an announcement to my great-great grandma in Ireland, informing her that her son Jon was killed in action. This was so tragic to the family, because he had recently boarded a boat and left Ireland at the age of eighteen to start work in England, but when the war broke out he said there was no way in hell he would fight for the English. So, he stowed away aboard a ship headed to America to fight for the United States in hopes of earning his citizenship. He did finally make it back to Ireland thirty-eight years later to see his mom one last time before she died, and when he walked in to her bedroom, she said, "Lord be to God, my Jonny boy has come home."

A week later, on August 23, 2006, it was my time to ship off—not as a stowaway—but in a white government van headed for Fort Benning, Georgia. It was the new Grant McGarry—I felt as if I had been born again—and being naive I did not fully know what I was embarking on, but I was ready to take on any task, one at a time, until I reached my goal. Before I shipped off I had had a going away breakfast that morning with family and a few close friends at a local diner in Tuscaloosa called Rama Jama's, located right next to the University of Alabama's Bryant-Denny Stadium. After breakfast I rode with my college girlfriend to her house with my parents in trail and said goodbye to her. I left her crying in her college apartment. It was very sad and I felt terrible but only for a minute because it was time to flip the switch and get on with my life. My parents were waiting in the parking lot to drive me to the recruiting station and drop me off. I ran out to the car and hopped in for a quiet car ride with my parents. None of us knew what to say, but the realization of what I volunteered for set in fast and heavy. There was nothing to say when we got to the recruiting station, so I just kissed my mom goodbye and hugged my dad in the parking lot. As I turned and walked into the recruiting station to report for duty, I thought that the next time I see them I will be a soldier and more of a man than anyone else I graduated with. As I took a seat in a chair by the pane glass window, I watched my parents drive away. It was an ominous but exciting feeling, and I couldn't wait to get this new chapter in life started. I was anxious. Shortly after my parents left, the white government van pulled up and I headed to the Military Entrance Processing Station, or MEPS, in Montgomery, Alabama. This was my last stop before going to boot camp. At MEPS I raised my right hand and swore my allegiance to defend the country against all enemies foreign and domestic for a third and final time. It was a proud moment that I experienced with a group of thirty strangers all going off to their perspective boot camps as well. Some had family there and some of these families were crying, but this was just a small step toward my goal so I did not see the reason for making a big deal out of it.

After our quick stop in Montgomery, I got back in the white van headed to Fort Benning in Columbus, Georgia, along with a half dozen other young Americans. All I had with me was the shoes on my feet, the shirt on my back, a Bible that I had bought a few weeks ago, and the bag given to me by the army for enlisting. Inside the army bag I had my army contract along with my social security card and birth certificate. The most important thing I had, which I was rubbing with my fingers, was new to me. It was the first chain/necklace I ever wore, so I was trying to get used to the feeling—a Saint Christopher medallion my grandmother gave me at graduation. I had no idea then how connected I would be with the medallion. As I continued to rub the Saint Christopher medallion, I looked out the van window and started to see mileage signs for Columbus, Georgia. My nerves started to build as we got closer, and I began to get a little nervous. This was the first time I asked myself "What have I gotten myself into?" Knowing it was too late to do anything, I just continued to rub my Saint Christopher medallion and thought about all the hard obstacles in front of me. As we pulled into Fort Benning and headed for Sand Hill, where Infantry Basic Training is held, I said a Bible verse, Philippians 4:6. I learned this verse in the fifth grade and had used it growing up to help calm my nerves prior to sporting events and anything else that made me nervous. As I sat there I recited, "Do not be anxious about anything, but in everything, through petition and prayer and with thanksgiving, present your requests to God." This was the first step in my enlistment to becoming an Army Ranger, and as I sat in that van pulling up to Sand Hill with a line of drill sergeants wearing their famous round brown hats, I thought to myself, if Pat Tillman can do this than why not me?

FORGING OF AN ARMY RANGER

*"People sleep peacefully in their beds
at night because rough men stand
ready to do violence on their behalf."*

- George Orwell

Almost four months later, after graduating army basic training and the Advanced Infantry Training Course, I graduated from the Army Airborne Course on December 13, 2006. With newly pinned airborne wings, which my father pinned on my chest, I was one step closer to becoming a Ranger. After the graduation ceremony, we were ordered to use our leave days over the upcoming Christmas and New Year's break prior to reporting to the next RIP course that was starting after the 2007 New Year. While on leave I flew out to Steamboat, Colorado—my favorite small town in the U.S.—where my Uncle Kurt Vordermeier has lived for as long as I can remember. It is a family pastime to go out to Steamboat to ski, and after being cooped up in Fort Benning, I wanted to get out and do something adventurous. There is no better place to get wild than Steamboat, Colorado.

All of my life I have been an adrenaline junky, and after not having had a drop of alcohol for four months, I wanted some chilly bravos (cold beer) and an adrenaline fix before reporting back to Fort Benning for RIP. It just so happened out of coincidence that my best friend from college, Charlie, was also going to Steamboat the same week. On the first day in Steamboat, after making a few turns by myself in the morning, I linked in with Charlie down at the bottom of the mountain at a bar called Slope Side for a few beers. After we had already had a few pitchers and shots of Goldschlager, skiers started to flow into the bar and the mountain was starting to thin out, so we decided it was time to get back up on the mountain and get one last run in. We went all the way to the top of the mountain, and as we rode to the top, I told Charlie about a back-country spot with deep snow and a great view that I had hiked to a few years ago with a local skier. After talking up the steep and deep terrain of the spot on the ride up, we decided to do it. I loved a great adventure, and even more, I love to ride deep untracked powder. I was in great shape and was not worried about anything, so I threw my board off and started hiking to the top, which is only accessible by foot. With liquid courage I was hard charging up the mountain, and after a fifteen-minute hike, I came to the access gate that read: "Danger! You are leaving the ski area boundary. You assume the risk of injury or death." Just below this descriptive sign is another sign with black skull and crossbones. This kind of sign was not a deterrent for me, but more of an enticing "good idea" sign. I stopped to catch my breath and read the sign for a second time; I was more motivated about this adventure than I was before I read it. I sat on top of my favorite and the most peaceful spot on earth and took in the view of the snowcapped Rocky Mountains. Sitting there, waiting on Charlie, I thought about how much I loved these rugged mountains and the vastness of the western outdoors. I continued to soak it all in, getting more excited about the idea of going down this cliff in front of me as fast as I could with my hair on fire, flirting with danger. Even though I hadn't done this in a few years, I didn't waste any time and strapped my board on. As I crept up close to the edge and peered over the steep drop, I got a little pucker factor and then dropped in screaming at the top of my lungs, "Whooo hooooo!" I was ripping through the trees and floating on the powder at high speeds, taking face shots of white fluffy Champaign powder which created an inexplicable high sensation; I never felt more alive. Without being able to see more than two feet in front of my face, I grabbed my board as

I flew off a ten-foot cliff with no view of how far I was going to
go until I hit the snow again. Only a few seconds later, I landed
in a white puffy cloud of snow and catapulted forward doing
a complete front flip in the snow. After completing the out-of-
control front roll, I popped back up like a spring standing on my
board and going at what felt to be about ninety miles per hour
passing by trees to the bottom half of the ridge until I rode out
into a valley with no trees. It looked almost like it were a snow-
covered lake. This was the first of two valleys that we would have
to hike out of for two more untracked descents through the back
country of Steamboat. I noticed immediately, though, that this
time there was not a snow-packed trail like the last time to lead
us to the next descent.

The trail out of the valley just disappeared. This was my first
sign that we could be in danger, but like most men, I didn't say
anything and just charged on in the direction that I thought we
needed to go. I knew that this was not good but didn't bother
to tell Charlie, because I didn't want to scare him and I was not
about to admit I got us lost. As night was fast approaching, I
continued to truck through the deep powder that was now up
to our waist. After an hour I finally stopped and Charlie asked,
"Are we lost?" By now the buzz we had had from the beers at
Slope Side grill had worn off and dehydration was starting to
set in. The temperature was dropping fast along with the sun
that was falling behind the mountains in the distance. After
an awkward moment of silence I said, "Yes, I do believe we are
lost." Without saying a word Charlie pulled out his phone to see
if he had service. Not to my surprise, he did not have service.
Charlie, still speechless, then post-holed about twenty feet to the

top of a knoll where he was able to get service. Charlie made a call out to his brother and told him we were lost. He asked his brother to get the number to the Steamboat Ski Patrol so that we could call them. He quickly typed the number into his phone and then hung up. Charlie followed up and called the ski patrol and then handed the phone to me. I gave the ski patrol guy on the phone an estimation of where we were. He then told me that this was out of bounds, and like the sign said, we entered at our own risk and that he is not able to provide aid and rescue to us. He then followed up and said that we would have to talk to the Rocky Mountain Rescue squad. Without wasting any time he gave me their number. As he was giving me the number, I was calling it out so that Charlie would also remember the number. After hanging up with the ski patrol, I called Rocky Mountain Rescue, and to my surprise a very nice and calm lady picked up. She informed me that if she and her team do so much as take a step out of their truck to come get us it will cost us each a $1,000! At the time Charlie was in law school and I was living off of E-4 specialist pay in the army. Neither of us had this kind of cash. As I continued to talk to this nice lady on the phone, she told me that it would be possible to make it out of there tonight and she gave me a lay of the land. Without a map I couldn't truly understand what she was explaining, but she mentioned a creek called Fish Creek. She said if we find the creek, follow it and it will lead us out to a parking lot where hikers park to hike that area in the summer. While I was on the phone, Charlie was using my snowboard and his skis to dig into the mountainside. He was starting to get cold and tired and was under the impression that we would not make it out. Covering the phone, I looked at Charlie and said, "Forget this. We are not paying a thousand bucks to get rescued." As I said this Charlie was continuing to dig and I asked him, "What are you doing?" He said, "I am digging us an igloo to sleep in." Before he spent too much energy on this endeavor, I quickly and sharply said, "I am not sleeping in the woods tonight." With that said, I told the lady with Rocky Mountain Rescue that I will get back to them in a little while. It was now about seven o'clock and completely dark. Without being able to see where we were going, I started to lead the way again into the unknown, post-holing every step in the snow that was coming up   to our waist. Every time we trudged up a ridgeline, our hopes and dreams were shattered when we crested the top and saw nothing but more snow and more trees with no sign of life whatsoever. It was a continuous mind game that was a complete let down every time. Not once did we see any lights of the town of Steamboat from the valley below, nor did we hear anything. We were encased in the complete silence created by the vastness of the Rocky Mountains.

After not making any headway and repeatedly getting let down, I felt hopeless and decided to stop and take a breather. Without knowing what to do, I stopped walking for the first time in over two hours. We stopped and talked things over, and Charlie tried to make a call but was unable to get any service. As we stood there I realized that we were soaking wet from head to toe and the crisp night mountain air was starting to take effect. I realized that if we didn't keep moving we could get hypothermia and frostbite. Without wasting any more time I picked up our skis and board, threw them over my shoulders, and continued to walk. We walked for what seemed to be an eternity and our speed of travel had dropped tremendously. At what might have been our final moment, a stream came into view. This was our first sign of hope and I knew that this had to be Fish Creek, which would lead us out to safety. We followed the stream until it disappeared under the snow, and I only found it when the ground came out from under me. I fell through a few feet of snow and landed in the ice-cold rushing and freezing cold water of Fish Creek. At first I was pissed that I was soaking wet, but after realizing I found our only saving grace to civilization, I didn't care that I was sopping wet. I crawled out of the creek on all fours, dusted myself off, and continued to walk—this time, with some adrenaline created by the freezing cold water. I noticed, however, Charlie was beginning to fade a little. Being that he was in law school and studying all the time, he was not in the best of shape, so I offered to carry his skis again to help him out. After grabbing his skis, we continued to post-hole in knee-deep snow, still with no clue where we were going. By now we had walked for over five hours in the waist-deep snow with no sign of life and our motivation to get out of the woods was fading fast. We had almost given up, but then finally we spotted a man-made bridge that crossed over Fish Creek. We knew with this sighting that we would make it out tonight. When we finally got up to the bridge, we saw packed trails and dog tracks everywhere. After post-holing for God knows how many kilometers, it was an immediate morale boost when we stepped onto the hard-packed snow created by snow shoes and hikers. We were so excited; I started to sing the cadence songs I had learned in basic training. We were finally moving at a pace that was getting us somewhere. We still had to battle the fact that Charlie was making this hike in ski boots, but with the new morale boost, he didn't care as much anymore. It was game time; we were getting out of here tonight. After hiking for about thirty more minutes, we finally made it out of the mountain only to be greeted by a car horn being honked repeatedly in the Fish Creek parking lot. Charlie's family was waiting for us. We were so thrilled that we forgot how tired we were and ran out of the woods to the parking lot. We gathered around with Charlie's brother and parents, laughing and telling stories about our journey. After a few pictures and some good laughs, we loaded up into the SUV the Barry family had rented for the trip and drove out of the parking lot. To our surprise, at that exact moment the Rocky Mountain Rescue squad pulled up in their Suburban. We pulled up next to them and we both rolled down our windows. The nice lady we spoke to on the phone earlier handed us two Gatorades, and because they did not have to step out of the car, we were not charged the $1,000 rescue fee.

After my adventure in Colorado, my grandparents Ken and Carol Vordermeier picked me up at the airport in Atlanta, drove me down to Columbus, Georgia, and dropped me off at the Army Airborne Course barracks in Fort Benning on January 2, 2007. I had anxiously looked forward to what was to come the next day since I had walked into the army recruiting station; it would be the day that I would be transferred and assigned to the 75th Ranger Regiment as a candidate for the next RIP, class 03-07. Class 03- 07 was to officially start the morning of January 4, 2007, and the night of January 3 all of the candidates for the upcoming RIP class continued to show up and grab a bunk. Each RIP candidate went straight to doing what he needed to do to get his mind right for the morning. I remember one of my roommates watching *Black Hawk Down* on his DVD player to get motivated, and as I watched over his shoulder for a few minutes, my nerves began to build with a feeling of excitement, but mostly anxiety. During my short career in the military I never heard one good thing about RIP. In fact, I realized I had never even seen an active duty Ranger wearing a tan beret or 75th Ranger Regiment Scroll. Realizing this as I lay in bed, I opened up a book I was reading called *Roberts Ridge* about the 1st Ranger Battalion's valiant efforts to save the body of a Navy SEAL thrown out of the back of a helicopter during operations in Afghanistan. As I continued to read I learned how a SEAL Team that flew to rescue their fallen brother—Neil Roberts—were forced off the peak due to two of the SEALs in the rescue element becoming wounded. The book began to pick up when the call was made to insert a Ranger QRF (quick reaction force) task force, which was located at Bagram Air Base. This QRF team of Rangers quickly got dressed into combat gear like a squad of firefighters going to fight a fire, loaded up on a Chinook, and flew straight to the fight in a second effort to retrieve Roberts. On the Ranger QRF element's approach to the target, the MH-47 Chinook helicopter they were in was shot down and three Rangers—Corporal Matt Commons, Sergeant Brad Crose, and Specialist Marc Anderson— were killed exiting the Chinook as they ran toward the fight. The remaining Rangers did not flee the fight, but instead they fought their way onto the objective at elevations pushing ten thousand feet until an additional squad of Rangers ran up the mountain as reinforcements so that they may complete the mission. As I laid wide-eyed like a kid on Christmas Eve trying to fall asleep, I thought about these Rangers and how heroic they were and realized that I was about to walk in the same footsteps as these amazing warriors. I hardly slept that night. The next morning came fast. Everything that I had done leading up to this moment was about to be tested and it was time to earn the coveted red and black Ranger Scroll.

To be an Army Ranger is a long and arduous road attempted by few and only accomplished by the elite. It is sometimes confusing to explain this "road less traveled" to a civilian who never served in the army, because there are many that claim to be an Army Ranger when in fact they are not. Sometimes people claim to be a Ranger because they graduated from Ranger School and wear a black and gold *Ranger Tab*. This does not make you a *modern day* special ops (operations) Army Ranger riding into battle on Little Bird and Black Hawk helicopters with your legs dangling off the side on a direct-action raid mission to capture or kill bad guys; this makes you Ranger qualified. You have to have served in the 75th Ranger Regiment to be a Special Operations Ranger and the only way to accomplish this is to receive a red and black *Ranger Scroll*, only awarded upon completion of the Ranger Indoctrination Program or the new and improved Ranger Assessment and Selection Program (RASP). As the two hundred RIP candidates lined up on the rocks in front of the airborne barracks, we saw a deuce-and-a-half pull up and two Rangers wearing tan berets stepped out. Everyone in the formation shut their mouths immediately and went to the position of parade rest. As the two

Rangers got closer, their presence alone intimidated everyone and you could feel it in the air. It was so quiet you could have heard a pin drop. I do not know what we all looked like, but I imagine that we looked as though we all had seen a ghost. The two Rangers walked up and the first thing out of one of their mouths was, "For now on it will be 'Roger, sergeant' or 'Negative, sergeant.' Is that clear?" The entire formation responded with a thundering, "Roger, sergeant!" It was so loud that it shook the rocks we stood on. The one Ranger cadre that was talking to us then said, "When I release you all from this formation, you will load your two duffle bags on the bed of the deuce-and-a-half truck and then [you] will be running to the RIP barracks." Without knowing how far we were going to run or how fast we would be going, we all shouted back at the same time, "Roger, sergeant!" He then said, "Fall out!" Immediately following was a mass chaos of two hundred soldiers running to the truck with their two duffle bags with everything they owned. As candidates began to throw their duffle bags on to the bed of the deuce-and-a-half, we all began to push and shove using our elbows to make our way to the truck in fear that we would be left behind. We did not know how far we had to go, but I could see that one of the cadre took off sprinting and the candidates who had already dumped their duffle bags were stretched out fifty to seventy-five yards behind him. Just simply not knowing what to expect was scaring everyone. I could hear guys asking open questions like, "Do you know how far we are going to have to run?" As I was shoving my way to the front of the line to throw my duffle bag on the bed, I mentally went back to when I was lost in the mountains of Colorado. I did not bother trying

to answer anyone or ask any questions, I just went into survival
mode and knew that I had to put one foot in front of the other.
Just like when I was lost I knew that at some point I will see a
sign that will boost my morale, and until then, I told myself,
"Don't stop." I continued to keep my head down as we ran a
mile, give or take, at a sub seven- minute pace in boots and army
fatigues, and to my surprise, it was over and we arrived to the
75th Ranger Regiment compound.

As soon as we got to an old three-story military barrack, I looked
up and saw the words SUA SPONTE (Latin definition: "of
their own accord") written in black bold letters on the third
floor just below the roof. "Sua Sponte" is the Ranger Regiment
motto; it was written there to remind candidates that the 75th
Ranger Regiment is a volunteer unit and you can quit anytime.
The 75th Ranger Regiment does not need anyone; it only
accepts those that survive selection and meet Ranger standards.
I gazed back down through the entrance of a tall fence blacked
out by mesh and noticed a handful of RIP cadre waiting for us
like caged pit bulls. As I crested the gates one cadre screamed,
"Start pushing Georgia!" I jumped down and was introduced
to my new best friend—a black concrete slab. I did not know
this at the time, but this would not be my last sight of the
black asphalt going from directly in my face to the distance
of my arms, back and forth, over and over, till my arms shook
like the legs of a scared man standing face-to-face with death.
It was then that the weak began to feel sorry for themselves.
Young, physically fit men were dropping like flies to the point
that one RIP cadre instructor asked, "Who else wants to quit?"
I just kept pushing   and didn't look up, scared that a cadre

would notice my wandering eyes and yank me off the blacktop asphalt. As I continued to push Georgia like a mad man, I could hear guys saying, "I quit," and others supposedly simply raised their hand out of pure terror. After hours of pushups, flutter kicks, mountain climbers, pull-ups, and reciting the Ranger Creed—or lack thereof since several soldiers did not memorize it prior to day zero—we finally stopped. We were called to the position of attention, ordered to fall into formation, and file into a classroom to in-process with now around 150 candidates. At this point both of my arms were so fatigued from all of the pushups and other exercises that my hands were shaking. Once we finally made it into the classroom, but before we even went through the paper work to in-process to RIP class 03-07, one of the cadre told everyone who had a seat to put his head down on the desk and for those standing in the back of the classroom, he ordered them to close their eyes. He then followed up and said, "If you want to quit, please walk out the door and wait outside." Again, more people quit out of pure intimidation of the Ranger cadres' presence. I am not saying I was not nervous, but we had not even done anything, yet soldiers were quitting out of intimidation and the thought of the unknown future that lay before us. As I laid my head down on the desk, I could hear what my friend from Alabama said, "They can't kill you." With this reassurance in the back of my head, I just kept my blinders on and my head down with my goal in my mind. I was so close but yet so far and quitting now was not an option. After we raised our heads and opened our eyes it was obvious many more young men quit out of pure uncertainty of not knowing what the immediate and distant future had in store for us while in

RIP.

The goal of day zero is to weed out those men who are uncertain about their decision of volunteering to be a Ranger. Being a Ranger is not for the weak and faint-hearted and the RIP cadre needed to get rid of them ASAP so that they would be able to better focus their time and energy on the men who have a chance at graduating. After all, one day it is possible that we would fight together with the cadre, and it is their job to send hardcore young men to Ranger battalions ready for war. The scare tactics inflicted on us by the RIP cadre worked flawlessly. (You cannot prepare for their tactics, which can only be conquered by mental toughness.) The Ranger Regiment has been perfecting this over many years of conducting RIP (now the RASP course) and only the strong and smart survive.

After in-processing we were all assigned a bunk, and this was the first time I met Ryan McGhee, who was assigned to the bottom bed of the bunk I was assigned to. McGhee and I would spend many waking hours in the field, enduring the cold January rain together with only bare essential clothing. Over the next four weeks we conducted land navigation, marksmanship, and combative training, and we endured the misery of RIP in the cold winter months together. We talked about the girlfriends we left behind and wondered what they were doing in college. Ryan McGhee would graduate and go to 3rd Ranger Battalion and serve his country honorably. While I was training for the 2009 Best Ranger Competition, I saw Ryan at the Fort Benning gym and he told me he was now engaged to his girlfriend. As we caught up and talked about lost time, Ryan was smiling ear to ear about his future. He seemed very happy. A little over a month later McGhee was killed in action on May 13, 2009, during Operation Iraqi Freedom.

After getting our bunks and wall lockers, we formed back up on the black asphalt in front of the barracks and were marched to the chow hall by a cadre for dinner chow. As we marched up to the chow hall, I could hear a C-17 taking off in the distance. Our RIP cadre said, "Do you hear that boys? That's the sound of men going to war." I looked off in the distance, and I was able to see a C-17 gaining elevation, rising above the Georgia pine trees, and taking Rangers from the 3rd Ranger Battalion to fight the Global War on Terrorism. Although I didn't know where they were going or the names of the Rangers onboard, the sound of the C-17 alone and the cadre's statement made the hair on my forearms rise, and I knew without a doubt I wanted to be on a C-17 one day going to war. That moment, along with not wanting to deploy with the regular army for twelve to fifteen months, motivated me to graduate, and I held this desire close to my chest, guarding it with my life. The cadre's comment was just another reminder of the big picture and why I was here. I wanted to kill enemies of the United States and I wanted to do it with the best. This was my opportunity and it was mine to take advantage of; I told myself there would be no excuses.

The next day started at 0600 hours with a physical fitness test, and anyone that did not meet the Ranger standard was dropped from class 03-07. Throughout the next few weeks we were tried, tested, and evaluated on our abilities to complete obstacle courses and long-distance forced road marches in boots with a sixty-pound ruck sack and a weapon, to effectively shoot and fast rope, and to demonstrate Ranger knowledge and history, land navigation, and more. What set me apart from the other Ranger candidates in RIP was the "Doughboy run," which is conducted on the last day. The Doughboy run is a long undetermined distance run and it was the culmination of RIP.

Having no idea that we were about to embark on the longest and fastest paced run of my life, I just stood in formation and waited for the task, conditions, standards, and time hack brief from the cadre of the day. To my surprise there was no brief, but instead we started sprinting in a gaggle of a formation with RIP students spread out all over the place trying to get their legs underneath them to work at the incredibly fast pace. My legs were not warm and they felt like Jell-O, and as we were sprinting off, I thought to myself surely we are not going to run at this pace for a long distance. I just didn't think it was possible. As I literally sprinted at a pace that I would normally run an 800-meter race, my legs began to flail and I started to look like an un-athletic nerd that had never ran a day in his life. Just like I had done throughout RIP, I maintained mental toughness, and to cope with the burning of my lungs and the pain in my legs, I just squeezed down on my thumbs as hard as I could trying to hurt them so that I would forget about the fact that I was running at a pace only comfortable to an Olympic long-distance runner. After about an hour of this, we came to a football stadium called Doughboy Stadium. As we approached the stadium I found a happy place in my mind that took me back to playing high school football; I thought about summer workouts with our strength and conditioning coach. In high school no one ever beat me running the stairs of the stadium, and I was not about to let anyone beat me today. I was determined to make a name for myself on this death run called the Doughboy run. I switched gears mentally and started hard-charging the stairs, churning my legs up and down like a robot and passing the younger Rangers in my class one at a time, and as we approached the end, I passed the cadre leading the run. I had my head down so I did not even realize that he was the cadre leading the run until he yelled at me for not paying attention. Once he put me in my place, he told me to look around and see that the closest Ranger in my RIP class was still a good distance behind me. Even though I was now ahead of everyone else, I did not let up. Instead, I pushed the cadre and ran so hard that at the end of the Doughboy run the cadre looked at me and said, "What battalion do you want to go to?" I said, "First Bat, Sergeant," and he said, "Roger that," and walked off.

On graduation day for class 03-07, sixty-nine Rangers pinned on a Ranger Regiment Scroll and donned a tan beret. I was awarded the PT (physical fitness training) Stud Award and the Honorary Colonel of the 75th Ranger Regiment. Colonel Ralph Puckett Jr. pinned on my 1st Ranger Battalion scroll. There were three awards given at graduation: the Honor Grad Award, the Leadership Award, and the PT Stud Award. My good friend, Benjamin Will, was awarded the Leadership Award, and like me, he chose to go to 1st Ranger Battalion in Savannah, Georgia. Only recipients of one of the three awards were able to choose which battalion he wanted to go to. The other graduates were assigned to a Ranger Battalion according to the regiment's needs. The 75th Ranger Regiment consists of one Special

Troops Battalion and three special operations battalions. First
Ranger Battalion, or 1st Bat as it's commonly called, is based
in Savannah, Georgia, at Hunter Army Airfield; 2nd Ranger
Battalion, or 2nd Bat, is based south of Seattle, Washington, at
Joint Base Lewis-McChord; and 3rd Ranger Battalion, or 3rd
Bat, is based in Columbus, Georgia, at Fort Benning, where the
headquarters of the 75th Ranger Regiment and Special Troops
Battalion are also based. It was an easy decision for me. I wanted
to stay in Georgia, and I liked the idea of being in Savannah
and away from Columbus. With that said, when I told the RIP
NCOIC (non-commissioned officer-in-charge) of my decision,
he was skeptical to send me to Savannah when he found out
I was from Atlanta. He literally looked at me and tried to sell
me on 3rd Ranger Battalion, telling me that I would be closer
to home. Without even being able to get a word in, the cadre
that lead the Doughboy run stepped in and told the NCOIC
the story about my performance on the Doughboy run. After
digesting it for a second and looking me up and down a second
and third time, he signed me off to go to 1st Ranger Battalion.
It was a nerve-racking couple of seconds while this was being
debated, because I really wanted to go to 1st Ranger Battalion
but did not want to come off as that guy. Nonetheless, I got
what I wanted and was Savannah bound. As for the guys that
quit or did not meet the Ranger Regiment standards in RIP class
03-07, they were assigned to the needs of the army.

After a few days of in-processing at Fort Stewart, I reported to
1st Ranger Battalion on February 14, 2007, which was also my
twenty-fourth birthday and the day that I consider my entrance
into manhood. When I and the other thirteen graduates of RIP

class 03-07 assigned to 1st Bat arrived to Hunter Army Airfield, we were picked up by a non-commissioned officer (NCO) working in the battalion headquarters office. After picking us up, we went through some more necessary paperwork, and we were assigned to line companies according to the needs of 1st Ranger Battalion. I was assigned to Charlie Company, also known as "Hard Luck Chuck." My good friend Alessandro Plutino was assigned to Bravo Company and my other friend Ben Will went to Alpha Company. Alessandro Plutino was killed in action four years later on August 8, 2011, in Afghanistan, and Ben Will was awarded a Purple Heart for being shot twice in the leg and once in the neck as well as a valorous award for killing the combatant who shot him at point blank in a direct action raid mission in Iraq just two months after arriving to 1st Ranger Battalion.

When I walked into the Charlie COF with four other new Rangers from class 03-07, escorted by the S-1 (personnel) NCO, we were introduced and left with the Charlie Company administrative NCO and then introduced to the highest ranking NCO in the company, First Sergeant Arrington. After the five of us told First Sergeant Arrington our names, he looked at us and said, "Rule number one in Charlie Company is always look cool, and if you don't know what's going on, revert back to rule number one and look cool." He also said Two Charlie eats their young so whoever comes here needs to be ready. As I stood at the position of parade rest while First Sergeant Arrington talked to the three platoon sergeants in Charlie Company, the squad leaders of first platoon, second platoon, and third platoon walked into the room. The platoon sergeants sized us up, looking at us from head to toe, each of them asked us questions one at a time. As I answered questions, which I thought might be trick questions, I tried my best not to make an ass out of myself and to just make a good first impression. Each platoon sergeant's first question was, "What is your PT score (Army Physical Fitness Test)?" Without hesitating I responded, "Three hundred, sergeant (300 is perfect score)." What I didn't know is that you could have a higher score than three hundred for credit of additional pushups, sit-ups, and pull-ups, and they wanted a candidate with a higher score than a three hundred. Being that I did not know this, I just reverted to rule number one and tried to look cool, but unfortunately I did not accomplish rule number one.

After being sized up by each platoon sergeant, I was chosen by Sergeant First Class Javez, the second platoon, platoon sergeant. Sergeant First Class Javez turned around and asked the squad leaders, "Who wants this guy in their squad?" As I continued to stand at parade rest starring straight at the white cinder block wall on the other side of the room, Staff Sergeant Bench from third squad asked me a few questions and then told Sergeant First Class Javez that he would take me. With that settled, Staff Sergeant Bench told me to follow him outside where the rest of Charlie Company was waiting in a company formation. It was a Thursday and the company was about to start a four-day weekend. Prior to long weekends there was always a safety brief, because when a Ranger gets a pass something crazy always happens. I briskly walked behind Staff Sergeant Bench out to the formation and fell in at the end of the line in third squad of second platoon's rank and file. In my duty uniform with my new 1st Ranger Battalion Scroll on my left shoulder and brand new tan beret, I went straight to parade rest and was immediately inspected by Specialist Kurtis Frasier and Specialist Josh Bevans. They told me to polish my DUI (distinctive unit insignia) on my beret with brasso to remove the gold so that it will be outlined in silver. This was the Two Charlie tradition and they gave me my first time hack as a private to have this task completed before the next work call. I would come to know these two tab Spec 4s (meaning Ranger qualified, wearing a Ranger Tab, and army rank of specialist, pay grade and enlisted level four) very well over the next few months while they tried to make me quit, to teach me, and to train me. Over time I would finally gain their respect.

First Sergeant Arrington and the company commander, Captain Ferrell, walked out and saved me from the wrath of Frasier and Bevans. We stopped what we were doing when First Sergeant Arrington called the company to attention. Captain Ferrell asked us to huddle around him so he didn't have to yell at us. Captain Ferrell went straight into the safety brief telling us and asking us to be safe over the weekend, because he needed each and every one of us for the upcoming deployment. He then lead into our upcoming training events and told us what we should expect when we get back from the four-day weekend. He began to speak directly to me and the other Rangers that arrived that day, informing us that we were about to go through the hardest and busiest part of the training cycle leading up to our deployment rotation, which was fast approaching. Once Captain Ferrell finished up, First Sergeant Arrington followed up and spoke about the conduct he expected his Rangers to uphold over the weekend. He then gave a broad overview about the upcoming training events leading up to our deployment to Iraq and said that we should use this weekend to relax and spend time with family, so that when we get back to work on Tuesday we would be doing what we need to do to get ready for the planned squad, platoon, and company training exercises coming up.

After the first sergeant wrapped up his brief up to the company, he called us to the position of attention in company formation and released us for the weekend. As I continued to stand at the position of attention, Frasier and Bevans walked over and told me to follow them back to the barracks. It was at this moment that I realized graduating RIP was not the hard part. In fact RIP was easy compared to what I was about to go through. With that said, I was also excited and ready to endure the long, arduous journey of becoming a modern-day warrior. I followed the two tab Spec 4's, Frasier and Bevans, to the squad room in the barracks for my initial counseling brief. That was when I noticed that we were actually following Sergeant Cousins. Once we got into the third squad's squad room in the barracks, Sergeant Cousins instructed me to take a seat. He first introduced himself and told me that he was the bravo team leader and then he told me that he was about to give me a platoon in-processing brief to start the counseling that every new Ranger in the regiment receives.

As a private in the Ranger Regiment you are put on a six-month probationary period and if you so much as fart wrong you can kiss your ass goodbye to the regular army. Sergeant Cousins started off by informing me of the additional duties that I must complete every morning prior work call. My additional duties consisted of, but were not limited to, buffing the first floor hallway of the barracks and picking up all trash in the barracks parking lot. The purpose of an initial counseling from your team leader is so that you are informed of everything up front. On day one you are told the standards of what it takes to continue to wear a Ranger Regiment Scroll, and if you cannot uphold what is expected, it will be documented in your counseling packet. If you receive more than one negative counseling, you can start planning to relocate to a regular army unit and new duty station.

After informing me of my additional daily duties and why I was being counseled, Sergeant Cousins then began to explain to me the standards of third squad, second platoon and the 1st Ranger Battalion so that I was crystal clear on what was expected of me from him and my chain of command. He also provided insight about what I should expect over the next two months of training in preparation for our upcoming deployment, telling me to be like a sponge and to soak everything up and retain it. He reiterated the importance of the training events that I was about to partake in and emphasized on how fast paced it will be, saying it is a sink-or-swim mentality. Sergeant Cousins told me that our deployment to Baghdad, Iraq, was set for April 5, which was less than two months away. Now knowing this, he said the only way I can get on that plane to Baghdad is to show him, the alpha team leader, and the squad leader over the next two months that I am able to perform to the standard. To sum it up Sergeant Cousins said that if I cannot perform to the standard that I would not be going on the deployment and that I would be released from the Ranger Regiment and would go to the needs of the army.

Even though I graduated from RIP and wear a Ranger Scroll, I realized that that did not guarantee my acceptance into the regiment. In the Ranger Regiment you had to earn your Ranger Scroll every day, and the day you get complacent could be the day it gets taken away. The Ranger Regiment is an ever-evolving volunteer unit and it is the only unit in the army that you can quit at any time. You can also be released for failure to uphold the Ranger standard (called released for standards, or RFS) at any time. For everything that we do, whether it is cleaning a toilet or conducting battle drills, there is a standard set in place, and if you cannot complete the task to the Ranger standard, you will be RFS'd and sent to a regular army unit.

After receiving the standards of what I would live by, Sergeant Cousins gave me an opportunity to talk for the first time and asked me two questions. He asked me if I played sports, and before he could say anymore, I blurted out that I played football and wrestled in high school. Without saying much more than a few words, he asked me why I joined the military. Like most young green Rangers I told him I joined the army because it was the right thing to do during a time of war, and I wanted to serve my country. I then went deeper and said that I volunteered to be a Ranger because I wanted to be with the best. Sergeant Cousins, Frasier, and Bevans all laughed and chuckled as my speech was kind of nerdy from the perspective of a seasoned Ranger.

After everyone in the room stopped laughing at me, Sergeant Cousins said, "Well, you are with the best and most of us in the platoon were wrestlers in high school and college, so we will see just how tough you are." He also said our squad members

love their job, and we are known as the "suicide squad." I didn't
know what that meant until he told me that every leader in the
squad has been shot. He said our squad leader, Sergeant Bench,
was shot in the femoral artery two deployments ago and dodged
death. My team leader—the alpha team leader—Sergeant Aaron
Hoffman, who left immediately after First Sergeant Arrington
released us, had been shot in the knee on the last deployment
less than seven months ago. Sergeant Cousins then finished
up, telling me he had been shot in the back, but the bullet
stopped in his ballistic plates after passing through his MBITR.
I immediately perked up and sat at the position of attention
as I realized that I was in a room of heroes. As I tensed up I
remember Sergeant Cousins telling me to relax, but after that
statement there was no relaxing. I was no longer playing BB-
gun wars in the woods of Georgia, and I was no longer playing
army trying to reach my goal to become a Ranger. It was at this
moment that it truly set in that I was an Army Ranger. Not to
mention I was deploying with the "suicide squad" in less than
two months. Lastly, to top it off Sergeant Cousins looked me in
the eyes and said something that still sticks with me today. He
said no man should be scared of another man, no matter what.
So act like a man, and I will treat you like one. If you do not act
like a man then I will not treat you as one. It was time to take
an even bigger step and man-up and answer the call. After all,
I enlisted and I made the decision to volunteer to be an Army
Ranger.

Once the in-processing counseling brief was over, I walked out
into the hallway of the barracks and what was a mad house
an hour ago was now a ghost town. All the Rangers that were

storming the halls had escaped and went God only knows where. As I followed Bevans and Frasier to my barracks room, they told me to take the weekend to get squared away because come Tuesday morning my ass was theirs. After they left my room I called Plutino to see if he was done with his in-processing. Luckily, he was also waiting to get out of the barracks. Without a plan I picked him up from the Bravo Company barracks and we drove to downtown Savannah with one mission and one mission only—get a beer on River Street. The first place we came to was an Irish bar called Kevin Barry's Pub. We went in Kevin Barry's, sat down at a table in the bar, ordered a beer, and ate dinner. There was not much said between us, as we were both digesting everything that had happened that day, but after a few beers we began to lighten up and we talked about everything and anything, from our new team leaders to our upcoming deployment. Looking back on that moment, we were so young that time stood still for just a moment and we had no idea what was to come in our future. After the Irish band finished, the night was a blur and time never stood still again.

The four-day weekend ended quickly, and on Tuesday morning the world that I once knew was no longer. The first lesson I learned that day was that as a private in Ranger Battalion, you are never right and that you will spend all day in the front leaning rest (push-up position) until you accept this and learn your job and the job of the Ranger appointed over you, and more importantly, until you earn respect. The second lesson I learned that morning is that when you do push-ups as a private, you do them with your feet elevated at a height above your hands, because as a private you have not been to "mountains"

(mountain phase of Ranger School). While I was doing push-ups with my feet elevated, specialists Frasier and Bevans grilled me about anything and everything, from Ranger knowledge and weapon specs to tactics, techniques, and procedures. If I got something wrong I continued to push; if I got something correct, I still pushed. It was a no-win situation and I just had to accept it. Specialists Frasier and Bevans went over everything with me that morning, over and over, until I reached a point when I eventually dreamt about battle drill six (enter and clear room). It was imperative to know this battle drill flawlessly, because it will save your life, and more importantly, the life of your Ranger buddy.

I soaked up knowledge like a sponge just as I was instructed to in my in-processing counseling brief. As I started to catch on and become proficient with the basics, second platoon started to conduct familiarization training (FAM). My first FAM was with the new regimental attack/transportation vehicle, the Stryker, which replaced the Humvee. The Stryker is an eight-wheeled armored fighting vehicle that the Ranger Regiment adopted as a mode of transportation for when helicopters were not available. It provided outstanding protection against rocket-propelled grenades (RPG) and had a ballistic up-armored shield under the engine that provided protection from improvised explosive devices (IED), or roadside bombs. As I was trying to take in everything, I pulled out my black pen and pocket notebook and started taking notes during the FAM so that I could operate it that day if asked. After a basic FAM of the Stryker, I received a familiarization class followed by a specific block of instruction from my squad leader on how to use the technology to operate the weapons system mounted on the vehicle. I was informed that operating this heavy weight, fully automatic, belt- fed, .50-caliber machine gun via the RWS (remote weapons system) would most likely be my job on deployment. Operating a .50-caliber machine gun mounted on a Stryker was comparable to sitting in the cockpit of a fighter jet. Second platoon became so proficient at operating the Stryker and using it to facilitate ground assault force missions that we would move out in a convoy of Strykers at 70 mph without headlights under the concealment of darkness using speed as security. To maneuver through Iraq, the drivers and vehicle commanders worked as a team using night optical devices (NOD)— or night-vision googles—and the built-in thermal screens to drive.

My next familiarization course and block of instruction was with UH-60 Black Hawk, MH-6 Little Bird, and the CH-47 Chinook helicopters. I was given a complete general overview class on each helicopter to prepare for helicopter assault force missions and was familiarized with the fast rope systems and weapons, and in the event of a crash, I was taught how to destruct sensitive items on each helicopter. Army Rangers are deployable by land, sea, or air and we are expected to be proficient at all ways of infiltration to complete a mission to the Ranger standard. Being a Ranger is not a job; it is a lifestyle, and the sooner you realized that the better off you were.

Everything in Ranger Battalion is based off of the crawl, walk, run approach. The crawl phase of classroom, familiarization, and tape drills was complete. Next was the walk phase, during which I trained countless hours in the shoot houses at Fort Stewart with my squad using blank rounds at first and then using live rounds and going over every possible scenario our chain of command could throw at us. Each of these events was taken seriously, and if you did not learn something every day, you were cheating yourself, and worse you were cheating your Ranger buddy. With this said, no one ever cheated their Ranger buddy. Bevans, Frasier, my team leaders, and my squad leader took our training seriously, and we worked harder than one could imagine. This was not an easy task to accomplish because of how new I was, but to my squad's credit I owe each of them a lot for what they did to develop me into a Ranger.

March was the beginning of the run phase for me. We (second platoon) and the rest of Charlie Company deployed on a training mission to Fort Bragg, North Carolina. This was the last scheduled training event and the culmination of the training cycle for Charlie Company before each platoon would deploy. The mission in North Carolina was to treat it as a miniature deployment. We slept during the day and operated at night just as we would do on our upcoming deployment. As soon as we got to our destination, we started working with a sense of urgency just as we will do on the upcoming deployment. We received missions from our chain of command and from there we went into action just like we planned to do overseas. As my squad leader always said, "Train like you fight." We planned, prepped, went over pre-combat inspections (PCI), and conducted mission briefs and operation orders, and then ultimately conducted the missions on the training grounds of Fort Bragg. After each mission we would conduct after action reviews (AAR) and fine tune everything to the smallest detail. In a Ranger platoon AAR

you had better have thick skin because nothing went unsaid, and
if you couldn't handle that you might as well quit. Like Sergeant
Cousins said in my in-processing counseling brief, all Rangers
are expected to perform to the standard, and if you don't, you
had better adjust your fires or kiss your ass goodbye.

Two months had passed and it was April 5 and second
platoon was deploying. For some this was their fifth and sixth
deployment rotations, but this would be my first. Not knowing
exactly how to handle this, I wrote a letter in the chance that
I should die and addressed it to my parents telling them that I
loved them and died proudly doing what I wanted to do. With
that said, I went through everything in my packing list once
more and then made a call home. My mom answered, and
without knowing what to say, we just kept it short and sweet.
I said, "It is time for me to go to work, mom." She understood
what that meant and she just said bravely be careful and call me
if you can. We were not allowed to tell our family and friends
the time and date that we were deploying, and we were not
allowed to tell them exactly where we were going. Even though it
was obvious that America was at war and had been for six years.
I was ordered to maintain operational security, and as a Ranger
private I was not about to screw that up. We were not at liberty
to tell family and friends the details, because we were executing
secret and top secret missions with intelligence that was only
allowed to be spoken about within the Ranger Regiment. With
the rules and guidelines set forth, it made for a weird phone call,
but it had to be done. After the phone call I powered down my
phone and left it on the desk in my barracks room. As I walked
over to the COF, I stopped by my Jeep Wrangler and put the

letter addressed to my parents in the glove compartment. My jeep was the only thing I owned besides some clothes, flip flops, and a bathing suit, so I knew that they would find it there. Once I got over to the COF, I signed out my M4, which was tricked out with a laser, flashlight, and other sensitive items attached to it from the company armorer. After signing out all of my personal gear, I compiled it neatly together in military fashion, dress-right-dress. As the newest guy in the squad it was my job to also compile all the squad equipment and have it ready to go when the rest of the guys got to work. I took the time to double and triple check everything before the rest of the squad arrived. Over the last two months I learned through repetition that it was best to get to work before everyone else and to take the time to stage everything for Frasier and Bevans to inspect. The easier I made it for them the better off I was!

As the hot Savannah night set in, I hung out with Vaughan and Plagge, my two Ranger buddies. Roland Vaughan was from Auburn, Alabama, and was deploying as well. Jacob Plagge, on the other hand, was staying behind to go to Ranger School. As we sat around, a staff NCO showed up holding a clip board. He asked for the platoon to gather around him for final manifest call (roll call). As we closed in and quieted down, he went through the roster of who was flying out tonight in the Two Charlie chalk. After going down the list, he got to my name and said, "Specialist McGarry." I quickly responded, "Roger, sergeant." I saw him put a check mark next to my name on the piece of paper he had attached to the clip board. Once he went through the list, it was confirmed that everyone was accounted for and we began to load up into the white government school busses waiting for us outside the company operating area next to what was called B. Co. Island (a little grassy area in the parking lot next to the Bravo Company COF), and we headed to the airfield on Hunter Army Airfield less than a mile away. There is no ceremony when Rangers deploy, and we do not even tell anyone where it is that we are going. We go in the night and we do not ask for sympathy. In fact, we love it that there is not a parade or civilians around to wish us off. We are in the business of killing the enemy, not to win the hearts and minds of anyone.

Most of my Ranger career was spent on-call in the chance that we had to answer a call and report at a moment's notice to take the fight to anyone we were ordered to destroy. When second platoon arrived to the airfield, we unloaded the bus and got into a platoon formation and laid our weapons cases in a platoon formation. While waiting for the C-17 (Air Force plane) to run pre-flight checks and for permission to load up all our equipment, we filed in line to get some army chow that was brought out for us in warm trays. After stuffing our faces and telling some stories about what we did while on leave, we were called over to huddle around our platoon sergeant, Sergeant First Class Javez. Our platoon sergeant informed us that the C-17 is loaded up and ready to go. He then said, "Squad leaders get on up and get your guys on the bird." We walked out onto the tarmac and loaded the C-17 with everything that our platoon was taking with us to Baghdad, Iraq—our final destination. We had everything on our person and loaded up in the bird that we needed to be mission capable once we were wheels down in Balad, Iraq, our first stop after a quick layover in Germany. I remember the smell of the jet fuel and the sound of the jet engines as I walked up the stairs and into the C-17 that night as if it were yesterday. My time had come; I was a Special Operations Army Ranger going to war to fight for the United States of America, and more importantly, fight with my brothers who were walking onto the C-17 with me.

FIRST DEPLOYMENT

"Let the enemy come till he's almost close enough to touch. Then let him have it and jump out and finish him up with your hatchet."

- Major Robert Rogers, 1759, 19th Standing Order

After an Ambien-induced sleep halfway around the world, I was awoken by an Air Force crew member working in the C-17. As the lights were being turned on, the pilot came over the loud speaker to tell us that we were entering into Iraqi airspace and to instruct us to buckle up in the very slim chance that we had to perform any type of an evasive maneuver. It was highly unlikely that this could happen, being that we had already destroyed the Iraqi Army in the initial invasion, but it is always better to be safe than sorry. Being that this was my first rodeo, I just started to do like the rest of the guys in Two Charlie and rolled up my sleep pad, mashed my sleeping bag into my aviator's kit bag, sat up in my seat, and looked straight forward. It is loud as hell in a C-17 and we were all wearing ear plugs to muffle the noise so there was not exactly a lot of friendly conversation going on. As I sat there I wiped the sleep out of my eyes and pulled out a book called Gates of Fire from my assault pack, which was given to me by my longtime friend Richard Bruno. Next, I heard the landing gear being lowered and the noise and vibration this created caused a very similar feeling to one that I get right before I jump out of a perfectly good airplane—a very nervous feeling! This was really happening. We are about to take the fight to the enemy. It was game time and to comfort this nervous feeling I thought about what my Uncle Mike told me over the phone before I left. He said, "Grant, trust your training."

As the wheels touched down on the Balad, Iraq, runway, we came to a screeching halt. After conducting a very fast descent landing that is only conducted in war zones or when training for such a landing, it took me a second to get my bearings back. Once I got my stomach settled, which I felt like I had left at about 30,000 feet, I started to get all my gear ready so that I could get off of this aircraft as fast as possible and be ready for anything I was instructed to do. I learned over thousands of push-ups, flutter kicks, mountain climbers, and wall sits to always try and be a step ahead of what Bevans and Frasier were going to want me to do. The side exit door of the C-17 swung open, everyone stood up, and we began to mass exit the airplane. When I approached the doorway I was taken aback by an unfamiliar smell that burned my nostrils. It was the stench of a war-torn Iraq. I stepped out into the dark night, walked down the steps, and took in my first deep breath of dust-filled air, which was so thick it felt like it coated my teeth. This was a new and unfamiliar scent that I would get used to over the next four years while operating in the Middle East. Being that it was April, it was not as hot as I expected it to be. In fact the temperature was very cool and pleasant. After smelling the burnt air, breathing in the dust, and moving away from the loud noises of the jet engines on the C-17, I noticed that there was a siren going off in the background. Immediately after I recognized a siren going off, I heard an explosion and just like that I earned a Combat Infantryman Badge for indirect contact. The next thing I knew Two Charlie was off to the races. Bevans and Frasier were in front of Specialist Randy Humphry and me and we were all running into the night. I didn't know where we were going so I just followed the leader. As a private I learned that it was best to keep your mouth shut and not ask any questions unless it was mission essential or something that directly related to me staying alive. With that said, I didn't ask where we were going or how far we would be running. I just followed them

to an old beat-up transportation bus that looked like it was
confiscated from the Iraqi military after the invasion, hopped
on, and grabbed a seat in the back where the privates sit. As we
drove off everyone was quiet and the only talking going on was
accountability of men and weapons and equipment checks. We
crossed over multiple runways until we pulled up to a massive
white tent that looked more like a hanger. I noticed that the
guys on the bus ahead of us were piling out and running inside
the massive white tent. When our bus stopped we all stood up
and piled out and ran inside the tent as well. Inside the tent
I fell into the platoon formation started by first squad. Once
Bevans, Frasier, and Specialist John Gumpf got an "up" from
Humphry (meaning that everything, including personnel, gear,
and equipment, was accounted for), Specialist Roman and I let
sergeants Cousins and Aaron Hoffman know that we were good
to go, and they passed it on to our squad leader that we were
up. Our squad leader then let our platoon sergeant know that
third squad was up. Immediately following, Bevans and Frasier
pulled me and the other privates in the squad aside and stressed
the importance of moving with a sense of urgency right now.
They told us that we are catching a ride on a Chinook directly
to our final destination—what is commonly known as the green
zone in Baghdad. Bevans then went on to tell us that we need to
continue to move with a purpose when we are wheels down in
Baghdad, because we are looking at a potential target (mission)
tonight, per the platoon leader, who was already in Baghdad.
As I soaked all this up like a sponge, I could still hear mortars
going off in the background. Then, the platoon pallet showed up
on a forklift and the privates of Two Charlie went to work. We

moved as a unit; we could have put a pit crew in NASCAR to shame. Everyone's voice was crystal clear and all communication was to the point. The "no bullshit" attitude from our chain of command set the tone.

Once we got all our mission kits and squad equipment unloaded from the pallet, the madness began. In the midst of our preparations, I thought to myself how cool this was to be in Iraq with an elite group of Rangers preparing for battle. I had dreamt about this and had wanted this for so long; I was finally living that dream. I jumped off of the pallet after throwing out the last kit, and I ran over to a pile of kits and located mine by the OD green name tag that I had sewn onto the carrying handle of my kit. Just as I was instructed, I grabbed all seven "mags" (magazines/clips) off of my kit, ran over to a bin full of ammo, and began to load each mag, one round at a time, until all of them were fully loaded with thirty rounds of 5.56, making for what we call a combat load.

As I put my mags back into my mag pouches in uniformity— all facing the same direction as I had trained to do. Each mag was placed just right so that in an event that I needed to do a mag change in combat, I would be able to grab one and insert it into my M4 out of muscle memory. After double checking everything I let Bevans know that I was up and ready to rock. Bevans shouted back, "Good. Now hurry up and get all your gear on for the final manifest call." I said, "Roger that," and in a few seconds, I had slipped my kit on over my shoulders, pulled my NODs out of my assault pack, and attached them to the mount on my helmet. Once I snap-linked a piece of paracord

tied to my night vision goggles via a bowline knot, I hooked
the paracord to a secure point on my helmet with a snap link
attached at the end of the cord. Double checking to make sure
they were on snug, I then threw my helmet on and buckled my
chin strap. Next, I pulled my weapon out of my weapons case
and began to check the optics, lights, and lasers on my weapon.
After checking my weapon, I pressed the selector button to
drop down my PVS -14 (single tube NODs) night vision to
make sure it was focused. I then grabbed the squad "donker"
(a one-man battering ram breaching tool used to knock out
door handles or to simply knock doors down) from the squad
equipment and set it down by my assault pack. I was ready to
go.

While we stood in formation I noticed an NCO from the 75th
Ranger Regiment Headquarters had begun to start the final
manifest roll call. As he went down the list calling off each and
every Ranger in the platoon and assigning us our Chinook, we
were finally good to go to Baghdad. Without wasting any time,
Two Charlie filed out of the white tent/hanger and loaded onto
the two buses that were to take us to the two Chinooks waiting
for us. As we were driving out to the Chinooks in the darkness,
and with sirens and mortar explosions still popping off in the
background, my buddy Randy Humphry looked over at me and
said, "I guess this is Iraq." I just looked back at him and said,
"Yeah, I guess it is."

A minute later we pulled up to the Chinooks and got off the
bus. I could hear the rotors warming up and the engine getting
louder and louder and then the twin rotors began to start

spinning, making for a thunderous "thud, thud, thud," until the rotors started to spin so fast that the Chinook just vibrated on the four rubber wheels beneath it. I ran onto the Chinook and went to sit down, and like an idiot, I sat down in a seat that lined the skin of the aircraft. To my surprise, I was ripped out of the seat so fast by Sergeant Cousins that my head spun. When Two Charlie went anywhere—whether it was in the states or overseas—privates and specialists without a Ranger Tab always sat on the floor, leaving the comfortable seats for the tabbed specialists, team leaders, and seasoned squad leaders. In Ranger Battalion there is a hierarchy and you had better know your place or someone will put you in it for you. As I was thrown down onto the floor of the aircraft and yelled at for even thinking I could sit down, I just shook my head out of disappointment like a beat dog. I knew better than to think I deserved a seat, and as I sat amongst the other privates, I began to unhook my snap link from my rigger belt to hook into the secure points on the floor of the helicopter. Due to the mortars still impacting inside the wire of the Balad FOB (forward operating base), there was a sense of urgency in the air that did not have to be explained. Through my night vision tube, I could see the flight crew working with a sense of urgency, checking to make sure the pallet with all our gear and luggage was loaded properly. Then it looked like the flight crew made a few radio calls, and in sequence the Chinook began to move forward and lift off the ground and flew toward Baghdad.

During the flight to Baghdad my shoulders were used as a foot rest, and I was pushed around repetitively by more senior guys who were trying to get comfortable until we finally landed in

Baghdad. It was the most uncomfortable helicopter ride of
my career and my butt cheeks and legs were completely numb
from not being able to adjust my sitting position. As I stood up
I began to get blood flow back to my feet, regaining feeling as
I tried to walk but looking like I had a load in my pants. Once
I got all feeling back, I quickly ran off the back of the Chinook
into the night once again. As we were running across the tarmac
to the opposite side of the airfield, I was trying to figure out how
to best hold the twenty-pound donker that kept hitting the tip
of my M4. Not paying attention to where I was going, I was
taken by surprise when a Chinook flew over my head. It had
taken off at the end of the airfield, and because I was too busy
worrying about the damn donker in my hand, I ran directly
underneath it. The twin rotors of the Chinook, which was about
twenty feet over my head, lifted my feet off of the ground and
carried me about two feet to my left in the direction of travel the
Chinook was headed. Not until the helicopter flew completely
past did I finally land back on the concrete tarmac. Luckily
and surprisingly, I landed on my feet and was able to regain
my balance even with the donker still in hand. As I gained my
center of gravity, I started running faster toward the rest of the
platoon, talking to myself out loud saying, "The hell with this
damn donker." I adjusted my grip on the handle of the donker
with my left hand, curling the arm holding the donker at my
waist, and I was finally able to run at a decent pace.

I continued to run into the dark night, still was clueless on
what was going on, but I noticed that all of Two Charlie was
loading up on and in a flatbed truck, white van, and an old beat
up black BMW. I hopped onto the flatbed truck with my team

leader and Bevans, and we began to drive off. I tried to revert to rule number one and look cool. As I sat with my chest out and head high, I noticed a platoon of Rangers from the 3rd Ranger Battalion standing off to the side of the flight line going through a final manifest call. These Rangers just finished a ninety to one-hundred day rotation and were going home to Columbus, Georgia. The first leg of the trip was on the Chinook we just got off of. I thought about how excited they must be to be able to go home after such an amazing accomplishment, but then I was reminded that I hadn't done anything yet.

After a short ride down a road lined with houses on one side and a twenty-foot wall on the other, we pulled into the gate and up a driveway of house number seven. As I looked around I noticed six Strykers under a long tin roof. Not knowing it at the time, but for the duration of my deployment those Strykers were going to be the means of my existence and life. The houses that lined this road next to the airfield housed the Iraqi Republican Guard prior to the invasion. Each of the seven houses lining the road housed a special operations unit. When looking at our house from the road, to our left was where a team of Green Berets lived, to our immediate right was where the Royal Airborne Infantry Unit from the British Army lived, and to the right of the British house a tank platoon from the 1st Cavalry was housed.

When the flatbed truck stopped, I hopped down and Bevans shouted at me to hurry up and follow him. As I ran up the driveway that leads to the front door, I passed an Iraqi interpreter sitting on a chair smoking a cigarette and gave him a head nod. After running through the cloud of smoke that did not smell too different from the Iraq air, I walked into the house where I would spend the duration of my first deployment. Surprisingly, the house was equipped with phones to call home, washers, dryers, a functional kitchen, and a TOC (tactical operating center) that had three flat screen TVs hung up on the wall to monitor satellite imagery and to be used by the platoon leader and platoon sergeant to pitch operations orders and mission briefs to the platoon. Later on I would find out that the backyard had a wooden shoot house for training on room entering and room clearing as well as a pool that me and the other privates would later clean out and fill up. There was also a volleyball court that would be manicured by the Two Charlie privates every day prior to the NCO vs. tab Spec 4 matches that were held every morning after the period of darkness.

Once we came to a bedroom, Bevans told me to drop off any gear that I wouldn't need for a mission. I threw my assault pack on a bottom bunk mattress, and as I did so Gumpf and Humphry claimed a bed as well. Sergeant Hoffman came in the room and told us that we are looking at a mission. Like we trained for, it was going to be the first of many joint operations with other Special Operations Forces. Immediately I thought to myself, "Where do I fit into this equation?" And just like always, I was told by my team leader what I was going to do. He followed up and told me to get out to the front yard of the house and link in with weapons squad and Corporal Wyatt. Sergeant Hoffman told me that I was going to be the .50-caliber machine gunner for Corporal Wyatt's Stryker, and I would be reporting to him whenever we have a mission involving Strykers from here on out.

I ran out of the house and into the dark, dusty Iraq night toward the Stryker closest to the house that was identified with a wooden placard zip tied to the RPG-protective armor surrounding the Stryker with the number six on it. The six was glint tape (infrared reflective tape) and 100-mile-an-hour taped (duct tape) so that it could be seen through at night. Before I even made it inside the Stryker, my Ranger buddy Private First Class Bryan popped his head out of the driver hatch and said, "Are you on this one?" I shouted back over the diesel engine, "Sure am." It was Bryan's first deployment as well and together we began to conduct a PMCS on the Stryker.

Bryan was the driver so it was his job to check all the fluids and make sure everything was good to go with the tires and anything else related to the mechanics of the vehicle. As the machine gunner it was my job to make sure the machine gun was good to go as well as the radio and all communications devices. So first things first—just like I was trained to do—I started up the RWS (remote weapons system) and then hopped up onto the roof through a small circular hole known as the gunner's hatch to check on the .50-caliber machine gun. After ripping off the cover and unleashing the beast, I noticed it was pretty dusty. Before doing anything else, I grabbed a rag and wiped her down and then picked up a bottle of CLP (cleaning lubricant protectant) out of a cage on the side of the Stryker and applied a light coat of oil all over the weapon with the rag. After wiping her down I pulled back the charging handle and sprayed two squirts of CLP directly into the moving parts of the

machine gun and then rode the bolt forward. After taking care
of everything up top, I could hear the RWS begin to boot up
and go through an automatic series of computer checks. Before
the weapon started to spin in a full 360 degrees on its own, I
jumped back down through the gunner's hatch. As I maneuvered
around my soon-to-be gunner's seat, I turned on all of the
radios. To my surprise, Corporal Wyatt showed up at about
the same time that I finished running the PMCS duties for the
.50-caliber machine gun.

Corporal Wyatt didn't say anything and went straight to work.
Before going through his routine inspections of the overall status
of our vehicle, he unslung his M4 off of his shoulder and laid it
on its side in front of a ballistic plate on top of the Stryker on
the front end of the TC (tactical commander) hatch. As I waited
for further instructions, our platoon sergeant and the rest of the
crew of Rangers we were taking to a fight started to load up and
grab a seat. At about that time Corporal Wyatt made a few radio
checks with the vehicles in the convoy and quickly ordered me
to raise the back hatch. I said, "Roger that," and turned around
and told the crew members that I was about to raise the hatch—
basically telling them to watch their hands and feet so they don't
get cut off by the hydraulic lift that was about to raise a door
that weighs close to five hundred pounds. Once it was closed I
shouted up through the TC hatch to let Corporal Wyatt know
we were good to go. Wyatt waited for his turn, and then came
over the radio and said, "We are good to go." We were ready to
roll. Immediately following Wyatt's radio call, the ground force
commander gave us the green light and the convoy started to roll
out into the night taking sixty highly trained Army Rangers to

seek and destroy the enemy.

As we rolled out of the gates of the house, passing by the airfield we had just landed in about an hour ago, I hopped up through the gunner's hatch and aircraft-loaded the .50-caliber machine gun and then hopped back down closing the hatch behind me, orienting the machine gun to the vehicle's six o'clock. As the trail vehicle, I was in charge of rear security and had an M2 .50-caliber machine gun with a max distance of 6,764 meters and a muzzle velocity of 3,050 feet per second. Once we went through jersey barriers leading us out of the green zone and into the red zone of Baghdad, Corporal Wyatt made an internal radio call telling me to charge the .50-cal, chamber a round.

Over the course of the next month and a half I went out on numerous missions as the .50-caliber machine gunner with Corporal Wyatt and Private First Class Bryan. Sometimes we would even go out twice a night. I learned a lot and soaked up as much knowledge as I could while out on target. More importantly, I learned a lot about direct action missions and the processes of setting the conditions and standards for a task force to surgically take down target buildings and compounds. I also became more proficient at Ranger combat battle drills from the platoon training that was conducted in the rocks out in front of the house we lived in by Two Charlie's specialists, corporals, and team leaders every day after the 1600 PMCS of the Strykers. When I was informed that there was a PT test coming up and Two Charlie was planning on sending two privates to Ranger School, my ears perked. The platoon takes everything into consideration during selections, from how you performed on target to how you handle yourself, but the difference maker is always the PT test.

A few days later I was walking back from KP (kitchen patrol) duty one morning listening to the annoying Muslim prayer that was blasted on loud speakers throughout Baghdad. I was thinking about how bad I wanted to have a chance at Ranger School. To my surprise the entire platoon was waiting for me to get back from KP so that we could start the PT test. With hardly any sleep due to the mission from the night before and having to do KP, I grabbed a "Rip It" energy drink and slammed it. A few minutes later we were off to the races doing as many push-ups and sit-ups as possible in two minutes and running five miles followed by max strict pull- ups. On fumes, I destroyed everyone and won the five-miler and did the most push-ups in two minutes out of all the privates. After the PT test my squad leader, team leader, and Bevans pulled me aside and said, "Good job, you are going to Pre-Ranger, and if you pass that you will go to Ranger School." He then followed up and said that I would be going home on the mid-rotator bird back to Savannah next week. Not knowing how to contain myself, I just said, "Roger, sergeant," and kept my mouth shut. My squad leader then looked me square in the eyes and said, "Don't come back without it." It was common for these famous words to be said before you left for Ranger School, because it was usually a one chance deal, and if you did not pass Ranger School you were RFS'd.

There was a sudden change in the mood of my squad. It seemed as if I had a little more respect from Bevans and Frasier. After all, it was their job to get me ready for Ranger School and to mold me into a Ranger. As I lay in my bunk trying to get some rack before the upcoming period of darkness, I felt a sense of accomplishment and was one step closer to becoming a respected Ranger amongst Two Charlie. During the daily poop meeting we received at the beginning of every period of darkness from Staff Sergeant Bench, we were told that Two Charlie was assigned as a QRF (quick reaction force) element for the Army's special mission unit. Unlike the past, I was actually on the manifest and my team leader told me to get my gear ready. After going over my gear and making sure I had everything, double and triple checking to make sure all my batteries were good to go for my weapon optics and night vision goggles, I was ready to be inspected.

After my team leader, Sergeant Hoffman, went over all of my gear, he handed me the squad medical bag and the collapsible litter and told me that I was going to carry this. The litter and med bag were combined into one huge shoulder-carried bag that you wore like a backpack, and as I grabbed the shoulder strap I said, "Roger that, sergeant." I then asked what my duties were for the mission. Without saying much, Sergeant Hoffman grabbed a GRG out of his cargo pocket and put it onto the table that was in the middle of our squad ready room. He pointed at a rooftop door and said, "You are going to fast rope on top of this roof here and link in with another Special Operations Forces unit and clear from the rooftop down to the main floor." As I continued to listen to my team leader, I thought to myself, "How in the hell am I, a cherry private, going to fit into a stack?" I began to get nervous and the look on my face definitely showed it. When Sergeant Hoffman looked up at me and asked if I was good to go, he busted out laughing because of the look of my face.

It was a huge joke and Sergeant Hoffman said, "There is no way in hell you are clearing a room with those guys. Instead, you are going to stay with me and do whatever I tell you, and all you need to know is that we are going to the flight line and will be staged and ready with a couple of Blackhawks, and if these guys get into a tic (fight) we are going to get called in. Basically, the mission is just be ready, and if help is needed we are going in." I felt like the world had just been lifted off my shoulders, and I couldn't help but laugh at myself along with the guys in the squad as we donned our mission gear and headed to the flight line.

A few days later I was packing my bags and getting ready to fly back to Balad on a Chinook with another private who was heading back to go to Ranger School with me. On my way out of the house that night to catch my flight home, my squad leader came up to me and said, "Go to the squad room and open the door and yell at the top of your lungs, 'I'm going to Ranger School and there isn't a damn thing you can do about it!'" My initial reaction to this statement was a smirk and a laugh, because I thought there is no way that he could be serious right now. Besides, they were sleeping and I just wanted to get out the back door without them even knowing. As my squad leader stood there staring back at me, I knew he was serious.

After a moment of silence I said, "Roger, sergeant," and slowly walked up to the hooch door where Bevans, Frasier, Cousins, and my team leader were sleeping. As I slowly opened the door trying not to wake them, I thought to myself "screw it," and screamed at the top of my lungs into the pitch black room, "I'm going to Ranger School and there isn't a damn thing you can do about it!" My squad leader started laughing hysterically, but I, on the other hand, ran straight out the front door as fast as I could screaming at my Ranger buddy to throw my luggage on the back of the truck. I knew it was only a matter of minutes before Bevans would be out in his Ranger panties screaming at me to do push-ups.

At that exact moment I saw my team leader come running out in his crocs yelling at the top of his lungs for me to start pushing. I was very surprised to see that he was the first one to make it out here and soon enough the rest of the squad followed. As I threw my feet up on the bed of the pickup truck, I was doing push-ups again. This time I was in full kit with my hands down in the rocks that made up the front yard of our house. After continuing to do push-ups and getting yelled at, I started to get nervous that I was going to miss my flight to Balad, and thanks to the air NCO (the NCO in charge of scheduling flights), he said that they had to wrap things up, but before doing so I did an extra push-up for the Airborne Ranger in the sky and shook my team leader's hand. I hopped onto the tailgate of the truck and headed to the flight line with a destination of Ranger School.

Before heading back home, I stopped in Baghdad and was assigned to the headquarters unit there while I waited to catch a ride home for Ranger School. I was starting to get antsy to get back and get Ranger School started when I heard that Two

Charlie hit an IED and my Ranger buddy Roland Vaughan was severely wounded. Vaughan was a .50-caliber machine gunner, but I had no idea what the details were or the extent of his injuries. I was feeling anxious to get back, but this news put everything into perspective for me and made me feel guilty that I was not there for my Ranger buddy.

I later found out that he was the vehicle two machine gunner and his vehicle commander, Sergeant Michael, pulled him out of the hatch after the explosion and got him to the platoon medic. Vaughan's life was saved because of how fast and efficient the platoon operated. Two Charlie had Vaughan evacuated and in surgery in less than twenty minutes. Vaughan would spend the next year in and out of surgery and rehab until given the opportunity to return to his platoon. Vaughan could have been medically retired from the army, but he wanted to come back to Two Charlie to finish out his enlistment, earn his Ranger Tab— which he did—and go back overseas to kick doors in.

I linked in with the support company of 1st Battalion while I was in Balad, and being that I was a private, I was assigned some details and guard shifts. Not knowing who I was supposed to report to, I just kind of found a routine for the few days that I was there and continued to do PT to maintain my fitness for the Ranger School PT test. Summer was almost in full force and the heat index in Balad was reaching almost 130 degrees. This dangerous heat was very obvious one day when another Ranger buddy and I were getting "smoked" for being late to a formation that we were never even informed of by someone I had never even seen. I began to get pissed and was tired of the games that you have to play as a Ranger private. This incident just fueled me to be more serious about graduating Ranger School. After close to an hour had gone by of doing repetitive elevated push-ups, rope climbs, and overhead lunges while holding a case of water jugs over our heads in 130-degree heat index, we were finally allowed to stop when my Ranger buddy passed out, tits up. What started out as remedial punishment for not being on time to a formation nobody told us about got serious real fast. Without wasting a second, the NCO ran to the medic station while I was pouring water all over my Ranger buddy trying to get his body temperature to cool off. When the medics came back with a gator, we loaded him up on a stretcher and hurried off to the medic's station. After an IV and an anal thermometer to get his core temperature, he came to and started to get color back in his face; he didn't remember a thing. Looking at my buddy, I felt pretty bad about what had happened and so did the NCO who was "smoking" us. I believe the NCO that smoked us was more relieved that he wasn't going to lose his job now that my Ranger buddy is ok. Thankfully, everyone was all right and my buddy was taken back on the gator to our hooch to recover. Our saving grace showed up the next day, and we loaded up on a C-17 headed for Hunter Army Airfield.

RANGER SCHOOL

"When we camp, half the party stays awake while the other half sleeps."

- Major Robert Rogers, 1759, 9th Standing Order

To graduate Ranger School, in my opinion, is seventy percent
mental, twenty percent physical, and ten percent luck. Due to
the lack of sleep, lack of food, and lack of comfort items, and
having to battle the elements provided by good ole mother
nature, graduating is a pain in the you-know-what. Not only do
you have these odds against you, but you also have the pissed off
RI (Ranger Instructor) grading your patrols and who have it out
for you and want to make your life a living hell. There is always a
chance that your RI might be in a fight with his wife and didn't
get any TLC the night before your patrol, and out of anger and
sexual frustration, he has already made up his mind that he is
going to give you a "No Go" (fail, do not pass) just because
he can. If you start to feel sorry for yourself in Ranger School,
you will most likely not pass a patrol and will end up having to
repeat a phase, or even worse, quit and never graduate. If you go
"straight through" (do not get recycled or have to repeat a phase)
Ranger School, you will spend sixty-one days fueled only by two
MREs (meals ready-to-eat), living in the woods, and sleeping in
the red Georgia clay, Blue Ridge Mountain dirt, and the black
water and sand of the Florida swamps.

Throughout your time in Ranger School you will only get a
few hours of rack a day—sometimes none at all. Every day
you will hump twelve to fifteen clicks (kilometers) with a
sixty-pound rucksack and lead men that are in a delirious and
confused state of mind. While you are trying to muster up
the strength to lead and motivate, you have only your Ranger
buddy to count on. My Ranger buddy was Pedro Lacerda up
until mountain phase when he was recycled for failing a patrol.
Pedro, a native Brazilian, and I became friends during Pre-

Ranger Course while sucking it up on the twelve-mile forced ruck march out to Cole Range for a field training exercise that all Ranger Regiment guys have to go through and pass before attending Ranger School. Pre-Ranger is about four weeks long and the culmination is a nine-day field training exercise to help us get ready for Ranger School. Although Pedro Lacerda was recycled in mountains, I got back in touch with him in 2009 while I was living and training in Columbus, Georgia, for the Best Ranger Competition. Staff Sergeant Lacerda unexpectedly died of a brain aneurism in 2010 after collapsing on a routine morning conducting PT with his squad-sized element of RASP candidates. Lacerda was known as the most lethal Ranger with his hands, winning the Gold Medals in Jiu Jitsu at the 1999, 2000, and 2001 Pan AM Games. He will be forever missed.

After passing Pre-Ranger, I got my packing list ready for Darby phase, the first phase of Ranger School, at the same barracks I lived in for RIP just six months ago. After going over the list and double and triple checking it, I was finally able to relax and get some rack before the early wake up call to report to day one of Ranger School. Just my luck, it turns out that the next three weeks were going to be hotter than hell. The temperature during my Darby phase was the hottest month ever recorded in Ranger School up to that point. It was so hot that on our first mission we would walk fifteen feet and have to stop and take a knee, because a Ranger went down as a heat casualty. This happened every thirty minutes on day one. We were losing so many Rangers to heat injuries that it seemed like it took us an eternity just to move a click. I am not sure what the exact statistic was, but it seemed that we would lose approximately two Rangers every kilometer we traveled during the day. Even worse, we would have to cross load and carry all the sensitive equipment that each heat casualty Ranger was responsible for to complete the missions. Having to hump someone else's stuff didn't exactly help morale. Instead, it increased the amount of weight for each of us who were still trying to survive and get a "Go." When the Ranger candidates were medevac'd out, it would be the last that we saw them. If you are documented as going down with a hot weather injury, you were not allowed to return to Ranger School or any other military school during the summer months, because you would be more prone to another heat injury.

It was so hot in August of 2007 that we didn't even care that we were pissing on ourselves. During our movements through the Fort Benning woods we got used to just hanging our locators out of our Army combat uniforms and commenced pissing all over our pant legs and boots as we walked. It was not an uncommon sight to see the leadership huddled in a circle taking a knee, looking at a map, and going over the plan and all the while a Ranger was just pissing on his pants and boots and carrying on like nothing out of the ordinary was happening.

Until Darby phase I had never experienced the feeling of salt crystals clogging my skin pores. On one particular mission I was getting down in the prone to pull security, and as I laid in what I thought was a thorn bush, I immediately jumped up. I had a prickly sensation that spread all over my body and it felt so terrible that I jumped up like one would if he were stung by a bee. I immediately looked down at the ground, grabbed my skin, and realized that there was no thorns or briar patch on the ground. I didn't fully understand what was going on and started to try and scrape my skin to get the sensation to go away. What I was later told was that the salt from sweat had clogged my pores, and as I was beginning to sweat again, the salt crystals were blocking the sweat and creating a stinging sensation. The pain only worsened until sweat was able to flush the crystals out, allowing me to perspire again.

Passing the Darby phase was not the least bit easy for me. In fact, it was the hardest phase for me due to the heat. My first graded patrol was a disaster and I, along with a few other Rangers, almost went down as a heat casualty. What was supposed to look like a lethal platoon of Rangers conducting an ambush and walking stealthily through the woods looked more like a group of zombies trudging through the woods and slowly going through the motions of an ambush like some kids playing army. You didn't have to be a rocket scientist to know that I was going to get a "No Go" for my patrol as platoon leader (PL). It was so apparent that I screwed up that when we finally got to our patrol base after a twelve click walk around midnight I didn't even bother trying to keep a security element awake. I just let everyone get some rack—including me— so that the next day we would be fresh and ready to go. After an MRE and some time to reflect on my worst day of Ranger School, I learned a valuable lesson. As the PL for actions on the objective, I was too worried about what everyone else was doing. I learned from this experience that as a leader you must trust that your men know and understand the plan to action the mission and tasks at hand. Completing the mission is best accomplished when you are clear and concise with the task, conditions, and standards when disseminating your plan to a platoon, squad, or team.

When we finally were told at the end of Darby phase who was moving on to the next phase, I was told I received a "Go" on my second patrol as squad leader and received the highest peer rating from my fellow Ranger buddies. While waiting for the Greyhound bus to take us to mountain phase with the rest of the Rangers that passed, I tried to heal a bad case of pitting edema in my legs, heat rash, and a pain and discomfort in my left groin that continued to worsen. The pain was a left inguinal hernia that I had assessed by a PA (physician assistant) on a cot in the Ranger School barracks who was going through Ranger School in the same company as me. When he mentioned that this could be bad enough to be "med drop" (release for medical issues), I couldn't believe it. As I continued to think on what to do, I told myself, "The hell with it … I don't care if it bursts out. I am going to graduate." Besides, I only had two more phases to go and I sure as hell didn't want to do Darby phase again. With that said, I just drove on and did not tell another soul out of fear that an RI would find out and force me to seek medical attention. I was not about to quit. Each day as I felt pain in my groin, I just reminded myself that I am one day closer to graduation. So, I hopped on the bus headed to Camp Merrill in Dahlonega, Georgia.

MOUNTAIN PHASE

"Don't Forget Nothing."

- Major Robert Rogers, 1759, 1st Standing Order

Mountain phase was a relief for me; the temperature had cooled off and the chow hall served the famous blueberry pancakes that I had been hearing about. Before the field training exercise with graded patrols in the Blue Ridge Mountains we had to get through a five-day mountaineering skills portion of what is called "lowers," which is evaluated and graded. In the lower mountaineering phase, we learned how to do everything from knot and rope tying, building rope bridges, and the basic fundamentals of climbing and rappelling so that we could conduct these skills as a team during patrols later in mountain phase. Before a block of instruction during "lowers," while I was maintaining my side lateral step through the chow hall with my eyes straight forward and not looking at anything but the kitchen wall in front of me, like I was supposed to, I tried to sneak an additional plate of blueberry pancakes. We were only allowed to have one plate of two blueberry pancakes, but I wanted more food and in my genius spur of the moment plan, I attempted to snag an extra plate of the delicious blueberry pancakes. I made it to the end of the line, and as I was about to do an about-face and head toward a seat in the chow hall, I was called out by one of the cooks. She screamed at me to stop and came out from behind the kitchen, grabbed both of my pancake plates, and threw them in the back of the kitchen like a frisbee. As my blueberry pancakes flew like saucers, smashing into the wall, I quickly straightened up as she threatened to tell the RIs. Instead of having the potential extra pancakes, I was left to having none. It was a hard morning with no pancakes.

The culmination of "lowers" was closing in on us and the dreaded knot test, which you have one chance at, was later that afternoon so I quickly forgot about the blueberry pancakes and moved on. After completing the knot test and earning a "Go," it was time to prepare for the upper mountaineering phase, which is a two-day exercise with the infamous "rescue Randy" mission on Mount Yonah. Randy is a two-hundred-pound mass of rubber that is dead weight to simulate a down Ranger. During the rescue Randy mission everything that you learned at "lowers" is put to the test, including getting Randy medevac'd off of the mountain with a nine line, a standard radio call format for calling in a medivac.

After a successful short stay at Mount Yonah with the mountaineering week in the past it was time to start the field training exercise. Everyone that has been to Ranger School always talks about how steep the mountains are in Georgia and how the terrain will destroy you. I use to camp and hike in the North Georgia mountains as a kid so I had an idea of what I was getting myself into. On our first mission we walked right out the backside of Camp Merrill near the Appalachian Trail, and I began thinking about when I went on a camping trip in middle school with my friends and our dads. I remembered finding MRE trash left by Rangers. As a young kid I had hoped that we would see a platoon of Rangers while we were on our hiking/camping trip, but we never did. I thought they were like ghosts that were most likely watching us as we sat by the campfire.

My trip down memory lane came to an end when my roster number, "187," was called after the first mission. My first graded position was as the primary assault squad leader on the second mission of mountain phase. I was excited to get after it right off the bat and was very excited that I got to be the assault squad leader. All the practice on the rocks in Baghdad, Iraq, on my first deployment was about to pay off. Unlike Darby phase I was a lot less affected by the elements and this time I had a clear understanding on how to lead my squad to conduct an ambush in a known area of insurgents located fifteen kilometers away from our current grid location.

Intelligence said that the insurgents would be at a known grid location between the hours of 1500 to 1700 the following day. With this in mind, our platoon planned to walk most of the distance during the evening and night and set in a patrol base so that we could clean our weapons and conduct an operations order for the upcoming mission. As we were approaching our patrol base, we were ambushed by combatants, and as the primary assault squad leader, I reacted to the ambush and got my two teams on line, and we assaulted through the ambush with bounding overwatch maneuvers, killing the combatants (with blank ammunition). As a platoon we fought through the ambush effectively without any casualties or fratricide. After conducting necessary post react-to-ambush tasks, we quickly moved out of the area and arrived to our designated patrol base location and set in security for the night. Once security was set and each individual was designated their sectors of fire, I began to fill out a sector sketch to reflect our squad's sectors of fire, including the fully automatic machine gun from weapons squad and our claymore, which was set out fifteen meters in front of us.

The nights seemed like they always took forever, but when you're in a graded leadership position like I was that night, time always flew by, and before I knew it I could see the RIs were starting to show up through the shadows of the moonlight. Before the sun rose the RIs were walking around trying to find a sleeping Ranger so that they could slit their throat with a red marker, or worse, simulate an attack and "blow us in place," because too many Rangers were sleeping while on security. My squad security was awake and so was the rest of the platoon; it was a perfect patrol base and there was not a throat slit. When there is a bad patrol base and the platoon is for some reason acting lazy, RIs will simulate with mortar rounds and small arms fire from the sleeping Rangers weapons, and the next thing you know we are having to pick up and move out to our designated grid location as an escape and evade maneuver, but luckily this did not happen today.

Throughout the remainder of mountain phase I was the RTO (radio telephone operator) twice and the medic once; I never had another graded patrol. Once we got back to Camp Merrill after completing the field training exercise, we received our one-on-one AAR from the RIs and I was informed that I was a first time "Go." My peer rating was not the highest in my class like it was in Darby phase, but it was high enough to keep me in the running for honor grad.

After the AAR a couple of Rangers and I, all of whom were up for honor grad, went to meet with the colonel for a meeting/interview.

The next morning everyone who got a "Go" loaded up on Greyhound buses and we headed to Dobbins Air Force Base. I took complete advantage of the bus ride down to Dobbins and slept most the way, trying to catch up on some rack. When we arrived at Dobbins Air Force Base in Atlanta to get rigged up with parachutes for the upcoming jump into Florida phase, an RI told me that it was the opening day of deer season. I thought how cool it would be to be hunting this morning instead of jumping out of a perfectly good airplane to start a new phase of Ranger School. Once we loaded up on the C-130s and flew to Eglin Air Force Base, I managed to watch the back of my eye lids again, despite the noise of the C-130's propellers. I don't think I fully woke up till the sudden jerk of my canopy opening on my descent into Eglin, and when I hit the ground I hurried to the assembly area and was immediately yelled at by an RI to get in a truck with the rest of the Rangers. As I waddled over to the truck with my parachute and gear, the RI shouted at me after a radio call he received and said, "Hey, dumbass, you jumped out on a red light." When he said that I was immediately surprised; I had no idea. When the jump light switched from green to red is still a mystery to me, because I think I might have walked off that C-130 with my eyes closed, just going through the motions. This was just more evidence of how tired you get in Ranger School; to think that I was half asleep when I jumped out of the C-130 is crazy now, but then it was just another day. Not thinking anything of it I just said, "Roger, sergeant," and moved out to the truck and off we went to Camp Rudder.

FLORIDA PHASE

*"If we strike swamps, or soft
ground, we spread out abreast,
so it's hard to track us."*

- Major Robert Rogers, 1759, 7th Standing Order

On day one of Florida phase, we went through the normal, dreaded "lay out" of equipment like we did in the beginning of the past two phases where the RIs would come around and check our gear to make sure that we had everything on the packing list. It was at this time that all the chewing tobacco was being hidden in random places and everyone was scared to death that they would be caught with their only saving grace while pulling security; mine was anything that had tobacco in it. If I didn't have tobacco I would dip the coffee beans found in an MRE to help pass time. If you were caught not having something on the packing list, despite any reason you may have for missing something as simple as a pair of socks, it went down in your file as a negative mark connected to your roster number. If you received too many negative marks, you would be considered for recycle. Once the pain of having to go through this process of making sure that all our equipment was dress-right-dress to the RI's standard and the inspection was completed by our new RIs, we quickly threw everything back into our rucks as if it was a contest to see how fast you could pack.

Finally, it was time for classes on the reptiles and amphibians that can be found in the swamps of Florida. Over the course of a day we were taught everything from emergency first-aid procedures in the chance we were to get bitten by a venomous snake while on patrol in the swamps as well as given the opportunity to handle the non-venomous snakes that the RIs were using to give the classes. While conducing classes like this in Ranger School was fun and informative, it was also a time for comic relief, because it never failed that Rangers would fall asleep in less than a minute after taking a seat. Looking around

the classroom, as I tried my best to stay awake, it looked like
Rangers were head bobbing. Some would fall asleep so hard
that their heads would smack the desk as if they were trying to
headbutt through their wooden desks. The last thing you wanted
to do was get caught sleeping, so in a matter of fifteen minutes
we were all standing up to stay awake.

After the conclusion of our amphibians and reptiles classes,
we went to the swamps and learned stream crossing methods
with rope bridges, techniques on how to insert and exit a
Zodiac (rigid inflatable boat), and how to maneuver Zodiacs
in the swamps and in the ocean. Due to the more in-depth
planning and complex missions that we were preparing for in
Florida phase, the RIs do not have to create as much stress as
the previous two phases; in this phase, the stress is created on
its own. Florida phase was the last phase and the culmination
of everything we learned to be as a leader, and it was time to
put our skills to the test. Our first mission was an airborne
operation, parachuting into an all-out raid mission. After a
successful jump—without jumping out on a red light—and
completing the mission as a team leader, I waited for my graded
patrol.

Halfway through the field training exercise my roster number,
"187," was finally called so that I could now be evaluated on a
graded leadership position. I was assigned to be the assault squad
leader. After navigating my squad's Zodiac through the bending
and winding river and through the swamp, we beached our
Zodiacs and began to maneuver to the target. My squad was last
in the order of movement, and when I noticed that the PL of

the mission had made the idiotic decision to walk the lead squad through an open field and not utilize the wood line as cover and concealment for security, I knew that if I did not stop this I would get a "No Go." Immediately, I got on the radio and tried to get the PL to get the platoon back into the wood line. The PL took it as a sign of insubordination and continued to drive on, eventually exposing the entire platoon in the open field. At this moment I knew I was a "No Go" and might as well have lit up a cigar, but I decided that I would try and make up for the effect of the PL's bad decision with my squad's actions on the objective.

My efforts to make up for this mistake were basically in vain, which was confirmed when my roster number, "187," was called for a graded patrol position as the security squad leader for the last mission of the field training exercise and for class 10/07 of Ranger School. I knew that this was a second chance and that I had to get a "Go." The pressure was on and if I didn't get a "Go" I would be recycled into class 11/07. Before my roster number was called, I was digging my fighting position in the patrol base talking to my Ranger buddy about what I was going to do when I graduate. It was a good morning. The remnants of Hurricane Humberto, which had dropped rain on us for the past two to three straight days, finally let up and we were in a good mood because it was the last day of Ranger School. Once my roster number was called, my mood changed and I took my aggression out with my entrenching tool (shovel) and beat it repetitively into the dirt like a mad man and did so for about ten seconds to get my frustrations out.

Everyone was on their last ounce of energy; we were all

exhausted and no one had any motivation. It was the most tired I had ever been and knew that I was also not at my finest, because just a few days ago I slept-walked in the patrol base from my security position and was supposedly talking to myself, but no one else had enough energy to know what I was doing. They all just thought I was walking the line. Needless to say, this kind of activity was of the norm by this point. We were all exhausted and ready for this Ranger School experience to be over. Knowing that everyone was unmotivated, including me, I had to immediately switch gears and do my best to get motivated, and more importantly, motivate my Ranger buddies. Our mission was to conduct a raid at a known area of insurgents with patrolling security at an insurgent compound. Our platoon would have to overcome a very strict timeline. If we were thirty seconds late everyone in a graded position would receive a "No Go." The good part about our infiltration is that we would be inserting via helicopter and to an HLZ (helicopter landing zone) approximately four kilometers away from the target. My squad was the lead element and would be responsible for navigating and getting to the target on time. Not only was my squad only half awake, but we were also beat up. One Ranger buddy in my squad had a busted bursa sac in his knee and could barely walk let alone run. Just a few days ago this Ranger fell asleep standing during an AAR that was conducted by the Ranger Training Brigade First Sergeant. It was a sight that I doubt I will ever see again and the first sergeant giving the AAR said that in all the years he had been in the army, he had never seen that happen. Everyone was laughing, but this Ranger was literally hurt. Usually people wake up and end up catching themselves mid-fall and do a little stutter step, but not this Ranger. He didn't wake up till he hit the ground and was rudely awaken when gravity took affect and his face and knees hit the pavement. He hit so hard that you could hear the crunch of his face hit the pavement that we were standing on.

These factors are why no one ever wants to rely on trying to get a "Go" on the last day of Ranger School. Just to make it clear, having a graded mission on the last day of school is the mythical kiss of death, because everyone else that is not being graded is already thinking about the beers they will get later tonight at the Gator Lounge. Not taking another minute to think about the odds against me, I went to work and planned out the mission with the rest of the leadership who were in the same boat.

The morning was going smoothly and the operations order seemed to be a success. As we loaded up on the helicopters and took off toward the HLZ, I got a sudden second burst of energy created by the thunderous rotors on the Blackhawk. Once we touched down everyone exfilled the helicopter with a sense of urgency and security was set in. Once the helicopters lifted off it was go time and my squad started to lead out toward the target. I paid close attention to my watch, keeping in mind the "no later than time" (NLT) set by the RIs; I knew we had to move out with a sense of urgency or we would not make it. We were moving out at a brisk walk, but I began to pick up the pace to almost a jog until I realized that the platoon was beginning to spread out with distances between each Ranger reaching almost twenty meters. This was way too far apart in the current vegetation and status of each Ranger. I began to get nervous that we would have a break in contact, so I backed the pace down a bit and let everyone catch up. Once we were all caught up, I began to pick the speed up again for as long as I could till I had to get my point man to back off again. We did this over the course of four kilometers. The platoon was like a massive human slinky and we did this all the way to the target building. The guys in my squad and most of the platoon were working hard, and I was so relieved that everyone was working for the guys in the graded leadership positions to get a "Go" that I totally forgot how tired I was. Once we got to the ORP (objective rally point) I set everything up to bring the platoon in so that we could drop our rucks and hit this target building before the NLT. Without wasting any time I immediately set-in near and far security to contain the target building and to keep anyone from coming into the target area. Once the assault was under way we would also make sure to keep "squirters" from being able to run out of the target area. After only a matter of a few minutes, security was set in and I radioed to the PL that we were good to go. The PL gave me a quick "Roger that," and the platoon commenced the assault on the target compound. From our vantage point we were able to watch the assault from our security position. Everything looked pretty good, but the best part was that when I looked down at my watch, I saw that we beat the NLT. Unless something terrible happens between now and the end of the mission I knew I was a "Go." As I continued to watch from our vantage point, it looked as though the mission went smoothly. Everything was secured and in a little over a half hour we began our walk back to Camp Rudder. This would be my last walk through the swamps of Florida, and as I thought about the last sixty days, all I could think about was getting a cold beer at the Gator Lounge.

Once we got back to Camp Rudder we were given some time to drop our equipment and get a quick shower before reporting to the RIs to do our peer evaluations. After our peer evals we would find out if we were a "Go." Everyone was pretty quiet, even though each man had a good idea if he was a "Go" or "No Go." It was obvious that we were all nervous, because no one wanted to do that again. As I sat there thinking about how bad it would suck to have to do Florida phase again, I tried to think about something else, but it all came back to this moment. Even though I was pretty sure I was a "Go," I tensed up like a tree when my roster number was called to learn my fate. I sat down in the RI's chair at the position of attention to receive my peer evaluation report; I was finally able to relax when the RI casually said that I was a "Go." When I heard it out of the RIs mouth that I would be graduating, I went into a state of solace. I almost felt like asking him to repeat that two letter word just to make sure I heard him correctly. Instead, I decided to keep my mouth shut in case that would make him change his mind.

After getting my "Go," I walked out of the RI's office and went straight to the Gator Lounge where the RIs were serving two beers to each of the Rangers who graduated. In the lounge the RI that graded my patrol earlier that day was working the bar and I noticed he had the Alabama game on. Alabama was playing the Georgia Bulldogs and the RI happened to be from Tuscaloosa, Alabama, so I watched the game and what was a two beer max per individual ended up turning into about six beers. This RI and I talked and watched the entire game, which Alabama unfortunately ended up losing. After being upset about the loss for only a few minutes, I remembered I was a "Go" and could have cared less. I went back to my bunk and passed out.

I do not know what the attrition rate is for Ranger School, because it differs for every class and is always changing with the times and the conditions of the each class, but I do know that when I started Ranger School there were over two hundred candidates on day one and on day sixty-one when I graduated on September 28, 2007, there were only fourteen of those two hundred original candidates in formation who went "straight through" to receive a Ranger Tab—I being one. The rest of my graduating class 10/07 of 102 "Qualified Rangers" were from previous classes that started Ranger School before the 10/07 class start date.

BACK TO BATTALION
WITH MY TAB

*"Nothing in the world can take
the place of persistence."*

*- Calvin Coolidge, 30th President of
the United States of America*

Ranger School graduation was a great day. My family drove
down from Atlanta and my dad pinned my black and gold
Ranger Tab on my left shoulder. After a good weekend with
family and friends and a quick pitstop in Jacksonville for the
Alabama vs. Florida State game, which we lost, it was time to get
back to Savannah and report to Two Charlie for work. When I
got back to my barracks room, I was greeted by my new barracks
roommate, Specialist Frasier, and he and I drank a beer and
caught up. Frasier informed me that I was no longer in third
squad and that I had been reassigned to weapons squad as an
assistant gunner for an M240 Bravo fully automatic, crew-served
machine gun. My squad leader was still Staff Sergeant Bench,
who had been promoted to the job of weapons squad leader
while I was gone at Ranger School and was now the second most
senior non-commissioned officer in the platoon, behind the new
platoon sergeant, Sergeant First Class Johns.

After getting a feel of what was going on in the platoon from
Frasier, I realized I had to make it known to my chain of
command that I had a hernia. After all, I wanted to get it fixed
ASAP for our upcoming deployment, which was only three
months away. Until I actually went to surgery, I was going to
train with the squad as if I didn't have a hernia. Not that I had
a choice in this decision, but if I could do Ranger School with
a hernia then I thought I could continue to train and get up to
speed in my new job with my new squad.

On my first morning back I caught up with the guys in Two
Charlie and was told that Roland Vaughan was recovering
quickly at Walter Reed Hospital in Washington D.C. from

wounds he sustained from being blown up in a roadside bomb four months prior and was taking advantage of his time by hanging out with the nurses. After some small talk with Plagge, Staff Sergeant Bench came into the squad cage and told us to get our rucks and weigh them in at fifty pounds plus a camelback. We all knew that this meant we were going on a ruck march for PT. Being that I just got out of Ranger School, a ruck march was nothing but a stroll in the park and I would have no problem keeping up with the squad. We hit a short five-mile ruck that turned into more of a conversational walk and talk about what is expected of us as a squad from our squad leader.

After PT I went to sick call to see Doc Osborne, our platoon medic. Osborne and the Battalion PA had me drop my trousers and then I proceeded to do the whole turn your head and cough drill. This was Osborne's first rodeo at detecting to see if a patient had a hernia or not, and with the PA's guidance he looked at me after I coughed and said, "You have a hernia." As quick and easy as that assessment was, I also got an appointment to see a surgeon at Fort Stewart in the next few weeks to schedule a date for surgery.

When I got back from sick call, the buzz around the COF was that we had a company stress shoot coming up this week. Weapons squad was always the unspoken underdog, because we normally are at the range shooting the big guns rather than M4s like the line squads. On the morning of the stress shoot, we were one of sixteen squads in Charlie Company to compete, and after listening to the course of fire brief from First Sergeant Arrington, we went over a game plan. Knowing that One Charlie would

go first and that we would be the last squad in Two Charlie to
go we had some time to kill. After watching One Charlie go
through the stress shoot one squad at a time, we were staged and
getting ready at the start point, strategizing last minute ideas,
and then the radio call was made from the range that third squad
was clear and off the range. It was go time. We were a mile
out at the start point, and at the sound of the buzzer the timer
started and we took off on our run in full combat gear. We kept
a decent pace but not too fast in order to keep our heart rate
down so we would be effective shooters. Everyone in the squad
was able to consistently keep together at the pace set by Staff
Sergeant Bench. As we approached the range, we pulled back on
the pace to prepare for the shoot phase of the stress shoot. Plagge
and I were right next to each other for the entire run, and as
we approached the first shooting stage we separated and walked
up to our respective lanes. Plagge and I were always competing
against each other trying and either one of us would have died
trying to beat the other.

The first course of fire was from the kneeling position. We had
a designated amount of rounds that we could use to engage clay
pigeons that were staged at numerous distances around twenty-
five meters. Every shot was crucial and a miss was a penalty
that added onto the total time it would take for us to complete
the course of fire. Once the entire squad was done with this
iteration, we sprinted to the next stage and I noticed that the
squad leaders from other squads in Two Charlie were running
alongside us to see how we did. It was a rainy day and as we
approached the next firing line that was conducted in the prone,
we all flew into the prone as water splashed everywhere. Shots

were already being taken down the line and you could hear the squad leaders in the background talking as we were destroying this competition.

After finishing the stress shoot we cleared our weapons and got our time and then we went back through each firing line to see how many targets we hit and missed so that we could add up our total score as a squad. There was a lot of bickering when it was determined that we were tied with another squad for the lead. There were still four squads from Three Charlie to go, but our time was impressive and would be hard to beat. The talking began and we were taking a lot of flak, which is normal when you are winning an event in Ranger Regiment.

We patiently watched all four squads from Three Charlie go through the stress shoot. We were still in the lead until we ended up tied with a squad from Three Charlie. With no better way to break this tie, it came down to a push-up contest between the highest ranking members from the two squads to see who could do the most push-ups in two minutes; winner takes all. Our squad leader pumped out push-up after push-up winning the tie breaker. It was a great day and made for a fun time to be back in Two Charlie. Days of training like this one is what made being a Ranger prideful. There is no other job on the planet that has company stress shoots with tie breakers settled by a push-up contest. A few months later each member of our squad who had participated in the stress shoot received an Army Achievement Medal. Mine read: for "Outstanding performance during squad stress shoot. Specialist McGarry's superior marksmanship at various stances and firing positions proved that he is an expert with his weapon. His actions contributed to his squad's win and reflect great credit upon himself, the 1st Ranger Battalion and the United States Army." After a good week of training, it was time to prepare for the upcoming training deployment. This year we were going to Fort Knox to conduct our platoon task force training exercises with the rest of 1st Battalion. When we got to Fort Knox it was controlled chaos while we got everything downloaded and ready to go for training. Everything seemed to be going smoothly as we prepared the Strykers that we would use in the upcoming training missions.

Prior to conducting the training missions, we had a range day scheduled. After a day of shooting on a flat range, we were eating some Army chow until it was time for the night iteration. We told a few Ranger stories while the sun went down and then we began preparing for a night shoot, getting our night vision and everything ready to go. This range day was a good break for weapons squad, because we were able to leave the big guns behind and were shooting M4s. After doing a few night shoot drills and qualifications, it was time for a little competition made up by the senior guys in the platoon. This was always the culmination of a range day in Two Charlie and competition is what makes you better and pushes you to bigger and better limits. Being that I was still a cherry Ranger in the platoon, it was a great time to try and push my limits and get better behind the M4. Plus, I was always trying to learn from the more senior Rangers in the platoon.

While we were going through the course of fire, one Ranger at a time, a few of the squad leaders went back to the barracks to prepare a meal. To our surprise they came back with a cooler of venison for a midnight snack. This kind of thing might not have been normal, but in Two Charlie it was actually the most becoming thing to do as a Ranger and it was not out of the ordinary. Cooking venison over a campfire after a day of shooting was like the icing on the cake. All we needed was a keg of beer and we might as well have been in heaven. We all cooked our venison snack on a stick as if we were roasting s'mores around a campfire. Rank and everything was put aside for a moment and then it was back to work.

After a successful training deployment we were back in Savannah and so was Roland Vaughan. Vaughan now known as "Bear," because when he was asked what his name was after being blown up and responded with "Bear," it stuck. Bear had finally been released from Walter Reed with a clean bill of health and was ready to get back on the line. His first stop would be to get back on jump status and then work to get a slot in Ranger School. It was great to have him back, but I didn't see him for long because I had to get to Winn Army Hospital to have my hernia fixed. Without wasting time, a nurse and doctor walked in and gave me some anesthesia and out I went in an anesthesia-induced sleep.

When I woke up the doctor said that I had a full-fledged left inguinal hernia and was now good as new, and so I went on my way. I was given convalescent leave by the battalion PA so that I could have time to heal. After a day or two of hanging in my barracks room, I drove back to Atlanta for Thanksgiving. I had planned to stay at my parent's house till Christmas day, which was when the battalion was slated to return from leave. After a great time hanging at home with family and friends, it was already time to head back to Savannah. Christmas day was a great day with the family, but when it was time to get back to Savannah the mood became very somber. This would be the last time that I saw my parents and brothers till I returned from the upcoming deployment I was getting ready to go on in two weeks. These kinds of goodbyes are always hard, and being that it was Christmas day, made it even harder.

At times like this you do not know what to say; you just have to hold your head high and assure your family that everything will be ok. Without a lot of conversation I hopped in my jeep and waved goodbye to my family and honked my horn as I drove off. They stood in the driveway waving goodbye, and I watched out of the corner of my eye until they disappeared in the rearview mirror.

ON THE LAST BIRD SMOKING TO IRAQ

"Somewhere inside we hear a voice. It leads us in the direction of who we wish to become. But it is up to us whether or not to follow."

- Pat Tillman

Before every deployment you have to go through a series of pre- deployment checks and the Army supplies you with some additional equipment. Depending on the time of year, you are usually issued some additional cold or hot weather combat uniforms and you could always count on getting a new Gerber/ multi-purpose tool as a little going away gift. After being funneled through the gear issuing facility staged by the Army, it was time to go get my pre-deployment health screen to get the all-clear and "good to go to war" blessing. The regimental PA who was doing the pre- deployment health assessment looked at me as he reviewed my medical record and said that he would not clear me to deploy due to my recent surgery. I stood there astonished. I had to grit my teeth being that he was the gatekeeper. The military is not conducive to two-way conversation when you are outranked, so long story short I just said, "Roger that," and moved out.

I immediately went back to the Two Charlie AO (area of operations) to let my chain of command know the bad news. I was sure that I was about to get some grief, but to my surprise my squad leader just said, "OK." I knew there had to be another way around this, so while everyone was packing up their bags and doing last minute stuff, I had my own mission and decided to go straight to the source. I called Winn Army Hospital and scheduled an appointment with the doctor who had performed my surgery. However, he was still on leave for Christmas/New Year and would not be able to see me till after my platoon deployed overseas. Two Charlie was on one of the first birds headed overseas on January 4, so I had some time to get on a C-17 headed to Iraq later that same week. It was an uneasy feeling for me when I was hanging with my buddies on New Year's Eve thinking about how they were all leaving and I might be stuck back in the states until the mid-rotator bird, which was scheduled a month and a half from now. On January 4 I watched from the company AO as Two Charlie loaded up on busses to head to the airfield to get on a C-17 and go to war.

The next few days were very quiet in the platoon AO, and I was now reporting to the non-commissioned officer-in-charge of the rear detachment, which usually just did beautification details while the Rangers down range fought the war. This was the last place you wanted to be, so when my doctor finally returned from vacation, I went down to Winn Army Hospital with a rehearsed speech in my head to get a signature that would let me go overseas. What I thought was going to be a hard sell turned out to be very easy, and without saying much the doctor signed a waiver clearing me to go to Iraq. With this paper I drove straight back to Hunter Army Airfield calling the Charlie Company rear detachment NCOIC and told him the news. He said, "Roger" and told me to get a haircut, pack my bags, and to keep my phone on me. I don't know why he told me to get a haircut, but I didn't ask, so I stopped to get my ears lowered before going to double check that I had everything packed that I needed to deploy.

A little less than a week after my platoon left I was boarding a C-17 on January 10, 2008, headed for Baghdad, Iraq. I was finally able to relax knowing that I would not miss out on a deployment with my brothers. It felt like a ton of bricks were lifted off my shoulders as the C-17 took off from Hunter Army

Airfield; I slowly drifted off in an Ambien-induced coma. When I woke up in Germany, where we stopped to refuel, I took about thirty minutes to walk around the concourse. In less than ten hours I would be in Iraq, but prior to linking up with my platoon in Baghdad, just like on my first deployment, I had to stop in Balad. To my surprise, when I landed in Balad it was freezing cold and there were snow flurries as I got off the plane. I couldn't believe it was as cold as it was especially as I walked past the area where me and my Ranger buddy were "smoked" like cheap cigars till he passed out on a day that had a heat index of 130 degrees just eight months ago. This place literally has the worst climate on earth and that same smell of dust and crap was just as fresh. I threw on my "fozzy bear" (a fleece sweater) and waited to see when I was slated to go to Baghdad.

There were no helicopters flying tonight due to the weather, so I was put up in a bunk until the weather passes. I hung out for a few hours with the other guys waiting to catch a ride to link up with their respective platoons and then I took a nap. I woke up to a private from the support company banging on my hooch door to let me know my flight was taking off to Baghdad in a few hours.

After getting settled into a bunk in the weapons squad tent, I was showed around the compound by some of the guys in weapons squad and then I put all of my mission-essential equipment into my locker in the ready room. Just like last deployment I was assigned to the last Stryker in the order of movement. Unlike last deployment though I had a new vehicle commander from the mortar platoon and I was the driver.

Knowing this I went and checked out the Stryker, and as I grabbed onto the rung to climb up on the hood of the vehicle, I felt a sharp pain in my left groin and was reminded that I was not completely healed from my hernia surgery. I would need to take it easy when climbing up here next time. As I checked out my Stryker and lifted up the hood to check the engine of what would be my new best friend for the next four months, I situated the driver seat and all the high-tech infrared screens like I liked it and got familiar with the vehicle, checking the fluids and making sure everything was good to go, and then I started it up to complete a PMCS.

This deployment was a lot different than the last. Our target was completely different and it was a joint operation between second and third platoon, Charlie Company, 1st Ranger Battalion, and a platoons of SEALs. This was one of the first times that a platoon of Rangers and SEALs ever worked side by side. You would have thought that it would have made for some growing pains to have to work with guys from different backgrounds, but it turned into a great experience in which we operated very well together. Being that I was still not one hundred percent from my recent laparoscopic surgery, I was trying to slowly get back into shape in hopes that I would be ready to go if I ever needed to do something besides just drive a Stryker. Missions were slim to none, though, and most of us were taking up playing a lot of video games, especially "Call of Duty." "Call of Duty" matches were intense and it was jokingly said that if you are not good at "Call of Duty" you don't know your job. So as we spent a lot of time fine-tuning our skills in the art of video games; our chain of command started to get antsy for something to do.

The op tempo of the deployment was so slow that we had time to completely take apart all five of the Strykers, clean them inside and out, and even drop a new engine in the Stryker I was driving. As we were putting the Strykers back together with new floorboards with immaculate undercarriages from pressure washing each Stryker once a week, it started to become an obsession to have these Strykers better than any others in country. You couldn't have found a better looking Stryker in all of Iraq. One would not believe how much junk we found underneath each of the floors of the Stryker. Everything from dip cans, lost gloves, Oakley lenses and a crawdad from what I only could guess came from the chow hall that a Ranger had lost while going out on a mission.

The highlight of this deployment was hopefully getting an opportunity to go fight in Sadr City, but a platoon of Rangers from 3rd Battalion went into Sadr City a week before we got here and killed over forty combatants so the Army was skeptical of letting Rangers back into Sadr City. I am still not completely clear on why it was a problem that 3rd Battalion Rangers killed so many combatants, because I thought that was the whole idea. After being in country for a month, we finally got some intelligence that gave us the green light to go into Sadr City, and everyone was saying it was going to be the fight of a lifetime. An old master chief from the SEAL Team gave a huge pump-up speech, kind of like a football coach would do before playing a big game, before we rolled out and then off we went, loading up on the Strykers like modern day Spartans. Intel told us that there were armed fighters on all rooftops, roadside bombs lining the streets, and some fighters even had night vision. With that information we loaded up for bear and rolled out.

The drive took about thirty minutes and we drove in black out with night vision at speeds of over sixty miles per hour; the adrenaline started to run through my veins. The new engine I had in this armored beast was allowing me to hit seventy miles per hour, and as I watched debris and streets fly by through the green tint of my night vision, we got the one minute out call from the vehicle drop off point. As we drove over the crest of a hill, we came flying into Sadr City looking for a fight, but to my surprise no one was there.

It was a ghost town, everyone had vanished. Even though no one was there I was still amped up with adrenaline, and even though I was just a Stryker driver, I was itching for a fight. As I watched my platoon and some SEALs walk past the front of my vehicle headed to the target building, I thought about how bad I wanted to be on the line with these guys, but just pulled security from my driver seat. I thought with any luck I might have an opportunity to run over a few terrorists, but unfortunately I only ran over the rock and debris that lined the streets. Instead of a massive firefight, we cleared the target building like ninjas of the night snatching up some terrorists in their sleep and were out before Al Sadr even knew that we were even there. I realized as I was driving that my incompetent vehicle commander (VC) had become more than just an annoyance during this deployment. He was an import from the regular army and was the kind that gave the army a bad name. He wore a nice set of scars up one of his arms from when he ate the blast of a breaching charge that was detonated in training by his team, because he rushed the door before it even blew up. This was just one of the instances that could go with the saying, "Here's your sign." This issue with my vehicle commander being incompetent finally came to a head when he tried to negatively counsel me for supposedly driving away from a gas pump without being ordered by him to move forward. As he was trying to negatively counsel me to cover his own ass, I thought to myself about what was going on.

Just like any other mission, we drop everyone off and then go to the gas pumps and top off our trucks. The standard operating procedure for this simple task for all vehicles is to have the driver remain in the driver hatch while the gunner fills up the trucks and while the VC usually is cracking jokes with other VCs over the net. After we topped off our tanks with some JP8 (also known as gas), I was ordered over the radio to "Go." Well, this was premature because the gunner was still on top of the vehicle, but I did not know this because I was in the hatch. The gunner almost fell off the back. This did not look good from the outside, and my vehicle commander immediately blamed me. After he finished ranting and raving at me over the vehicle internal radio, he said, "McGarry, shit falls downhill and if the weapons squad leader says anything to me, I am going to blame you." Trying to keep from wanting to jump out of my driver seat and beat his face in, I just gripped on the steering wheel and didn't say a word. I drove back to park the Stryker and put this behind me. I just thought about how I didn't like being a Stryker driver, and even worse, I couldn't stand the VC. Once we got done shutting everything down and putting everything up, my vehicle commander told me to meet him at his hooch. So I did and not surprisingly he said, "I am going to negatively counsel you for driving without being ordered to drive." I looked at him and noticed he was holding the counseling form and I said, "No, you are not and I am not signing that piece of paper."

The time to head back home to the states was getting closer and it couldn't come fast enough, because I would now have to deal with the drama of bucking the system with my VC and not signing his little negative counseling form, which made for a quiet vehicle when on a mission. As the redeployment window drew near, the exciting topic about the future manning/platoon roster started to spread. This was the time to start planning for the next training cycle and the next deployment. Just like all businesses, people get promoted and new jobs are created when people leave, so it was time to start thinking about who Two Charlie would have in regards to men and see how to best reorganize the platoon after guys get out of the Army, get promoted out of the platoon, or leave to do other things in the military. I took this as an opportunity to get off of the Stryker and requested to be slotted to go to the sniper section tryouts when we got back. Sniper and reconnaissance section tryouts always take place when everyone gets back from deployment.

I was surprised to find when the future manning for Two Charlie was disseminated that I was slated to be promoted from specialist to corporal and become a machine gun team leader in weapons squad. Not only was I being promoted, but a new squad leader from first squad named Staff Sergeant Schantz was taking over weapons squad, so I started to second guess my decision to leave Two Charlie. A few days later we were training at the demo range doing a basic breacher course, and when I was working on my charges that I would later blow for training purposes, my platoon sergeant came up to me and said, "Heard you want to go be a sniper," and his tone was one of that made you feel like you were almost quitting. Not that I had any inclination of wanting to quit, I just didn't want to spend another deployment on a Stryker while everyone else got to kick doors in. At about that time my new squad leader, Staff Sergeant Schantz, walked up and said, "If you are nervous about being on a Stryker again all next deployment, I can assure you that you will not spend the entire next deployment on a Stryker." I told my platoon sergeant and new squad leader to pull my name for the upcoming sniper section tryouts. That was the end of that conversation. I never once looked back on my decision and am thankful that they talked me out of becoming a sniper.

DOWNTOWN SAVANNAH

*"Rule number one: Always stick
around for one more drink. That's
when things happen. That's when you
find out everything you want to know."*

- John Berendt, Midnight in the Garden of Good and Evil

When we landed we were greeted by Vaughan, who was now back on jump status and would also become the assistant gunner in my machine gun team. Without wasting much time we all got unpacked and Plagge and I headed toward the historic district of Savannah with no plan but to grab a beer. It was springtime in Savannah so we were cruising the streets looking for a good spot to grab a drink. Because, after all, we had just gotten back and we needed to cut loose and catch up from all the opportunities we missed to drink a beer. We found a cool spot we had never been to before called The Six Pence Pub and walked straight to the bar, sat down at a stool, and ordered a draft beer. After a couple beers we started cutting up, talking about anything but the past deployment. Plagge and I were both looking forward to being gun team leaders. It would be our first leadership roles and we couldn't wait to get after it this training cycle. Even though we were still in weapons squad, we had a great new squad leader and an awesome group of guys in the squad.

There were a few older couples, who were on vacation, sitting next to us at the bar and they overheard our conversation. They were very intrigued that we were Army Rangers and more intrigued that we just got back from Iraq a few hours ago. What started out as an informative conversation about what an Army Ranger does, quickly turned into more beers and Irish car bombs. The couples at the bar were awesome and didn't let us pay for a single beer. They even gave us twenty bucks to get a cab, which we used to take us down to Buffalo Wild Wings in City Market of the historic district. At the restaurant, we ran into our new squad leader sitting at a table on the patio with his wife, their two dogs, and my first team leader. We quickly walked over to their table, pulled up a seat, and continued to act as if we had just gotten back from Iraq, ordering beers and embellishing on the deployment and what to expect this upcoming training deployment.

What started out as only a few Rangers quickly multiplied. More and more Rangers from Two Charlie were showing up in pairs and pulling up a seat around our table ordering beer after beer. All the guys that we just spent the past few months with sharing tents, showers, and hooches with were now there. It didn't take long for us all to be back in a group hanging out again. If you find one Ranger you can bet that a Ranger buddy is within hand grenade range. It was embedded in us from the beginning to always travel with a buddy and it carried over into life outside of work. After all, being a Ranger is not just a job, it is a lifestyle. What started out as a day cruising around Savannah ended into a long night of partying and making up for lost time that by now is a little foggy.

Once we all dried out from the platoon bar crawl, it was time for a two-week block leave, but just like that, we were back to the grind. The first order of business—like every training cycle—was to conduct airfield seizure training and an actual airfield seizure. The airfield seizure is an Army Ranger specialty and it is taken seriously. For this specific training cycle the company airfield seizures would be conducted at "The Rock" (the Hunter Army Airfield tarmac/ runway and surrounding areas of concrete landing zones) and the battalion airfield seizure would be executed at Fort Benning. It was never fun to land on the tarmac, and the potential to get injured at Hunter was pretty high, which is why it was coined "The Rock."

I was the number one jumper for the company airfield seizure, and when the jumpmaster looked at me and said, "Stand by," I waddled up to the door carrying my reserve on my front with my ruck between my legs and my MK-48 on my side. Once I heard "Go" shouted by the jumpmaster over the loud noise created by the wind and engines of the massive C-17, I jumped out into the darkness, and as the C-17 flew away, the night became still and almost so quiet you could hear a pin drop. I was the number one jumper and as I quickly descended, I saw more and more Rangers' parachutes open on down the line of the tarmac.

I began to prepare for my landing, but as I was falling through the sky preparing to land like a sack of bricks, I realized that I was going to land inside the target building if I didn't slip away. The target building was just wooden walls with no roof and was constructed specifically for this airfield seizure training exercise. As I looked down I could also see the Op-For (opposing force, or role players, playing the enemy) congregating inside with weapons. Wishing that my Beretta M9 had blank rounds, I would have killed everyone in the house, called it a day, and radioed the company commander telling him that I killed and secured everyone in Two Charlie's objective and that we are taking it back to the house for a beer. I knew that I didn't have a lot of time to slip away and was still going to close to the target building. But, I didn't want to G2 this and I also didn't want to be the guy that had it way too easy. After I finished packing my parachute, I decided that I would move out of hand grenade range from the building—plus a few extra—to make for a more realistic support-by-fire line. Once I staged my parachute five meters off to the side of the runway like we were instructed to do in the brief, I got my machine gun up and ready because it was a training environment. As soon as I did this Vaughan, aka Bear, my assistant machine gunner, showed up with five hundred rounds of 7.62 ammo. Once Vaughan linked up his five hundred rounds to my one hundred rounds, we were ready. We laid down in the prone, scanning the building for potential targets. Plagge's assistant gunner showed up and the weapons squad leader was right behind him.

Then, it was just like taking candy from a baby. An armed roaming guard walked out of the target building to see what was going on, and we lit him up with blank rounds and started receiving more from Op-For in the windows. We continued to lay down a cyclic rate of fire. Plagge was still trying to make it to our position as we began to get low on ammo, so our squad leader grabbed ammo from Plagge's assistant gunner and gave it to Vaughan. Without hesitating Vaughan had that ammo linked into what was initially six hundred rounds to the remaining two hundred, and we were back up with five hundred rounds of blank ammunition and continued to suppress the building while the line squads of Two Charlie tactically maneuvered to take down the target building. As the platoon approached the building, Plagge showed up and quickly got his machine gun up and we shifted fire to the right half of the building and started to "talk the guns" to mitigate the amount of rounds used at a cyclic rate of fire. We continued to shift further right until we were almost directing our fires behind the building. The platoon entered to clear the target building and we then line-lifted fires (ceased fires) to allow the platoon to conduct the clearing of the target building and what would have been dead bodies if this were the real thing.

After many nights at the range and training exercises in Fort Campbell, Kentucky, Vaughan and Plagge's assistant gunner went off to Ranger School. That exact same day we got two new guys. In addition Frasier, the third machine gunner, who was the senior machine gun team leader in the squad, returned to Savannah as well. Frasier had been gone for most of the training cycle, attending advance army schools and was back for our upcoming deployment. The new guys arrived fresh out of Ranger Indoctrination Program. This would be the first time that I would give an in-processing counseling and was excited to take on training the new guys. After learning a little about eighteen-year-old Kevin Hanley, a wide-eyed young kid, I realized that this was going to be challenge. Unlike our other new Ranger, Dave McNeil, who was a little older with more life experiences and whose entire family had served or is serving in the military, including his brother who was a tried and tested Ranger in a different company in 1st Ranger Battalion. When Dave heard the news in 2007 that his brother was shot in the back of his helmet and the bullet ricocheted down his back, he was immediately motivated to join the military to get revenge as well as get in the fight with his brother. Up until now I never really had to take on training a brand new private, and I was excited for the challenge that lay ahead with the young eighteen year old … at least I thought I was.

BALAD, IRAQ

"Energetically will I meet the enemies of my country. I shall defeat them on the field of battle for I am better trained and will fight with all my might. Surrender is not a Ranger word. I will never leave a fallen comrade to fall into the hands of the enemy and under no circumstances will I ever embarrass my country."

- Command Sergeant Major Neil R. Gentry, 5th stanza of the Ranger Creed

On the first mission of my third deployment, I was loaded up on a UH-60 Black Hawk with my old squad, third squad. John Gumpf was still in third squad along with Sergeant Cousins and Randy Humphry, but there was a new squad leader and a few new faces since the last time I was in the "suicide squad." The new squad leader of third squad was a blonde-headed, fearless Ranger known for his tough and honest attitude and chiseled physique. As a corporal and machine gun team leader in weapons squad attached to third squad as a rifleman with a radio, I was jacked up. Unlike the past two deployments, I did not have to worry about conducting a Stryker PMCS every day. Even better, I didn't have to drive the assault element of Two Charlie to the fight like I did in my last deployment in Baghdad.

Instead, on this night I was an assaulter on primary assault for the first time and I was carrying an M4 with four mags of thirty rounds of 5.56, one M67 fragmentation grenade, a Beretta M9 with two mags, a lock-busting charge, an MBITR, and a can of Copenhagen long cut. As a machine gun team leader, I would still be required to hump the MK-48 (lightweight, fully automatic, belt-fed machine gun firing from the open bolt position with a 7.62X51 MM NATO round) with my assistant gunner, Private First Class Kevin Hanley, when it was third squad's duty to be the security squad walking point and when the mission called for it. But in this exact moment, the MK-48 and a Stryker were the last things on my mind. This was one of our first missions—if not the first—since we had returned from Al Asad, Iraq. It was fun and all to work with those guys, but the Two Charlie morale was very high now that we were back in Balad operating with a complete package of helicopters designated to us from the 160th Special Operations Aviation Regiment (SOAR). Not only was it my first direct action raid on primary assault, but also it was the first mission period for Daniel Escobar. Private First Class Escobar was a highly respected "private" (new guy) and was liked by all of the senior leaders in the platoon. Escobar was a natural leader and held himself confidently. His initial appearance was one best described as tall, dark, and handsome. Over the course of the 115-day deployment in Balad, Escobar and I became good friends. His family was from Columbia, but like me, he was also born in Fort Lauderdale, Florida. Prior to enlisting in the army, Escobar went to the University of Central Florida where he played college volleyball. He was dedicated to his volleyball team and spent most of his time at the University of Central Florida on the court. When he was not playing volleyball, you could find him in the Orlando bars majoring in "chasing woman." Escobar was not lost and he was not in trouble; instead, he was inspired by his older brother to join the army. His older brother, Sam Escobar, served in the army and was wounded by an IED while operating a machine gun in the turret of a Humvee. When Dan heard the news that his brother Sam had been wounded in Iraq, he changed. He was motivated to serve his country just as his older brother had.

As the rotors started to pick up speed and spin so fast that I could no longer see the actual rotor blades themselves, but only a constant blur, the "60" (Black Hawk) began to vibrate on the rubber wheels touching the tarmac. Once this familiar feeling started to take place, I could see the two pilots through my night vision goggles going over last minute checks and preparing to take off. After the crew members operating the mini-guns in the doors on both sides of that "60" finished their pre-mission inspections, it was time. Escobar lifted up his fist for a fist bump and in return I gave him a fist bump; it was on. This was the first fist bump of many that would turn into a tradition before every mission, but tonight it was even more special because our cherries were getting popped. In addition to our "load out" of weapons and ammo, Escobar and I were both carrying climbing ladders for breaching and overcoming obstacles. To keep them out of the way we had them tucked up underneath our legs and resting on the back bench wall where we were sitting. The more senior Rangers in the squad and platoon who were riding on the Black Hawk were riding in style with their feet hanging off the side of the "60" and just flapping in the wind. As I looked over at them I could see my weapons squad leader, Staff Sergeant Schantz, sitting in the doorway checking to make sure his EOTech light was on, and at that exact moment we started to move forward.

As the "60" picked up speed we lifted off of the ground, and the cool October breeze started to hit me in the face making my cheeks flap in the wind. I felt an onset of adrenaline as we banked hard left and headed toward the target building thirty minutes away straight line distance. On the ride I went over the plan in my head making sure I knew exactly what to do and where to be. The crew chief test fired his mini-gun and out of pure surprise I almost jumped through my skin. My senses were so heightened, and I honestly had no idea that he was about to test that lethal and loud weapon so it took me a second to gather myself. It was kind of a relief though, because the startle the mini-gun created got all my nervous jitters out and I was now even more ready to go.

As we continued to fly toward the target building, I could see through the night sky the rest of the platoon that was on a Chinook MH-47 in front of us about fifty meters and off to our left. On the Chinook MH-47 there was the secondary assault squad, the security squad and the enablers of the mission, as well as the dog team, radio operators, and forward observers. Everyone on this mission was a Ranger; we were mission capable on our own and we did not need to pull any enablers from other special ops units or regular army units. That is what makes a Ranger platoon so lethal and amazing. As we got closer to the target building, Sergeant First Class Johns, our platoon sergeant who was riding between the "60" Black Hawk crew chiefs, plugged into the "60" Black Hawk radio to listen to sit-reps (situational reports) from the pilots over the "net" (radio) and gave us a three minute call. Everyone took this into consideration and started their last minute to-dos before being infiltrated into a fight.

The basic scheme of maneuver for the mission was not too complex. After all, we had the best pilots in the military taking us to the fight, and we were going to use that to our advantage. The pilots were to touch down their respective helicopters in an offset two ship infil (infiltration) in the front yard of the house. Once we (Two Charlie) got our boots on the ground, we were going to make a fifteen to twenty yard sprint for the front door, bringing American hate and 5.56 with us as we booted in the door. As I went over a few last minute checks to make sure everything was good to go with my equipment, I reached down and gripped the ladder with my left hand while still holding the pistol grip of my M4 with my right hand. My right hand was where it had been so many times before … with my thumb lined up on top of my safety selector switch ready to manipulate at a moment's notice and my trigger finger outside the trigger well ready to go into action at the drop of a dime.

On our way into the suburban area where the target building was located, I got my bearing on where we were as I looked through my NODS, seeing everything in green. Out in front of us I could see a pulsating infrared sparkle provided by the ISR platform shining on the rooftop of the target building. At about the same time Sergeant First Class Johns came back over the net MBITR and said, "one minute." As we all echoed this back flashing up our index fingers, Escobar looked over at me and gave me a head nod confirming that he was good to go. I looked over at Escobar and gave him a head nod as well. I then bent over and grabbed the D-ring of my "safety line" that was attached to the skin (floor) of the aircraft by a bungee cord which was attached to the riggers belt around my waist to keep me locked in and safe. It was somewhat of a pain in the ass to get unhooked prior to fast roping or trying to get off a bird in a hurry, but it was a necessary evil to keep you from being tossed out of the door in the chance of an evasive maneuver. In the worst case scenario—if we were to be shot down—your safety line could keep you alive.

As I still glared out the door of the Black Hawk through my NODS, the helicopter began to flare as it prepared to land, and immediately following a rush of dust was kicked up in the air. It came rushing into the aircraft and for a second I lost complete sight of the target building in the midst of the Iraq dust. We came to an abrupt stop, and we were all jolted forward as the Black Hawk touched down. At that exact moment I unhooked from the bird, grabbed my ladder, and jumped off the bird, keeping my head low and out of harm's way from the rotors. I started to sprint for the house that was now back in sight about twenty meters away and still marked by an infrared sparkle. To my surprise the ground was slippery and the ruts of the freshly tilled ground made it hard to get my balance; I began to slip and slide all over the place. While I struggled to balance, the ladder began to flail as it was pulled   up with the updraft caused by the Black Hawk rotors pushing the "60" back into the air to fly away. I finally gained my balance and could see that Escobar had been struggling with the same issue so I didn't feel as bad for slipping in the mud. Once I finally made it out of the freshly tilled wet dirt and onto more solid ground, I began to pick up my speed and got right behind Sergeant Cousins and our squad leader in the stack leading up to the front door, and seeing that there was no need for the climbing ladder, I threw it in the dirt and out of the way. The ladder was made out of carbon fiber, which made it very light, and had rubber ends to keep it from making any loud noises, but I was glad to finally ditch that and get both hands on my M4. At about the same time third squad's bravo team, who rode on the Chinook led by Sergeant Michael along with Humphry and Gumpf, showed up to boot the door in.

As Humphry reared back with the Thor's hammer (breaching

tool) in hand, he continued to wrap it around his torso winding it up like a cork screw and then let the fury of American hate unleash as he plowed through the door and stepped out of the way for the rest of us to enter. Humphry was probably the biggest guy in the platoon—an ex-defensive end for the Washington Huskies—so bringing this door down was nothing but another walk in the park for him and at seeing the ease with which he knocked it down, it looked as such. Once the door flung open, all the assaulters that were spread out immediately collapsed, and like caged horses at a horse race, we Rangers sprinted through the "fatal funnel" (doorway), getting our muzzles into the house and into its interior rooms as fast as we could, eliminating the time it would take for any potential combatant to grab an AK-47 and defend himself. The idea behind entering and clearing a house is simple: get to the terrorist behind the closed door before he gets his AK-47, but what happens to make sure we succeed is very detailed and fast paced. I followed in trail behind the squad leader and Sergeant Cousins and then I peeled off to the left and entered and cleared a small rectangular-shaped room with women and children in it. After I cleared my primary, secondary, and tertiary sectors of fire with Sergeant Michael, he ordered me to stay there and lock down the women and children. I responded with a quick "Roger" and locked them down to make sure they would not move. They all began to scream and cry at the tops of their lungs. Without saying a word, I aimed my M4 right in their direction, which was in my opinion as good as knowing Arabic. It was short and sweet and the communication was crystal clear. After all, it worked every time.

While I was stuck in this room by myself guarding the women and children, the rest of the assault element continued to clear the house with violence of action and dominating each room they entered. I waited for the rest of third squad and secondary assault to start back-clearing through the house, double checking each room by clearing it one by one for a second time the same way they cleared each room the first time. There is a reason for everything in the army and usually, if not all the time, the reason behind it involves bloodshed and sometimes the loss of life. While the rest of the assault element was making sure that we did not miss anything, I knew that the secondary clear of the house was almost done when I started to hear chatter on my MBITR from team leaders saying that the back-clear was complete. I knew it was time to start preparing to separate the men from the women and children. Being that this room had the women and children and no men, it made my job easy. As I started to search the women, Escobar came over to help me and pulled security while I searched each woman, one at a time. I was looking for anything that would be evidence pertinent to putting the males of the house in prison. It was customary for these women to hide stuff where you would least expect and did not want to look. For sanitary purposes, I always kept my gloves on for this portion, because their armpits and body parts usually smelt so bad that it almost knocked me over.

After checking all the womens' pockets and their dishdashas, it was evident that they did not have any weapons, phones, or anything pertinent on their person. After I completed the searches, I left Escobar to guard the women and children and jumped in with the rest of third squad and started ripping up and turning over everything in the house, looking in every possible hiding place and any nook and cranny I could find for sensitive materials that could link these terrorists to acts of terror and crime. After a few minutes we were done, and in the matter of an hour we had everything we came for. No shots were fired and hardly a noise was made. We were like ninjas in the night who came and left before anyone knew we were there.

Missions like this would be the norm for the next 115 days. Two Charlie was operating like true modern elite warriors under the concealment of darkness, and our greatest attribute was our leadership, who instilled a disciplined mentality amongst the platoon, making us all improve in every facet of our job. Even better, we never once had to use the Strykers for a ground assault force mission during this deployment. Instead, we went out on over sixty helicopter assault force raids. Each time we went out, we improved and got even better than we were the previous mission. Two Charlie was pushing the limit going out every night— sometimes twice a night—hitting multiple targets and compounds, capturing and killing terrorists from central to northern Iraq. We were at the cutting edge of close-quarter combat tactics, conducting simultaneous explosive breaches, entering and clearing buildings without making a noise every night, and we did not get hit once.

Operating out of Balad was one of—if not the—best times I had in Ranger Battalion … and possibly my life. Even amongst all the action there was comic relief and a few incidents in which I just happened to be in the spotlight. On one particular mission, for example, third squad was on primary assault and we were

going explosive. I was attached to bravo team and we were
around the corner about eight feet away from the front door
and waiting like caged pit bulls for the charge to blow down the
door. The countdown was followed by an incredible thunderous
explosion that ripped the metal door right off, and the
overpressure blew out all the windows that led up to the front
door. As I ran to the front door at a flat-out sprint, I realized that
alpha team still had not all made it through the doorway. I tried
to put on the breaks and slow down. To my surprise, not only
was the slab of concrete covered in glass, but it was also as wet as
a slip-and-slide and what happened next is exactly why you don't
run near the pool. My legs went straight up in the air. Out of the
corner of my eye I could see Gumpf watching me take flight and
then gravity took over. As I came down I put my left hand out to
catch my fall and as soon I hit my fourth point of contact a piece
of glass went straight through my glove and into the palm of
my hand. I ripped out the glass and my hand began to spit out
blood like some kind of miniature hose. I then quickly grabbed
the fore grip of my rifle with my hand to use it as a compress
and then got back in the stack and followed Gumpf up the stairs
to the second floor.

In trail behind us was the platoon sergeant, third squad's squad
leader, and the weapons squad leader. When Gumpf and I came
flying into a room on the right of the hallway, there were two
fighting-aged males fast asleep. Even though we blew up their
front door, shattering all of their windows and running in like
mad men with a warrant, they were, amazingly, passed out.
Gumpf and I immediately removed them from their beds and I
detained one of them for battle interrogation.

As soon as the building was clear, I linked in with Doc Osborne and he quickly cleaned up the cut with some antiseptic, threw in four staples, and off I went. A few days later Osborne let the new medic, Specialist Vetter, who was being prepped to be the lead medic for Two Charlie, take the staples out. According to the PA, I got pretty lucky that I didn't hit any nerves in my hand, but nonetheless I was back at it without skipping a beat.

Not only were we going out on missions every night, but also I learned more about fitness than I had ever even imagined. My workout partner and I, Troy Jenkins, turned into complete beasts. If we were not the fittest in the platoon at the time, we were definitely in the top five. At the end of the deployment, Troy brought up his desires to compete in the Best Ranger Competition and asked me to do it with him. I figured with all the functional fitness, Gym Jones, and CrossFit workouts we had been doing that there would be no better time to try than now. Like any other type "A" personality, I also selfishly really wanted to see where I measured up, and I wanted to go after the title of winning the Best Ranger Competition. After pushing our goal through our chain of command, it was approved and Troy and I were slotted to go to Columbus, Georgia, to train for three months for the Best Ranger Competition upon our return from the deployment.

STATESIDE

"For those who have fought for it, freedom has a flavor the protected will never know."

- Unknown

As soon as Two Charlie got back stateside from Balad, Iraq,
I pinned on my sergeant rank and was promoted to bravo
team leader in second squad under Staff Sergeant James Ross.
Immediately following, Troy Jenkins and I—like most every
other Ranger—went out for a few beers, which always turns into
a crazy event, especially when you have not had a single drink
in over a hundred days. When you compound that with the fact
that you just got back from war and that you are ready to try
and catch up for lost time, there is no telling what could happen.
Some of the craziest stuff you can't even imagine takes place, and
if you weren't there you just don't understand.

Our first stop was the Ranger hangout/watering hole in the
downtown city market called Wild Wings for a pitcher of beer.
After a couple of pitchers and flirting with the waitress, we
decided that we needed tattoos. So in true Ranger fashion it was
going down, and not only was it happening, but it sounded like
the best idea ever. We drove over to the tattoo shop in Savannah
that stays in business mostly because of Rangers. I had no idea
what I wanted, so I walked in and at the last second decided to
go with the Ranger Crest. About thirty minutes later—no longer
buzzed from the pitcher we drank—I had some fresh ink on my
inner right bicep. Once Troy's tattoo, the angel of death, was
finished we both paid up and headed back to the bars. Not really
sure what happened after that … all was a blur. It was not till
the next morning when I was brushing my teeth that I noticed I
had a tattoo on my right bicep. I took it in and then went back
to brushing my teeth like nothing happened and headed out for
Columbus, Georgia.

When I got to Columbus and reported for Best Ranger, I
was in the best shape I had ever been, and during this time I
learned even more about how the body can be pushed and how
extreme my breaking point was. On the first day I ran five miles
in thirty-three minutes then went straight into two minutes
of push-ups, two minutes of sit-ups, and max effort of strict
pull-ups till I couldn't do anymore. Immediately following, our
coach, Jeff Strueker (more commonly known for his actions in
Mogadishu, Somalia, as the leader of the convoy sent back to
base to take a wounded Ranger out of the fight), had us conduct
a twelve-mile ruck with a fifty-pound pack and I did it in less
than one hour and forty-five minutes. I think I would have
been better off doing the competition that day, because over the
course of the next three months I trained hard   until I injured
my left knee on an eight-mile run only a few weeks out from the
competition. After the first of many Cortisone shots to come
from the injury, I was not able to recover and still to this day feel
the pain whenever I overdue it. Not finishing the Best Ranger
Competition was more painful than the injury, but I had to
suck up my pride and drive on. Even though I did not have the
outcome I had planned and envisioned, the Best Ranger train-up
and competition was a great learning experience on many fronts
and it helped develop me into an even better Ranger. A year later
I tried to get approval to give Best Ranger a second attempt, but
because of the importance and focus of training for Afghanistan,
it was neither the time nor the place to take the time off from
training with my team for that which would be needed to train
for the Best Ranger Competition. I never attempted it again.
What was more important and necessary was for me to train my

team and to not put my wants before our mission. After all I was now a Ranger team leader and some say that this job is the pinnacle of a Ranger career!

THE NEW GUYS

"Have your musket clean as a whistle, hatchet scoured, sixty rounds powder and ball, and be ready to march at a minute's warning."

- Major Robert Rogers, 1759

When I returned to Savannah from Columbus after the Best Ranger Competition, I got right back in the mix with my squad, second squad. But before I even went back to work I was informed that we got a new guy in the team, Ethan Gronbeck, who had recently graduated from RASP. Ranger Battalion can be a gossip ring (which is usually fueled by privates and the bull crap that they think and make up) that would rival a cheerleader squad in high school, but the information it provides is actually accurate nine out of ten times. After seeing young Rangers come and go over the years you get pretty good at being able to size up a new guy in a matter of five minutes. It is almost as if you can determine who will make it and who won't just by a first impression. In Gronbeck's case, I knew he would make it by my first impression of him. He was a quiet and confident Ranger.

Staff Sergeant Ross assigned Gronbeck to my team as the M203 gunner and over the next few months we would do everything together. Specialist Ethan Gronbeck was from West Bend, Wisconsin, and his grandfather served in the 6th Ranger Battalion during World War II, and it was his dream to keep the tradition going. Specialist Gronbeck had always wanted to serve his country and was motivated to do so even more when his older sisters signed up to serve. At age seventeen—before Gronbeck graduated from high school—he enlisted under the delayed entry program.

After graduating from high school, boot camp, and infantry training in 2006, Gronbeck was assigned to his first unit out of Fort Lewis, Washington. He became fast friends with Chris Wright and Aaron Kleibacker. Gronbeck, Wright, and

Kleibacker were all in second platoon, Alpha Company, 1st Battalion, 25th Infantry out of Fort Lewis. The unit as a whole was later reassigned to Vilseck, Germany, and the three of them went with the unit. In Germany, their unit fell under a new chain of command and was changed to 2nd Stryker Calvary Regiment. They immediately began to prepare for a fifteen-month deployment to Iraq. When Gronbeck, Wright, and Kleibacker were not training for Iraq, the three young men were out and about traveling Europe, living wild and free going from place to place by train, getting tattoos, and living in the moment without a care in the world.

Once the three of them were finally settled in and accustomed to a fun lifestyle in Germany, Wright was sent to Sniper School in preparation to their upcoming deployment. When Wright returned from Sniper School he was assigned to a sniper section that attached him to first platoon. Despite the separation, the three of them remained close, and while on their deployment, Wright, Kleibacker, and Gronbeck decided they wanted to be in the elite 75th Ranger Regiment and wanted to attend RASP together. They decided that they only would do it if the three of them could go as a group. This would be Wright's and Kleibacker's second attempts at RASP. (When they went through it the first time—in 2005—it was called RIP). As a testament to Wright's character, he withdrew from RIP on his first attempt to go home to be with his dying grandfather. When Wright left RIP on emergency leave, Kleibacker thought it would be the last time he saw Wright, but only a month after Kleibacker arrived to Fort Lewis, Wright showed up and then Gronbeck's arrival followed a few weeks later.

By 2008 each one of them had been in the army for a while and
they were all due for a promotion. But after pushing the request
through their chain of command to go to RASP to try out for
the Ranger Regiment, they were each told that they would not
be promoted to sergeant prior to their return from Iraq if they
choose to go to RASP. Because, their chain of command told
them, the Ranger Regiment would not accept an NCO into
RASP. Even though the three men really wanted that promotion
and the pay raise, they were more determined to be Rangers, so
they turned down the promotion and re-enlisted for four more
years to become Army Rangers. The three of them would later
find out that their chain of command screwed them out of their
promotions to sergeant to try and keep them from leaving. But,
they never looked back. Together the three of them took the
road less traveled, one that many would not dare to attempt, to
become Army Rangers.

These three guys spent every moment they could together and
were excited that it was finally time to take the leap of faith
together and go big. In RASP one of the cadre, Christian
Twyman, who happened to be from Charlie Company, 1st
Ranger Battalion, took a liking to these three young men who
so boldly stuck out from the crowd. It was not just that they
wanted to be Army Rangers that attracted Twyman, but the
confidence and pride they each exuded as well as their strong
bond. Like most everyone who heard the story about what the
three of them did to get to Ranger Regiment, Christian was
inspired by their sacrifice and couldn't help but to want to help
them. Twyman, an experienced and seasoned Ranger and a
good friend of mine, was working on a temporary assignment

as a cadre for RASP by request. As the class finished up and was preparing to graduate, Twyman listened to where Gronbeck, Kleibacker, and Wright wanted to go and helped the three of them get assigned to Charlie Company, 1st Ranger Battalion so that they could stay together.

After they graduated RASP, out-processed from Fort Benning, and reported to Savannah for in-processing, Gronbeck and Kleibacker were assigned to Two Charlie and Wright was assigned to Three Charlie in Kevin Pape's team. I remember when they arrived and the buzz that their story created amongst Charlie Company. We couldn't believe that someone gave up a promotion and re-enlisted to go to RASP. The three of them were some of the first Rangers we ever had to show up as privates who had already served in the regular Army, which made them a different breed. Because, to be honest, we Rangers are spoiled when downrange, but it is something earned by those who wear the Ranger Scroll. It was a breath of fresh air to have someone who lived the life in the regular army. Also humbling, each one of them had been in the Army longer than I had and now they were taking orders from me. I remember thinking for a quick minute about how that must feel for them and then remembered that we all volunteered and that they still did not know Ranger SOPs (standard operating procedures) and if I thought too hard on this, I could fail them because being a Ranger private is not exactly a fun-filled lifestyle, and I will never forget what it was like. I made sure not to be like Bevans, whose leadership was immature. Their story was a cool one that I respected, but honestly at the time, I did not think too much about it. I was just glad to have some motivated guys ready to take the fight to the enemy.

Over time it was apparent that Gronbeck was working hard to be a squared away Ranger, and even though at first he came off as a very quiet Ranger, he eventually opened up. Gronbeck only needed to be told how to do a task once and then he was able to perform the task to the Ranger standard every time. He was a smart, confident, and a hardworking Ranger, and what I respected second to his story of how he got here was that he was not afraid to ask a question if he didn't understand something. He was eager to learn and he would eventually fit in well with the other guys in the squad and platoon.

After another long and arduous training cycle that was very different from ones in the past due to the shift in focus from Iraq to Afghanistan, we made some great adjustments on how we planned to fight, and as a whole, we were ready to go to Afghanistan. Like all the other training cycles and cumulative training events, we were worn out on training and ready to put what we had trained for to the test. It was always an exciting time to have the training cycle behind us and to shift gears to get ready to deploy, but what was even more exciting for me was that this would be my first deployment as a fire team leader.

AFGHANISTAN

*"Then I heard the voice
of the Lord saying,
'Whom shall I send?
And who will go for us?'*

And I said, 'Here am I. Send me!'"

- Isaiah 6:8

Once we landed on the rocky desert landing strip in
Afghanistan, we got everything situated in our hooches and
ready room, and in only a few hours Two Charlie was mission
capable. Once we were acclimated, it was game time! Two
Charlie had been in Afghanistan for only a day or so (less than
a week ago we were in Savannah) and we already had a mission.
Our mission was to invade and destroy a terrorist training camp
located in some of the steepest and roughest terrain Afghanistan
has to offer. Our mission was in the Hindu Kush mountains
near the K-G Pass (the Khost-Gardez mountain pass) where it is
commonly knowledge that the Taliban and Haqqani network do
most of their training. This stretch of mountain peaks that make
up the Hindu Kush push eleven thousand feet and more. The
terrain is treacherous and steep and consists of boulders, rocks,
small shrubbery plants, and trees scattered throughout. Hardly
any of the ground that make up the mountain range made for an
easy place to fight. Throughout the Hindu Kush mountain range
the locals have many networks of trails. The K-G Pass itself is
considered the highway to hell to those who spent time there.

Two Charlie's mission was to fly in at night on two MH-47
Chinook helicopters through the mountain pass. The plan was
to have the helicopter pilots drop us off in the low ground at
the base of the Hindu Kush mountain pass and from there we
planned to walk up and over a mountain that would give us high
ground to look into the terrorist training camp from above.

On our ride in on the Chinook, I was looking out the window
through my night vision goggles and staring at the treacherous,
steep mountain sides that were literally fifty meters away on both

sides of the Chinook. I couldn't get over how steep and rugged they were and was completely fascinated by them. Its sheer presence was scary, and when I thought about how we were about to be dropped into this terrain, I realized just how much of a risk factor the terrain is. The terrain was so rugged that it was almost just as much of a threat as the Taliban fighters hiding out in the mountains themselves.

After banking left and right repetitively at high speeds and going up and over the contour of the fingers and back down in the saddles while staying away from the mountain peaks of the Hindu Kush in the Chinook, it was finally time for Two Charlie to get inserted to seek and destroy our objective—the terrorist training camp. As the Chinook flared, I prepared my wrist Garmin so that I would know where we were going. It was a slow landing, which was unlike your typical landing in Iraq. Once we finally touched down, everyone was anxious to get the show on the road, so we all had no problem sprinting out the back of the Chinook, that is, until you realized that the ground was not meant to be sprinted on. The HLZ was like a dried up river bed full of rocks and massive boulders, some the size of a Volkswagen. So what started out as a sprint, turned more into a leap of faith as we navigated through the dust created by the twin rotors of the Chinook and the rocks and boulders. Once I finally got far enough away, I took a knee and looked down at my Garmin while the rest of Two Charlie did the same. The Chinook started to take off, and just as the loud noise of the most powerful helicopter we had to our disposal began to bank off the mountain side walls as it flew away, calmness set in. I looked down at my Garmin to double check that I was going to be going over this massive mountain in front of me, because I honestly didn't believe that we were about to do just that. As the dust settled I stood up and I literally felt like I looked straight up into the sky—to the point that I almost got dizzy—trying to see the top of the mountain that we were about to walk up and over. I shrugged my shoulders to make sure my kit shoulder straps were adjusted and ready for this climb, and I gave Gronbeck a nod to let him know that we were about to climb over this massive beast. Like any tough Ranger would do, he just gave a nod back, but because he was carrying a SCAR-L (Special Operations Forces Combat Assault Rifle, L for light) with a grenade launcher on the bottom as well as the squad litter and med bag on his back, on top of nine rounds HEDP grenades, and seven mags of 5.56, I am sure he was not exactly thrilled that we were about to climb hand over fist.

As the platoon started to slowly make its way up this mountain nearing toward ten thousand feet above sea level, we started to feel pain that is only replicated through complete muscle exhaustion. At the halfway point we started to cross load the litter and took turns carrying it up the mountain to give Gronbeck a break. To make sure that everyone was fresh and ready to lay waste to the terrorist training camp, it was imperative that we not burn out a man in the team. As a squad/team you are only as fast as your slowest link. We also wanted everyone to be ready to go, because we were secondary assault for this mission and would need to be ready to move fast, think clearly when engaging combatants in a terrain and environment that they know like the back of their hands, and destroy the enemy. Not to mention they only wear sandals and bed sheets to keep themselves light and agile so that they can maneuver quickly through the mountainous terrain. However, this is why we trained the way we did and do train as hard as we do, because it is our job to go where others are afraid to go or simply can't go. This is why we take our physical fitness seriously and tonight it is paying off. This is the hardest terrain Afghanistan has to offer and we were moving efficiently and fast enough to get to the target at the desired and planned TOT (time on target). The worst part about the mission was yet to come, though.

We reached the military crest of the mountain ridgeline after climbing up for almost two hours hand over fist, slipping and stepping over small rocks and boulder-sized rocks. We set in the conditions for assault, but as each of us stared down through our NODs, it was apparent that the terrorist training camp was abandoned. After gearing up for what I thought was going to be a shootout similar to the O.K.-Corral, the mission was a dry hole (nobody there). We actioned a mission on some bad intelligence and got all excited about nothing and were let down. It was the beginning of the deployment and we had a long way to go; at least we got the first mission of the deployment under our belts.

Even though this mission appeared to be a dry hole, we still had to execute the mission and we had to execute it flawlessly, because who knew what was hiding in the trenches and in the two homes/shacks that looked to be a place of bed down. After silently descending down the mountainside and into the terrorist training camp, Two Charlie spread out abreast, keeping fifteen meters between us and staying on line, keeping a Ranger buddy to the left and right in each of our peripheral vision. The conditions were set for the most effective raid an enemy (who was not there) would have ever seen. I slowly stepped one foot at a time, rolling from my heel to my toe, with my rifle at the high ready, and through my nods I was searching high and low, left and right, for targets of opportunity. Once the platoon pushed through the abandoned valley that once housed terrorists and the grounds that they used to train on, we pushed out to a safe limit, created a perimeter, and prepped for exfil (exfiltration). We had to go all the way back down to the valley we had landed in and no one was excited about this, not to mention how slippery those rocks were and how unstable every step was; going down would be a battle in itself. Looking back later that day, I wasn't sure how we actioned such terrible intelligence, but at that moment, I knew this wasn't the time to think about it. The only positive about the mission was that we made it out safely with no injuries, and we now know what the terrain is like, but to take the risk to walk through the mountains of Afghanistan on bad intelligence is sometimes sadly part of the job and is just as simple as it sucks. During the AAR there was definitely some heated words sent out toward the intel guys asking them what their processes were and what happened. In light of this we made many changes and our platoon sergeant got to the root of the cause. He had us instill our own ISR watch to double check their work from this time forward.

About a month later, after going out on a couple dozen more missions, it was obvious that Gronbeck was ready to become a junior leader in the platoon, but he would have to pass Ranger School to do so. Gronbeck had been exceling in all facets, from fitness to learning the tactical ways we operate, proficiently enough to be a Ranger leader. It was going to be a hard void to fill when he left, but it was a necessary process that needed to happen to keep developing the platoon. So just like me, Gronbeck was scheduled to leave on the redeployment mid-rotator bird back home to Savannah. A few days after deciding to send Gronbeck to Ranger School, Staff Sergeant Ross came rushing through the door, slamming it behind him as always, and told us, "We got a new guy coming to the squad from Three Charlie named Chris Wright." Gronbeck perked up and looked very excited that his best friend was joining him and second squad. Sure enough Wright showed up on our hooch doorstep with everything he had in his duffle bag and with his ruck sack on his back that night in September 2009. From what I had heard from my chain of command, Wright had recently beaten up a private in the other platoon over an issue I was not ever clear on nor cared about. Also, his team leader, Sergeant Kevin Pape, had given him multiple opportunities to better himself, but Wright kept getting into trouble. He was a problem and it was just not working out, so it was a call made by First Sergeant Kevin Led to move Wright to our platoon and it just so happened that second squad needed to plus-up now that Gronbeck was going to Ranger School. Even before Wright showed up Staff Sergeant Ross told me that Wright would be in my team and once he gets here to get him spun-up for our next mission.

I told the other guys in the squad to make room and get a bunk ready for Wright. After he dropped his bags by his bed, I told him to get all his mission essential gear out and to follow me.

We immediately got him set up over at the Two Charlie ready room and after squaring him away with a locker, I witnessed him and his buddy Kleibacker exchange some high fives. There was definitely a morale boost amongst the three of these guys now that Wright was in the same platoon. But, due to the sense of urgency instilled upon me by Staff Sergeant Ross to get Wright ready, I told him and Kleibacker that they will have plenty of time to catch up later. After getting Wright's locker all squared away and showing him where we store the ammo, frags, and everything else that he will need, I showed Wright around our compound and told him what he needed to know immediately in the chance that we roll out on a mission tonight. During the time I got Wright all squared away, we talked and got to know each other. I told him about me and what I expected of him and he told me all about his background and upbringing.

Christopher Wright was from Tollesboro, Kentucky. He was twenty- two years young and was full of life and energy. Wright weighed in at about 170 pounds and stood at about 68 inches tall. He was very muscular and had an arm full of fresh patriotic and memorial tattoos in remembrance of his friends who were killed in combat on their fifteen-month tour in Iraq. What I noticed more than anything was that Wright was fired up for a second chance, and I think that seeing his two best friends, Gronbeck and Kleibacker, was a real morale booster for him. Not only was he fired up to see them and catch up with them, he also didn't waste any time getting to know the rest of the guys in the squad and was not afraid to tell some good stories about his experiences in Three Charlie, his time in Germany, and just his day-to-day life. Wright was a young man, in shape, full of life, and he could tell a story with the best of them. Two Charlie's second squad was glad to have him.

A few days later Gronbeck flew back stateside to go to Ranger School. On his way off I gave him a "drive on" Ranger Tab to sew onto his patrol cap to have for motivation, and like my squad leader told me, I told Gronbeck "don't come back without your tab." Gronbeck looked at me and said, "Roger, sergeant," and then loaded up on the C-130 and headed home. Over the course of the rest of the deployment we went out on some more missions and Wright fit right in, taking up the slack for Gronbeck and not missing a beat. Just like Gronbeck, Wright did great on target and worked hard every day to improve himself as a Ranger.

LIVING THE DREAM

"No matter whether we travel in big parties or little ones, each party has to keep a scout twenty yards ahead, twenty yards on each flank and twenty yards in the rear, so the main body can't be surprised and wiped out."

- Major Robert Rogers, 1759

In December 2009 we redeployed home to Savannah just in time for Christmas. Every year there are people that come and go in Ranger Battalion, but this was a hard year to watch some of our leaders who I had become friends with leave for different reasons. Some moved on and accepted new jobs in Ranger Regiment, others went to go do more secret squirrely stuff within special operations, and some just got out of the Army. It is just the way of the Ranger Regiment; when good leaders go, new ones step in, and this year I stepped into the alpha team leader position and my best friend Rooster took over second squad from Staff Sergeant Ross. After almost ten years of service to his country, Staff Sergeant Ross decided to get out of the Army to settle down and start a family.

Although we just got home, it was time to get back to training and get back to the grind, because we were deploying again in seven months. When we got back from deployment there was a new guy waiting for us—Private First Class Tristan Wales, and we had to get him ready for the training cycle before going home for Christmas and going on leave. Wright had been stepping up and did great on the deployment. He immediately took the reins to help get Wales ready for the upcoming training cycle. The word amongst the platoon was that Wright would be the next to go to Ranger School, and he was not about to let up now. Just like he did overseas, Wright continued to show his desire by being resourceful and taking on any task without having to be told. But, before he was able to completely take care of Wales, Wright had to go over to his old squad's cage and clear out his locker. Once he got all squared away, he immediately went back to helping out the new guy Wales.

Christmas leave came and went and before we knew it, we were back to work. First order of business was to get Wright sent off to Ranger School ASAP so that he could earn his Ranger Tab and be back in time to deploy. In just a few days Wright had his entire packing list complete for Ranger School. We went over some last minute preparations and sent him off to take the battalion PT test to compete against all of the other Ranger privates trying to go to Ranger School. It was not a surprise when I heard that Wright did the most pull-ups and beat enough eager Rangers full of piss and vinegar for a spot in the next Pre-Ranger Course prior to the upcoming Ranger School class, which started in three weeks. Before Wright left—just like I did with Gronbeck—I told him to not come back without his Ranger Tab and gave him a "drive on" tab for motivation. Everyone in the squad gave him a few motivational pep talks and some words of encouragement to get it over with so that he can meet us in Afghanistan in a few months, and just like that, he was gone and headed to Columbus, Georgia.

My second order of business was to get myself ready for Emergency Medical Technician-Intermediate (EMT-I), which was starting soon. In no time, everything was under way and I found myself sitting in EMT-I with my good friend from RIP Alessandro Plutino. Not only was Plutino in the course, but Escobar was also attending. Together we took the course on and engaged ourselves heavily to learn as much as we could to be more effective on the battlefield. It was a condensed course that lasted five weeks, and in those five weeks we covered material that takes a civilian program six months to cover. After completing forty hours of clinical time riding along in an

ambulance as well as working in Savannah hospitals and passing
the practical National Registry exam, we were ready to go back
to our respective platoons.

When we returned from training, Escobar and I were surprised
to find out that he was transferred from third squad to second
squad and promoted to second squad's bravo team. It was a very
exciting time, but as we prepared for the upcoming deployment,
I was met with a challenge and that challenge was Private Wales.
Wales was a PT stud but he was a scatter brain when it came to
training missions. He was the complete opposite of Gronbeck
and Wright; he was not respectful of military rank and he
thought he knew everything. Over repetitive re-training and
blocks of instruction to help develop Wales, it was obvious to
everyone in the platoon that his mindset was just not one of a
Ranger. Wales liked the idea of being a Ranger and could stick it
out, but he was not ready for combat.

Wales quit a month later, but the course of events that took
place around his departure was crazy. We, Two Charlie, were
on a training deployment at Fort Bragg, North Carolina,
conducting final training operations before our upcoming
deployment to Afghanistan. Coincidentally, I was instructed not
to be on this training event due to a concussion I had gotten a
few days prior on the new obstacle course back in Savannah. I
was commando crawling across a rope that was approximately
fifteen feet in the air. Just my luck the knot that secured the rope
was not taut and while I was crawling across, the rope dropped
about five feet flinging me to the ground, and according to my
squad's account, I landed on my head. After watching me fall

and land, my teammates said that they knew I was concussed when they saw my head bounce off the dirt. Once I came too, I was told to see the doc and sure enough I was diagnosed with a minor concussion.

Not thinking too much about the concussion or what had happened, I deployed anyway with my company to Fort Bragg. On day one, we shot rifle and pistol on the flat range. It was an easy and fun day at the range, but Private First Class Wales was acting weird and didn't seem to be having a good day. After asking him repetitively what the problem was I saw tear drops fall down his cheeks from behind his dark-lensed Oakley sunglasses. I didn't know what to   say. I had not seen anything like this in my time at Ranger Battalion and couldn't believe what I was witnessing. At that exact moment the ever so calm and cool Escobar showed up. Without knowing what else to say, Escobar asked him, "What's the matter?" And just as fast as he let out some tears, Wales said, "I quit." Wales admitted to both of us that he just wasn't cut out to be in Ranger Battalion and wanted to go to the regular army. Having said this, I told him to go to the platoon formation, clean his weapon, and just hang out and wait for us to finish our platoon training.

The next day was a normal hot spring day in North Carolina. Being that today would be the first day of our four consecutive training days of day and night missions, it was a relief that Wales was not in second squad any longer, because after all we were a volunteer unit and didn't want anyone that was on the fence about being a Ranger. With a strong squad of Staff Sergeant Rooster as the squad leader, me as the alpha team

leader, Escobar as the bravo team leader, and Gronbeck as the
SAW (squad automatic weapon) gunner along with a fill-in
(Garret Fritz) from another squad for Wright while he was at
Ranger School, we were good to go and had all that we needed
to fulfil the training deployment. After we geared up and went
over the mission brief, we walked out to the vehicles to do some
last minute PMCS before we rolled out. These new vehicles that
the army adopted, called the MRAP (Mine-Resistant Ambush
Protected vehicle), which most of us had never been in before
and had only seen from a distance when the regular army drove
by in a convoy, looked like a rollover waiting to happen. Having
been in weapons squad as a private, I knew how the concept of
operations works with the vehicles and convoys, but I only knew
the vehicle we used in Iraq, the Stryker. We were not the least
bit happy to use this new vehicle. In fact, most guys were mad
that we had to train with the MRAP; I being one. As we began
to load up I thought how awesome it was that Wales was not in
the vehicle with us. If he were here today I would have probably
had to hold his hand the whole way to the gun turret where he
would have been standing and acting as if he were operating a
mounted .50-caliber machine gun. Being that we were running
this mission without Wales, we did not have a gunner, which
was not an issue. I looked up to the driver's seat as I low-walked
into the back of the MRAP, and I noticed our driver was a young
Ranger who was with us on our last deployment but was still a
Ranger private trying to make his way.

The specific MRAP that we were on had four racing seats lining
the skin (sidewall) of the vehicle, and when I reached down
to lower the bottom portion of the seat so that I could set

my fourth point of contact down (butt), I noticed a six-point seatbelt harness that looked more like something you would see in NASCAR. With all my gear on, it was not easy to get my shoulders into the harness, but with my unfamiliarity of the vehicle and the unknown, I didn't hesitate strapping up. Escobar, on the other hand, who stood over six feet, was having issues getting the straps to fit over his shoulders and was not holding back on how pissed he was about the seating arrangements. As I looked directly across the vehicle to him—like we were in some kind of space ship—I couldn't help but laugh a little as he struggled to clip the shoulder straps, which were barely long enough for him. At that moment Rooster looked back and said, "Ya'll better be all buckled up." There was something in the air and it just didn't feel right.

As we slow rolled out the gate, I heard over the radio that we were good to go. At that moment we started to pick up speed. I was not able to see out the front windshield, but I was looking out the back window of the heavy outward swinging metal door. These vehicles were designed to move at a slow speed, but that is just not how Rangers roll. When we drove to a mission in a convoy of Strykers, we traveled at speeds topping out around 70 mph. We used speed as a safety measure. That is not how the MRAP was built, and as we picked up speed this top heavy vehicle started to sway. As we crested the top of a hill on a windy road, I yelled up at the driver, "You better slow down or you are going to kill us!" Sure enough, after we crested the hill and began to go downhill we started to sway back and forth, which caused the driver to swerve back and forth more rapidly in an attempt to get the vehicle to straighten out. A few seconds

later I could hear Rooster instructing Private Franks to ease off
the gas and gain control. Rooster was trying to calm the driver
down so that he would not make a juristic move. Just then
Rooster yells, "Hold on!" I was not able to see in front, but it
did not take a rocket scientist to figure out that we were about
to roll over. Immediately I remembered what we were trained
to do in a rollover and threw my hands to the ceiling of the
vehicle to brace myself for impact. As we started to roll toward
the passenger side, I could feel my side (the driver side) of the
vehicle begin to rise and as I started to look down at Escobar, I
slowly realized that we were about to crash—the passenger side
was completely below the driver's side. I have never experienced
what happened next, and so it is difficult to compare it to
anything, except to compare it to being stuck in a dryer. As we
rolled I could see gear going everywhere, including the twenty-
pound donker floating in the air, and when it impacted into
my ribs, I knew it was not floating, it was flying at an incredible
rate. Luckily I didn't feel much of anything at the time, thanks
to the protective plates guarding my vitals. Once we made a
complete roll I felt like we might be okay, but to my surprise we
picked up speed. I could only think to myself about how bad
this is about to be; I couldn't believe that this was happening. I
had always heard horror stories about being in a vehicle rollover,
but I never thought that I would be in one. That thought only
lasted for a second as we were catapulted into the next roll. It
felt as if we were in a NASCAR accident. The second roll was
estimated to be about ten feet in the air from the speed and
force of the first roll. This time we hit the ground so hard that
Escobar's and Fritz's seats both broke from underneath them and

their tail bones were slammed into the floorboard of the vehicle, nearly breaking their tail bones and backs. The estimated ten-foot jump made by an eighteen-ton vehicle was later confirmed by the Military Police investigation as well as by the guys riding in the vehicle behind us. As soon as we smacked the pavement in the beginning of our third roll, I thought we were never going to stop rolling. It was no longer as if we were moving in slow motion. I tried to look out the back window, but I could only see a flash of light coming through the window. Then, just as fast as it started, we stopped.

Dazed, I could only make out that the engine was still revving at a high RPM. I could hear Fritz screaming at the top of his lungs, and as I looked down at Escobar, I noticed that he could not move. In my normal fashion—when things go wrong—I shouted, "God dammit!" Without thinking, I undid my seatbelt, which had me suspended and dangling in the air because my side of the vehicle was on the upright side. I immediately slammed into Escobar and he let out a pissed off grunt as I fell into him. This sigh of annoyance with me was completely understandable, but I wanted out of the vehicle. Before doing anything else, I helped him get his shoulders out from under the straps; thankfully, he had managed to clip himself into the six-point harness seatbelt despite his size. Hearing Fritz still screaming at the top of his lungs, I began to get annoyed and told him to shut up, but then I noticed his eyes were still shut and that he was screaming out of pure terror thinking that we were still rolling. I went over to him, told him to open his eyes, and I unbuckled him. To his surprise, we were stopped. I told Fritz to help Gronbeck get out of his seatbelt and went to the back to open the door so that we could get out. There was an overwhelming claustrophobic state going on and I felt that we needed to get out. I began to hear Rooster screaming for help in the front. Not knowing what the exact issue was I ran out the back end and saw that we had crashed into a massive pine tree, which had kept us from rolling another one hundred yards down into a ravine. As I crested the vehicle and ran to the front, I saw Staff Sergeant Cousins running down the hill and screamed at him that Rooster is messed up and he is hurt; we need to get them out of the vehicle ASAP. We both jumped up on the driver side door, which was upright, and looked through the glass. Franks was laid up on top of Rooster, and from the looks of it, he must have come unbuckled in the roll. The door was mashed shut and we couldn't open it, so Staff Sergeant Cousins grabbed the Hooligan tool off of my back to pry the door open. Once we finally got the door open, we noticed that Jenkins was already in control and had cervical spine control of Franks, who was paralyzed from the waist down. Franks could not move his legs. Seeing that Jenkins had everything in control up in the front of the vehicle and after getting a verbal confirmation from Rooster that he was okay, I hopped back down and ran to the back of the vehicle to check on the boys. Escobar and Fritz could not stand up and could barely get on all fours. Their backs hurt so bad that I swore they had broken something, but surprisingly they did not have a priapism or any indications of a broken back. Once the rest of the platoon arrived, they immediately took control and we all just sat down and started to take our kit off. The medics showed up next and gave us all fentanyl lollipops and that was all she wrote. As we were triaged and strapped into straight boards, I saw Franks get carried out the back door of the MRAP on a straight board, loaded into an ambulance, and rushed out. It was then that I found out that he was paralyzed and that all of the bones in his neck were broken; the only thing keeping it together was the skin around his neck. Later, Franks began to get feeling back in his feet and was soon able to move his toes and legs thanks to Jenkins taking c-spine control immediately and not letting go. Franks was later able to walk and after six months living with a halo drilled into his forehead and braced onto his shoulders, he was almost as good as new.

Rooster and I we were triaged and put into the same ambulance, and as we finished the fentanyl lollipops Rooster started to crack me up. He was telling the medics that he was an American Jedi and going on and on about only God knows what. The kicker was that Wales was not with us today and thank the Lord he quit, because if he would not have quit the day prior, he would have been the top gunner in the well of the vehicle and would have either been thrown out into the woods or onto the street and crushed by the eighteen- ton vehicle. I believe there is no way he would have survived. After finally being released from the hospital, Rooster and I were picked up by our platoon sergeant and on the way home we picked up a can of dip. We were taken back to the training compound to get some rack and relax. Escobar and Fritz were back as well. Both of them were still so sore in the lower back and tailbone region that neither could stand without walking like an old paratrooper hunched over, grabbing for anything to brace themselves with.

When I walked into the compound the first person I saw was

the last person I wanted to see. Wales came running up to me
and said, "Sergeant, can I talk to you?" I said, "Sure, Wales, what
is it?" He said, "I am sorry about what happened and hope you
are doing okay, but I think the Lord is talking to me; I want
to be a chaplain's assistant." I sharply responded, "Great, I will
get it taken care of. Now go away and leave me be!" Wales said,
"Roger, sergeant" and ran off. Once I got to my room I shut the
door and passed out from the fentanyl lollipop residual earlier.
The next morning I and woke up in a world of hurt. My ribs
from where the donker hit me were black and blue, and I had
the worst case of dizziness spells imaginable from the concussion
added on top of the concussion I had had the week prior, which
made for a bad cocktail in my brain. After months of dizziness
I was diagnosed with benign positional vertigo, which I tried
to treat with the Hallpikes Maneuver. Talk about a drunken
nightmare. Benign positional vertigo is something I don't wish
upon anyone and is downright miserable when it goes down.
Basically the calcium deposits in my left ear were knocked loose
and when they travel through my ear canal sometimes they will
touch the nerve endings and create a spinning sensation only
comparable to when you have been over served at the local
watering hole and try to go to bed and then end up feeling like
you are falling down into a spiraling death trap that results in an
immediate projectile vomit that most Ranger privates and avid
beer drinkers can relate to.

During the two months before our next deployment, Rooster
and I spent most of our time hanging out at the house chilling
on the back deck. We built a fire pit and would sit around
drinking and burning wood from the backyard until we had

no more sticks to burn. We then had the genius idea one night
to rip out the fence and burn the wooden planks till there was
nothing left, which was fine because we now had a mission ...
a mission to build a new fence. The next day we were up bright
and early and headed straight to Home Depot to buy everything
we needed to build a new fence. A few hundred dollars later
this new mission was about to start, and we were not going to
stop till it was completed. Like any Ranger, though, we had to
stop and get some beer before we built this fence, so on the way
home we picked up a case of Coors Light and we were off like
a prom dress. Drinking beer and building a fence is like mixing
oil and water; it just doesn't mix. When we were finally done
later that day, it was obvious that the leveler we were using must
not have been working, because our fence was not the least bit
straight. It was definitely not human error; I am sure the fence
was crooked not because we were drinking, but because the
leveler was broke. That's our story and I am sticking to it.

We had a few more weeks of fun in the backyard confines of our
newly erected and stained fence from Home Depot and then
it was time to get ready to deploy. Neither Rooster, Escobar,
Gronbeck, nor I had been to work in almost two months and
Fritz had been transferred to third squad with Staff Sergeant
Cousins. So second squad was running pretty slim in numbers,
but not in regards to fitness and health; this was the least of our
worries, because in second squad it didn't take us long to get
back to "manimal" (beast mode) status. On our first day back
to work we were going through our stuff when I realized that
the barrel of my M4 was crooked from the infamous rollover.
I do not know when but at some point my M4 turned into a

projectile flying up to the front of the vehicle. The barrel must have been the first piece to impact a solid surface. This is just a testament to how fast things were flying around inside the vehicle and how out of control we were. We were literally at the mercy of God, and if it were not for the tree that stopped us we would have rolled another one hundred feet to our death.

As I was staring through the barrel amazed, Rooster walked in and said Wright is being sent home from Ranger School. I looked up at him in even more amazement. I was shocked, and honestly at first I was confused and mad. But when Wright came back and explained what had happened, he said to Rooster and me, "I can't let ya'll deploy without me." I looked back at him and said, "Well it's good to have you back and glad you are coming with. Now go get everything unpacked and let's go work out." Second squad was back and we were all accounted for, and wouldn't you know it, we even got two new privates from RASP. What was even more impressive was that these two privates, Blaise and Sesh, were squared away and ready to go. Each morning we were doing squad PT and in only a week we were almost back to where we wanted to be. After a few weeks of getting all back together and going over everything under the sun with Blaise and Sesh, we were informed by our squad leader Rooster that we were going to Jalalabad, Afghanistan. It was game time!

Just like every other deployment, it was time to pack bags, load the pallet, and prepare for block leave. This time was different though; there was a different feeling in the air. I remember when we finished packing the pallet, we were looking at the wall of heroes who had paid the ultimate sacrifice outside our squad cage that the boys (Wright, Blaise, and Sesh) had made with scripture from the Book of John 15:13. Standing there, we began talking about the buttstock number on Sergeant Robert Sanchez's M4 and ran through theoretical "what if" scenarios. Sanchez was killed in action in Afghanistan on October 1, 2009, and his M4 buttstock was twenty-two. Significantly, this number is our squad leader's call sign, which represented our squad as a whole. As we continued to talk, we were also looking at the picture of Anthony Davis who used to be second squad's squad leader back when our squad leader, Rooster, was a specialist. He and Rooster were good friends. Rooster looked at Wright and me and asked if we were ready to go overseas and kill bad guys. We both responded "Roger, sergeant," and just like that the subject changed. We started to tell war stories as we waited for the company safety brief before being released for block leave.

It was the start of block leave and on the morning of June 1, 2010, one of our Ranger brothers who was already deployed, Sergeant Jonathan Peney, was killed in action in the Kandahar province of Afghanistan while rushing to aid a wounded comrade on a rooftop. Peney was a medic and his selfless, heroic actions defined the epitome of what it is to be a Ranger. I got a phone call that day from Rooster telling me to alert the guys in my team and to make sure that they knew the news. It was a sobering day and I took the time to reflect on what had happened, what we were about to get into, and let the reality of war soak in. This was not the first time this happened right before my platoon deployed. Last deployment, as my previous squad leader, Staff Sergeant Ross, and roommate were packing

up last minute items at the house we lived in, we were informed
that Private First Class Eric Hario and Staff Sergeant Jason
Dahlke were killed in action. Although we should have been
enjoying our time with family and loved ones, hearing the news
of a fellow Ranger's death did not make us relish our time at
home and hold those we loved even closer. Instead, it made the
time allotted for relaxation even harder. I know I can speak for
most Rangers that news of a Ranger's death just makes you want
to kill more. It angers you to the point that you almost see red; it
made me anxious and eager to get back to Savannah to be with
the guys.

A week later leave was starting to wrap up, and I said my
goodbyes to my parents and brothers and started the trek back
to Savannah on one of the most boring roads ever, I-16. During
the four-hour drive from Atlanta to Savannah, I went over in
my head possible scenarios that I might face in combat in the
upcoming months. I went over SOPs, radio calls … anything
that I could think of. There was not a thoughtless moment in
the ride to Savannah; my mind was flooded with hundreds of
possible scenarios. It was a nervous type of feeling that can only
be related to a feeling you might get before a big game, but just
like my uncle told me before my first deployment, "Trust your
training." After all, this was our Super Bowl. It was time to put
our training to the test and do what we Rangers do best. In case
you don't know what Rangers do best, I will tell you: we are
masters of the raid and we take pride in killing the enemies of
the United States of America. We are defenders of the free world.
We are the ones that make sure we have freedom. If defending
these principles meant sacrifice, I was ready and I knew that the

guys to my right and left were ready too.

OBJECTIVE LEXUS
AUGUST 11, 2010

"Readily will I display the intestinal fortitude required to fight on to the Ranger objective and complete the mission, though I be the lone survivor."

- Command Sergeant Major Neal R. Gentry, 6th stanza of the Ranger Creed

It is the beginning of August in 2010 and it is the peak of fighting season in Afghanistan. As an alpha team leader with Two Charlie, I was exactly where I wanted to be, an FOB (forward operating base) in Jalalabad, Afghanistan. Jalalabad is the capital of the Nangarhar province and was formerly called Adina Pur as documented by the 7th century Hsüan-tsang. Located in eastern Afghanistan at the junction of the Kabul River and Kunar River near the Laghman valley. Already 2010 had been the deadliest year yet for U.S. troops in Afghanistan, and we had arrived a little over a month ago on the 4th of July to spearhead the surge. Thus far in 2010, 266 U.S. soldiers, sailors, Marines, and airmen had died compared to 317 total U.S. deaths in all of 2009. By the end of the year sixteen Rangers will have paid the ultimate sacrifice making it the most costly year in the 75th Ranger Regiment's history. Knowing these statistics at the time and that there was a lot of action going on made it imperative that we get out on direct action raid missions to diminish the Taliban (TB) network. Two Charlie, being a seasoned special operations platoon of Army Rangers, was exactly who the U.S. needed on the front lines. We were a tight-knit group that had evolved into one of the most elite fighting forces ever to walk the planet, and we loved nothing more than to go out on direct action raid missions to capture or kill TB and Al-Qaeda (AQ) insurgents. Every time we were put to the test, we brought violence of action with us and nothing short of perfection. The men of Two Charlie were once again ready to answer the call!

On August 11, 2010, I was hanging out in second platoon's TOC with Staff Sergeant Rooster, the squad leader of second squad; Staff Sergeant Wyatt, first squad's squad leader; and Staff Sergeant Cousins, third squad's squad leader. As we were talking about college football and who we thought would win the National Championship this year the PL and PSG (platoon sergeant) walked in and said we had a mission. We all stopped talking about football immediately and listened to the PSG. He gave us a broad overview of what we were to do that night and said, "Second squad, you will be security to the west side of the compound, and third squad you will also set in security, but will be the security element to the east side of the compound." He then told Staff Sergeant Wyatt that first squad will be on the QRF and his squad will loiter around overhead in the Chinook and will only be inserted if back up is called and needed. As the PSG was talking about the mission, he was going around to each of us handing us a GRG. After our platoon sergeant was done giving us an overview of Objective Lexus, he said the brief is at 1500 over at the Pit (where the SEAL team conducts mission briefs). I turned to Staff Sergeant Rooster and asked if he wanted anything specific. He said, "No, just get the guys ready as usual."

With that said, I immediately turned and walked out of the TOC and ran to second squad's hooch where the guys were hanging out playing "Call of Duty" on the squad Xbox. I ran into the hooch and said, "Hey, we got a mission. Start getting ready and have everything on and be standing outside of the ready room in thirty minutes. We have a brief at 1500 zulu (Greenwich Mean Time), and I want to knock out PCIs and go over the squad plan before we walk over to the Pit for the mission brief." Escobar, Wright, and Gronbeck jumped up and began to hop into their combat uniform like firefighters would when called to fight a fire. As they were doing this our squad leader walked in and pressed play on the IPod to listen to the squad's ritual song "Rooster" by Alice in Chains. As the song started to blare throughout the room, a calm sensation set in and our senses started to enhance. Everything started to smell a little stronger and the dusty and dirty environment of Afghanistan became a little clearer. We slowly changed from a state of going through the daily routine to becoming American Jedis.

On this specific deployment/rotation, second platoon was assigned to a joint task force based in Jalalabad, Afghanistan. The task force was comprised of Special Operations Rangers from the 75th Ranger Regiment, Navy SEALs, Air Force Pararescue, and the 160th SOAR. The Ranger Regiment is an elite fighting force that can sustain its own missions and operate solely on its own, but sometimes, whether we liked it or not, as a special operations unit that falls under the Special Operations Command we deploy with other special operations forces units under this same chain of command. Although we have the capacity to conduct our own missions, we also trained for joint missions to build cohesiveness with the special operations community so that we could work alongside each other, or in some cases even work for one another as a facilitator to a specific mission.

It was 1450 and Escobar, Wright, Gronbeck, and I, along with all of the other guys in the platoon headed out tonight, were out in front of the Ranger TOC on the rocks going over the broad scheme of maneuver for Objective Lexus with a GRG that I had gotten from the TOC. Using a flashlight, I showed the guys the target building primary assault was hitting tonight. I explained that we were on security tonight and showed them the tentative spot to the west of the target building where we were going to set our squad in to. To the west of the target building we would be able to provide overwatch on surrounding buildings that were just south of the target. We would also be able to have eyes on a building to the southwest of the target. In addition, this spot had great cover and concealment from trees and brush that would mask our movement.

After giving the guys a FRAGO (fragmentary order, mission brief), we went into PCIs, checking all our gear and mission equipment to make sure each of us was ready to go. Most of us were armed with an M4, and combined we were carrying over 630 rounds of 5.56 in magazines of thirty rounds. Specialist Christopher Wright was equipped with a combat load of 210 rounds for his M4 and nine rounds of 40-mm HEDP grenades for the M203 grenade launcher attached to his M4. Specialist Ethan Gronbeck was carrying the SAW, armed to the teeth with five hundred rounds of linked 5.56. A combat load is a specific amount of rounds required for each weapon system. Second squad was known to be a little heavy on the trigger so we always carried more than a combat load. I used to always say that it is better to have it and not need it than to need it and not have it. In addition to our round count, we were armed with M67 fragmentation grenades, smoke grenades, and concussion/flash bang grenades.

Escobar double checked everyone, and I sent out a radio check over the MBITR to my squad leader to make sure my radio was up and working and to also let him know we were ready to go over to the Pit for the operations order. Staff Sergeant Rooster came back over the radio and replied, "Roger." A minute later he walked out of the TOC in all his mission gear, and we followed him over to the Pit for the brief, which was going to be given by the SEAL chain of command. On the way over, no words were said; we just walked with our heads high and chests sticking out and with our weapons slung on our shoulders ready to do business. The SEAL NCO-in-charge of the platoon said that the brief was going to be a "broad brush," which was normal for this specific SEAL platoon. We then went into a roll call to get an "up" from each squad leader representing their guys from both second platoon and the SEALs. The mission statement was to conduct a raid on high value targets (HVT) positively identified in order to disrupt the terrorist cell network in the area. The insurgents we were after were positively identified, tracked by intelligence and ISR assets, and currently still accounted for in the target building. Our helicopter package was two Chinooks and we would be inserted four kilometers from the target building so that we could walk up and use the element of surprise and silence to our advantage. Start point was 1530 zulu and TOT was 1700 zulu. When the mission brief was over, I made sure I had the correct infil route loaded into my handheld and wrist Garmin, which the SEALs also intended to use, and then linked in with my squad as we went over a few specifics on how we were going to set in security and also to see if anyone had any last second questions. With that said, we were all on the same page and good to go.

Second platoon loaded up in buses, and we rode out to the

flight line located just outside the walls of the compound
but inside the Jalalabad FOB. We rode over to the flight line
without uttering a word; guys were busy checking their NODs,
oiling their guns, and some were just staring out the window
into the darkness going over the mission in their heads. As we
pulled up to the flight line, you could hear the two twin rotor
MH-47 Chinook helicopters start to warm their engines. This
creates a high-pitched noise that to me was so familiar that it
triggered something in my body as another reminder that it's
game time. As the engines warmed up, the rotors started to
spin slowly and then very quickly until they reached top speed
to the point that the helicopter almost vibrates as it sits on the
tarmac. The smell of the jet fuel and the sound of the Chinook
and its massive rotors made the hair on my arms rise up; it was
my favorite part of the mission. Knowing that we were about
to ride out on one of these awesome state-of-the-art helicopters
with thirty of my best friends with a mission to capture or kill
bad guys is something that only a special operations warrior
can understand to its entirety. As we all started to download off
of the buses, we put our NODs down and viewed the world
through a green tint. Once I got off the bus I walked over to
the side to take a piss. I always had to get a pre-mission piss out
of my system. I buttoned back up and faced a safe direction to
charge my weapon and chamber a round. With my camouflaged
Petzl headlamp, I double checked to make sure my 5.56 round
was actually chambered and seated properly by slightly pulling
back the charging handle and using my headlamp to see the
brass casing glisten in the light. Once I saw that the round
was actually chambered, I let the charging handle go forward

and then firmly pressed down, locking the bolt forward in the star chamber. As I looked up and started to walk toward the Chinook, I brought my weapon around to my chest with my right hand on the pistol grip and slowly used my left hand to shut my dust cover. These were all steps and processes I took— just like everyone else was doing at that same moment—to eliminate the chance of a malfunction.

After going over my personal pre-mission necessities, I gathered up the guys, got a head count, and sent a radio call to Staff Sergeant Rooster to let him know we were up. Second squad was once again "armed for bear" on a planned direct action mission with the most elite modern-day warriors doing what we Rangers do best and that is conduct a raid in order to capture or kill wanted HVTs to deplete the TB network. Without saying anything over the radio, Staff Sergeant Rooster raised his left hand to signal for me to come over to him and bring the squad. We had trained and operated together for thousands of hours and saw eye to eye on everything so most of the time we didn't even have to talk, we just got it done! Being that we were the security squad element, we were leading out tonight, so we would be the last to board the Chinook and when we land we would be the first off. As we walked up the ramp of the Chinook, we each found a spot to sit and then I snapped in with my D-ring (mountain climbing Karabiner) that was attached to a foot-long bungee cord as well as attached by a medal clasp to my riggers belt by a metal clasp hook. As the Chinook picked up altitude it slowly turned and hovered over the tarmac and then at the drop of a dime the 160th SOAR pilots flying the Chinook tipped the nose down and took off at full speed to the infil HLZ.

In flight to the infil HLZ, the Chinook crew members were going over their routine checks on the mini-guns and 240B machine guns, test firing them into the Afghanistan rock and dirt and making sure that everything was good to go before getting close to the HLZ. On the ride out to the target I went over in my head the infil route and distinct landmarks on my GRG that would help me know where I was in regards to where the target building was located. As we started getting closer to the HLZ, Staff Sergeant Rooster came over the radio and said, "One minute!" With that call I started to button everything up and pressed the power button on the wrist Garmin GPS device that I would use to lead the way to the target building. Staff Sergeant Rooster then came over the radio and said, "Thirty seconds!" We all sat up and took a knee; I kneeled on my left knee, placed my M4 on my right thigh, and held my pistol grip with my right hand with my shooting/right index finger outside the trigger well and my thumb on my safety selector switch. This was a position that my right hand was always in out of muscle memory. I bent down, grabbed my D-ring with my left hand, and got ready to unhook from the floorboard of the Chinook.

As the wheels of the Chinook touched down, I unhooked and then ran out the back of the Chinook and took a knee in the midst of the dust and small rock being kicked up by the rotors. I began to scan through my NODs the valley that we had landed in and hit the light button on my wrist Garmin to get oriented before I stepped off. As a Ranger team leader walking point, it was my job to make sure we got to the target building on time at the planned TOT without getting lost. I got my bearings and the Chinook started to lift off and flew out into the darkness.

As the sounds of the rotors and the noise of the Chinook went away into the night, so did the dust and debris kicked up by the Chinook. While I acclimated to the silence interrupted only by the sound of our feet crunching down on the rocky terrain, which I heard through my Peltors (protective headphones attached to MBITR radio via radio cord), I pulled out my Oakley lens cleaning cloth and wiped away the dust film off of my NODs and took off my goggles and attached them to the Velcro on the back of my helmet.

Second squad was in trail behind me with Staff Sergeant Rooster right next to me serving as my eyes and ears while I navigated for the assault force. It is usually a boring mission when tasked as the security element, because every special operations warrior wants to be on primary assault kicking down doors and killing the enemy. But even though it was boring, you never got complacent and you took everything serious because complacency kills. At the end of the four-kilometer infiltration movement over the rocky terrain of Afghanistan, we began the familiar process of setting in security and making sure the conditions were set for the assault element to do its job. It was all pretty routine at that point. As I was moving silently through the Afghan foliage, I found a dried up wadi (creek bed) just outside of the target building that would conceal our movement. My intent as the alpha team leader walking point was to find a good spot with cover and concealment that provided clear sectors of fire for my squad to set in and provide overwatch. I walked through the Afghan brush and trees with my team of Rangers behind me, including my squad leader, platoon leader, and a team of SEALs. I crept out from the concealment of the brush and walked into an opening, using the wadi to mask my movement, and I identified three roaming guards approximately twenty feet away in a grove.

Two of the roaming guards were carrying AK-47s and one had an RPG launcher strapped to his back. I immediately put my infrared laser on the closest enemy combatant armed with an AK. All of the second squad Rangers and the SEALs providing security for the joint task force assault element identified a target and acquired them with their infrared lasers without saying a word. Each of us had our infrared lasers aimed center mass on a roaming guard's chest. Once we had an ambush line set, a volley of precision fire immediately followed from all of second squad simultaneously, including me, Staff Sergeant Rooster, Corporal Escobar, Specialist Wright, and Specialist Gronbeck. Gronbeck, the SAW gunner, was laying down the "scunion" (slang for shooting effectively at a rapid rate) on the remaining fighters. I could see Gronbeck getting after it as his machine gun started spitting fire from the muzzle. As he was laying waste to the combatants, Wright and I were engaging at a rapid rate of fire while lying in the wadi to keep our bodies concealed from the incoming rounds that were two feet above our heads from additional combatants coming out of the target compound. We were able to peak our heads up enough while keeping our body in the wadi with our M4s secured on the mound of the wadi bank. Rooster, Wright, Escobar, and I suppressed the additional combatants that were appearing out of the target compound into the grove with our infrared lasers placed directly on the combatants' chests. From the opposite side of the target compound, third squad's M203 gunner fired a

40-mm HEDP grenade right into the center of the combatants finishing them off.

At that same moment Rooster and I realized there were rounds coming from behind us. It was obvious at this point that we were also taking effective fire from our rear, because every third round was a tracer round flying over our heads from our six o'clock. The tracer rounds were lit up like a ball of fire ripping and popping over us and leaving a fire trail as the round passed over. I immediately rolled over onto my back, keeping my entire body in the wadi, and placing my M4 perpendicular on top of my chest and pointed it to our six o'clock. I was able to see through my NODs that the rounds were coming out of a crop field. As I continued to search through my NODs for the combatant on the machine gun to positively identify him, my squad leader stood up and ran over to the platoon leader. Staff Sergeant Rooster wanted to update the PL on what kind of radio calls he needed to be making to the other elements on the mission as well as to gain a better understanding of where the other elements were in relation to us. As Staff Sergeant Rooster ran through the blaze of bullets, Wright yelled, "Rooster, get the fuck down." With the tracer rounds ripping and popping all around us, I couldn't get small enough! I continued to keep the better half of my body in the wadi with my head up, but after seeing Staff Sergeant Rooster almost get shot in the head multiple times as he ran to the PL, I opened up at a cyclic rate of fire into the crop field. The additional fire that was coming out of the crop field was a combatant with an RPK (hand-held machine gun). Realizing we were in a classic Polish ambush, I now had to get the squad turned around and suppress the machine gun position at a cyclic rate of fire.

The original three roaming guards were already eliminated and nothing but a thing of the past. As a team leader it was my job to get the guys refocused on the automatic machine gun fire coming from behind us. I first yelled at Wright to make sure that he knew what was going on, and just like I had expected, he was already engaging the machine gun position. I ran through the bullets still flying through the air over to Gronbeck and grabbed his shoulder, telling him to lift his fires as he continued to lay waste into the now dead roaming guards. Escobar, Gronbeck, and Wright were now all effectively suppressing that machine gun position. As we continued to take fire, Staff Sergeant Rooster and the PL set up an L-shaped ambush over the MBITR with the squad of SEALs that made up the other half of the security element. Once the L-shaped ambush was set we continued to engage the insurgent at a cyclic rate of fire and we were now way more effective. We continued to engage until all fire had ceased from the machine gun position.

To prepare for the ambush, we picked up and were moving our flank to get on line with the SEAL team, and in the process of us making a run for it, Wright and I heard that familiar noise made only by bullets that call for the saying, "That was a close call." As the rounds flew directly over our heads, we moved faster and we were more agile than what should be humanly possible. Without saying anything we both jumped back down to the ground taking cover behind a mound of dirt. We both landed on our asses and slammed our shoulders into the dirt. We simultaneously looked at each other and started laughing out of pure joy and adrenaline ... we were having fun! After all, this is what we trained for and it was time to fight and dance with death. We both loved a good adrenaline rush and there was nothing like the high of a firefight when you have the advantage. Meanwhile one of the SEALs armed a grenade and threw it about fifteen feet into the crop field right where the fires were coming from and where the insurgent was hiding out. This was a surprise to us, as it is customary to yell "Frag out!" so that the other members of your element know where the explosion originated; however, this was not relayed to us. This same SEAL, with another one of his buddies, walked into the field and positively identified that the lone insurgent was dead.

After effectively negotiating the Polish ambush that we had walked into and eliminating every Afghan terrorist in the fight, we spotted headlights on a vehicle headed our way. The vehicle was a white pickup truck and was identified by our ISR assets a few kilometers out but was headed away from us. The truck was monitored by ISR during the duration of the mission. Even though at the time the white truck was too far away to be considered a threat, we kept our eyes on this vehicle and made sure that it did not get within a range of the target compound that would be considered a potential threat. It was our job as the security element to ensure that all avenues of approach leading up to and in the target area were secure while the joint assault force of Rangers and SEALs strategically took down the target building with violence. While we, the security element, fought through the Polish ambush, the building was cleared and secured. Second squad was feeling good, as there were no friendly casualties or injuries sustained, and second squad was responsible for the elimination of four enemy combatants.

As the security element, my squad of Rangers and the SEALs were tasked with being first to move out to the HLZ to lead the way for extraction. After consolidating inside the bordering walls of the target building, I stepped out to lead the way with second squad for about one kilometer in distance to a flat plateau, freshly tilled by the local village farmers, that was just big enough for the two helicopters to come in one at a time. As we set up security and the rest of the element lined up for extraction, which is the most vulnerable part of any mission, I noticed a MAM (military- aged male) walk out of the corn field onto the edge of our HLZ about fifteen feet behind us. Staff Sergeant Rooster, Staff Sergeant Cousins, Corporal Escobar, Gronbeck, and Wright also saw the MAM. The sun was now cresting over the mountains so we were no longer using our NODS and night optics. We had switched over to our EOTech rifle sights and overt red lasers. As the interpreter was telling him to get off the field, tension started to build, because the MAM was not responding. Earlier on this deployment we had been briefed on an enemy TTP (tactics, techniques, and procedures) that was very familiar to what was happening. It was reported that insurgents were sending a lone person out to draw attention from and distract assault forces to prep an ambush on HLZs exactly like the one we were on. The MAM was doing nothing but staring back at six muzzles as if he did not care that he would die. After repetitively telling him to leave the area and put his hands up where we could see them, he squatted into a crouched position and put his hand in his dishdash. No one said anything; we all opened fire and put 5.56 into his chest and face. His actions—not listening to the interpreter and putting his hands where we could not see them after being told to raise his hands—were enough to meet the rules of engagement and we had to put him down. We were not about to wait to see what it was that he was reaching for; he could have pulled out a gun or even worse clacked off a suicide vest under his dishdash. This MAM executed a jihad mission. He knew that if he were to disobey the orders given to him by us and our interpreter he would die. As rounds continued to impact his dead body, he literally convulsed from the bullets impacting his body and brain matter sprayed across the dirt. His mission was to die. He and his terrorist cell planned and expected this result. (It was confirmed later that he was an insurgent, and he was part of a terrorist cell.) This was just the first stage of an ambush to distract us at our most vulnerable point when security was limited and while we were preparing to run and board the inbound/landing MH-47 Chinook. What we didn't know at the time was that a group of insurgents was gathered in the compound to the north of us. Simultaneously, as the shots were taken by our task force to eliminate this MAM on the HLZ, the first Chinook landed to pick up the "first stick" (personnel assigned to helicopter manifest) of our task force consisting of Rangers and SEALs. Once we lifted our fires, the silence signaled the insurgent group to ambush our task force and the Chinook Helicopter.

As the helicopter touched down on the HLZ, the compound located up on the hill above us about one hundred meters away opened up on us with RPGs and small arms fire (SAF). Two RPGs ripped over our heads, coming within about two feet of the tail of the twin rotor aircraft and only a few feet over our heads. A crewmember on the Chinook began to open up on the compound with the mini-gun (there is nothing "mini" about it) along with the M240 machine gun that was located and fixed in a window on the rear of the aircraft. As the "first stick" of Rangers and SEALs hastily boarded the bird, Wright and I ran up to an embankment along with Rooster and our platoon sergeant. We slammed into the embankment with our shoulders at full speed and immediately started suppressing the enemy's fortified fighting position, focusing on the elevated machine gun nest shooting down on us. I could hear the popping noise of the bullets as they passed over my head, and at that moment the Chinook took off from the HLZ. A calm, quiet sensation set in when the noise of the helicopter's rotors and machine fire faded as the helicopter quickly flew away into the distant sky until it was no longer in hearing distance. We now only had half the men we started the mission with, but we were still taking fire from the enemy. I gave Wright a fire command, ordering him to shoot one of his 40-mm HEDP grenade rounds into the machine gun nest located on top of the wall of the compound. Just as Wright and I had done so many times in training, he methodically loaded and fired from the M203 grenade launcher attached to his rifle. Surprisingly, the first round was a miss, impacting twenty meters short and a little to the right. Without asking him why he missed or what the problem was, I just repeated myself: "Wright, again one round, HEDP!" Wright shouted back, "Roger that!"

We had trained for this, so there was no need to create more anxiety or tension by yelling at Wright for missing. We were professionals, and yelling at him would only add more frustration to the task at hand. I trusted Wright with my life, and I knew he was about to come through. He loaded the next 40-mm grenade round and stood up with complete disregard for his own safety. He was now exposed from his waist up with enemy bullets flying all around us and impacting the ground in front of us. Wright paused, took a deep breath, angled his weapon at about a forty-five degree angle, and using the day sight attached to the rail of his M4 he zeroed in on the muzzle flashes and squeezed the M203's trigger. As soon as he let that round fly, he took cover and began to load another. His well-aimed round was a direct hit into the fortified machine gun nest, blowing bits and pieces of rock into the air and ceasing the machine gun fire. All the way down our fire line, I could hear the SEALs cheering, elated that Wright single-handedly took out the enemy machine gun nest. They literally were jumping up and down in amazement!

Wright's shot suppressed fire from the compound for only a short second though. An AH-64 Apache attack helicopter flew in overhead toward the target and began to engage the target, unleashing hell. In the morning sky, I saw two more RPGs streaking out from the center of the compound toward their assailant in the sky. The Apache banked left and then right, dodging the RPGs with apparent ease. I told Wright to send another grenade round into the center of the compound. Wright once again responded, "Roger that." As soon as he let that one go I said, "Again!" Wright continued to send three more 40-mm grenades into the center of the compound with expert precision. After the seventh grenade and the sixth direct hit from Wright's

well-aimed 40-mm HEDP grenades slamming directly into
the center of the compound, Staff Sergeant Rooster ordered
us to run to the lower side of the HLZ to cover the rest of our
element in case of a possible flanking movement by the enemy.
Immediately, Wright and I complied; we picked up and sprinted
toward the lower side of the HLZ.

Once we arrived, we found a pile of rocks that was only about
six inches high. We lay down in the prone position on our bellies
behind the rocks, leaving just the tops of our helmets and back
exposed to any enemy combatants that might travel up the hill
below us. The most prominent and likely avenue of approach
leading to the HLZ was a dirt road. Meanwhile, we could hear
the hellacious gunfight unfolding behind us. Wright and I were
pissed that we had to leave the firefight, but after thirty seconds,
we saw a white pickup truck headed our way. We were pretty
sure it was the same pickup from earlier in the mission that ISR
identified, but we were not positive. We started to zero in on it
to see what the pickup was about to do. As it drove into a clear
view, we had a vantage point from two hundred yards away—
the maximum effective range for Wright's M203, but a very
effective range for us to utilize our M4s. Once the truck came
to a complete stop, the doors opened and the driver stepped out
along with a few guys piling out of the back passenger side door.
As they got out of the truck, we scanned through the magnified
optics mounted on top of our M4s looking for weapons. At
first glance we did not see anything, but simultaneously we
started to hear rounds fly a few feet over our heads. Wright
and I could hear the rounds as they made the very distinct
noise that one would only know if they have ever been shot at.

Wright said, "Are they shooting at us?" I responded sharply: "Yes." Immediately, more rounds flew over our heads and then the driver reached back in to pull something out of the truck. We saw through our optics that he was reaching for an AK-47. As soon as I saw the weapon, I opened up with a burst of 5.56 and instantly killed him. I could hear the truck's glass windows shattering and the metallic thuds of rounds hitting the chassis. Wright was joining in as if we were archers on top of a castle just lobbing precision-fired shots one after the other and not letting up. We had them pinned down and we were picking them off one at a time. Those same noises we heard directly from the impact of metal on metal when hitting the truck were echoing off the mountain range, producing a chilling effect.

The remaining Afghans were pouring out of the truck and trying to escape the death trap as if this truck was a Taliban clown car! At an elevated position, Wright and I had the drop on these guys and it was like shooting fish in a barrel. As Wright was continuing to lay waste into the combatants with 5.56 from his M4, I gave him a fire command to shoot one more of his high-explosive grenades at the truck. "Wright, one round HEDP, white truck, two hundred meters." Immediately following, I gave a quick radio call to my squad leader telling him to "get over here." Again, as Wright had done so many times before, he replied with "Roger that." After going through the motions earlier, he was a well-tuned machine and pulled his second to last round out from his kit and loaded it into the M203's breach. Wright got up on a knee, and with only a split second of dialing in his aim, he let it rip. Rooster ran to our position along with our platoon sergeant. As they arrived to our fighting position,

Wright's HEDP round impacted between ten to five meters in front of the truck, spraying shrapnel into the truck and enemy combatants–dead and alive. Wright and I continued to suppress the vehicle along with our reinforcements—our platoon sergeant and Rooster. There were now dead bodies lying all over the place, including one guy laid out on the ground in front of the vehicle in a black dishdash, who had foolishly tried to make a forward maneuver to our fighting position for cover.

Comedy always seems to work itself into even the most serious of situations. This firefight was no different. As a couple of SEALs were running to our fighting position, one tried to take a light anti-tank weapon (LAW) off his back, which resulted in him tripping and falling right on his face. He immediately was back on his feet, dusting the dirt off and deciding to leave the LAW on his back and now acquiring and engaging targets with his assault rifle. He joined the four of us laying waste to what, at this point, had increased to fourteen dead terrorists and one very shot-up truck. As we lifted our fires in order to reassess the situation, we noticed a "squirter"—an enemy combatant attempting to flee—sprinting away from the truck toward a rock. Immediately, the five of us opened up, and just before he made it to the rock, the squirter stumbled and fell due to the amount of fire that struck, paralyzed, and killed him in his attempt to flee. The total insurgents killed coming out of the truck was fifteen EKIAs (enemy killed).

At this point there was finally a sense that maybe the HLZ was secure enough for a helicopter to fly in and pick us up. As if fate were playing a cruel trick on us, at that very moment

the compound on the north side of the HLZ started firing
at us again with SAF. The six of us quickly ran back to the
embankment where we had found cover earlier in the firefight.
On my run across the HLZ, I changed magazines and realized
that I only had two left out of the original nine. I tried to put
the now empty magazine into my cargo pocket, but there was
no more room. I had to open up the dump pouch on my battle
belt to put the empty magazine in there instead and in the
process my clear lens Oakleys that I had taken off earlier in the
fight fell out of my cargo pocket and into the dirt. I quickly
retrieved them and threw them into my dump pouch along
with the magazine. It may seem odd to pause in order to pick
up a pair of glasses in the midst of gunfire flying all around
you, but a Ranger never leaves his equipment behind. "Care of
equipment" is literally in the Creed that we all lived by. I also
received a round count from Wright and told him that we will
be conserving his last grenade round and not to shoot it unless
we are being charged. I remember one of the SEALs (the one
who had fallen earlier) was upset with me for not having Wright
shoot that last round at the truck. It being in the heat of the
moment, I told him, "I will manage my team, and you can
worry about yours." My thought process was that if we get stuck
out here on this HLZ all day, there is no telling what we could
be facing later today, and I did not want to use our last 40-mm
HEDP grenade unless we absolutely had too.

As we were taking cover, it was broadcasted over the radio that
our exfil helicopter was two minutes out. While waiting for our
extraction bird, we continued to engage the compound and
suppressed into the fortified fighting position to keep their heads

down and to not allow the enemy to gain momentum and fire power on our position. The 160th SOAR pilots with complete disregard for their own safety were inbound and the noise of the rotor blades thudding the air never sounded so sweet. As I turned to see the Chinook flying toward us in the morning sky with its mini-gun and M240 firing at a cyclic rate of fire (as fast as they can shoot) I knew we were going to be just fine. The rounds from the Chinook were eating up the compound wall and chewing through the rock, sending fragments and dust everywhere. Besides being one of the coolest things I have ever seen, it provided the warmest feeling of safety I have ever felt.

Being at the end of the firing line with Wright and Rooster, the noise had increased behind me from the rotors of the Chinook indicating to me that it was almost time to run toward the ramp. I unattached my custom goggles, which I had fabricated for the extraction portion of missions to keep the flying dirt kicked up by the rotors out of my eyes. As the bird completed the landing sequence, the sound of its mini-gun and unrelenting barrage of lead on the side of the compound pouring down fire was music to my ears. Before we stood up I switched out my magazine to my last full mag of thirty rounds and ran to the helicopter, shooting until I expended my last round into the muzzle flashes that were still visibly coming from the compound. All of our team dove onto the Chinook and laid out near the tail of the aircraft as the helicopter thundered away from the still hot HLZ. Seeing the tail gunner on the M240 machine gun expertly handling the business of protecting the bird gave me a safe feeling. Wright and I eventually crawled over a layer of brass casings of 7.62 rounds that covered the floor of the aircraft

into seats toward the front of the aircraft, with high fives and
fist bumping going all around. We made it out alive, smiling
ear to ear! Resting my head back on the chair, I started to smell
the roses and take in what had just happened and realized how
effective and deadly only four Rangers can be. I imagined what
it would be like if we had the entire platoon there with us. As I
daydreamed, the Chinook began its approach back to the FOB
and we started our descent. At the abrupt feeling of the wheels
touching down, I sat forward and unhooked my safety line from
the floorboard of the Chinook. Once we came to a complete
stop, I walked out the back of the Chinook stepping on a layer
7.62 casings from the 240 Bravo covering the floorboard of the
aircraft, which kept my feet from touching the aircraft itself,
and then stepped out onto the tarmac to see the rest of Two
Charlie waiting on the back of a pickup truck and in the buses
that we use. As I walked over to them, Escobar stuck his head
out the window and the high fives of a great mission and "atta
boy" comments began to take off. Each of us were so jacked. If
we were in the states, we would have gone straight to a bar to
tell war stories and talk about the events that just took place,
but in Afghanistan it was time to conduct an AAR and prepare
for the next mission. The EKIA count from small arms fire for
Objective Lexus was fifty dead insurgents, give or take a few. (I
am not spot on with this, but I do remember it to be around
fifty.)

DOWNTIME

"And because that boy said those words, and because he died, thousands of other young men have given their lives to his country."

- Edward Everett Hale

After Two Charlie downloaded all our gear and threw it into
our designated cubbies and lockers in the ready room, we went
straight into the mission AAR in the TOC. The AAR was fast
but we went over everything to include the good and the bad
individual actions as well as the overall operation. During the
AAR, Wright and I were given positive feedback from Rooster
for our great communication and for accurate shots with
Wright's M203. In total Wright shot eight rounds of 40-mm
HEDP rounds and seven were direct hits. However, Wright and
I did have to discuss that missed first round, and after talking it
out, we realized that he had not accounted for the hill that he
shot into. Most of our training was done on flat ground, and
out of muscle memory, Wright zeroed in and did not account
for the incline. This was not just Wright's fault; after all, I am
his team leader and I am ultimately responsible for the actions
of my team. I should have directed Wright to account for the
incline/hill that he was shooting into in my fire command. As
a team leader it was my duty to accept the good and the bad
without emotion and to take the constructive criticism from
the AAR and go back to the drawing board with the team to fix
our shortcomings and to work on the basics to become a more
proficient, more elite fighting force. I led under the concept
of the four pillars of leadership taught to me by my previous
platoon sergeant: coach, train, mentor, and retrain. Mixed in
with these four pillars is the infamous motivational piece, and as
a team leader, I always found how to best motivate each one of
my guys. Some Rangers needed to be yelled at to get motivated
while others simply just needed to be told what to do once and
motivated themselves. With that said, Wright and I hashed out

what we needed to do differently in the future. I was going to incorporate in my fire command to adjust fires due to a hillside or whatever obstacle may affect the distance of the grenade shot. Not only did we practice what we learned, but we also made sure to spread the knowledge gained throughout the platoon through the Ranger gossip network, which travels faster than the speed of light. After the AAR, I told the guys to just go through their normal routine, clean their weapons and gear before going to bed, and when we wake up we will get together and go over more drills and tasks tomorrow with Blaise and Sesh, the new guys in our squad. Rooster was planning on taking them out on their first mission ASAP, and it was me and Escobar's job to get them ready.

After we wrapped up the AAR, Rooster and I went back to the hooch to change into our PT gear and hit the gym. We got out of our mission gear and hung everything up on the nails we hammered into the two-by-four posts of our bunk beds. Once everything was prepped and ready to go at a moment's notice, I got into my Vibram FiveFingers minimalist shoes and threw a scoop of my pre-workout supplement, Jack 3D, into some water, grabbed my IPod, and headed to the gym. Rooster and I walked in to find Wright on the pull-up bar with his legs out at a ninety-degree angle doing L-shaped pull-ups. Wright was a pull-up beast who could do over twenty straight strict pull-ups after a five-mile run without so much as moving a hair on his head while keeping his body straight as a board. Wright had amazing core strength and had a chiseled physique that would rival any fitness freak. Rooster and I got a quick kettlebell complex workout in that we had gotten from the Gym Jones workout

program designed specifically for special operations warriors
deployed overseas to better facilitate core and leg strength   to
help with the rough and rocky terrain that we fight in. It was
always a competition between Rooster and me to see who was
stronger and faster. We pushed each other to the max every day
and we never settled for mediocrity. It was a fun but respected
egotistical competition that neither of us ever wanted to lose
at. We took our fitness in second squad seriously. Prior to the
deployment we had a workout regimen that would have gotten
us ready to climb Mount Everest. As a squad we ran five miles in
less than thirty-three minutes every Monday morning to sweat
out the weekend's activities and festivities and then we would
do two Mountain Athlete workouts a day up until Friday. On
Saturday we would do a recovery workout followed by some beer
drinking on River Street in Savannah.

After the workout we went back to the hooch to get out of our
FiveFinger shoes and to link in with the rest of Two Charlie at
the chow hall. Even though it was actually morning and the rest
of the military was eating breakfast, we operated in the cover
of darkness and ate our meals aligned with our sleep pattern.
So this morning we were eating the beloved surf-and-turf, and
being that we worked extra hard last night I treated myself to
two pieces of pecan pie. It is said that vampires see more daylight
than a Ranger does on a deployment in the Global War on
Terrorism, so getting to experience some daylight this morning
was good for morale. After a tough steak and a decent lobster tail
at the chow hall, the entire platoon went back to our respective
squad hooches to throw in a dip of Copenhagen, hit the
showers, and conduct squad family time. Family time in second

squad usually consisted of our favorite TV show Dexter or a game of "Call of Duty." We took the "Call of Duty" multiplayer game about as seriously as we took our jobs. We actually went so far as to hang sheets up in the middle of the room leading up to the TV so that no one could screen watch and cheat. Sometimes "Call of Duty" matches would get so heated that there would be intense arguments ending with controllers thrown into the wall. Tonight we decided to go with the squad's favorite movie, A Perfect Getaway. Escobar introduced this movie to me over the training cycle when we were on CQ (control of quarters) one night. (CQ is the worst thing to be volunteered for; it is a twenty-four hour mandatory watch of the Ranger barracks to make sure young privates are not coming home drunk from the bars and bringing in the general's daughter for some late night fun or throwing beer bottles throughout the barracks and making a ruckus. Even though there was a CQ presence, these kinds of things still always seemed to happen.) We loved this movie because the main character was a cocky veteran who had served in a special operations unit in the Carolinas and referred to himself as an American Jedi who is extremely hard to kill. This stuck with the squad. Being the "cocky, arrogant Rangers" that we are, we began to refer to ourselves as American Jedis who are extremely hard to kill.

Before the movie was even over, we were all passed out, and just like any other day at 1400 zulu, our alarm clock went off and it was time to get back into action. Once we got up, the second squad privates, Sesh and Blaise, started their morning chores of cleaning up the room and making real, authentic Columbian coffee that Escobar's mom sent to us on a regular basis. On the way out the door, Rooster, Escobar, and I grabbed a cup of Columbian coffee and headed to the TOC for the daily brief to get an idea of potential targets that we were looking at actioning tonight, or in some cases, lack thereof. In this case there was nothing worth taking action on, so we would revert to training. Although there was nothing for us today, our PL was referencing some ideas that he had to get us some targets in the Pech Valley at a place known as Command Outpost (COP) Michigan. Without thinking much of it, Escobar and I went to the chow hall to get some breakfast and talk about what we were going to do today.

We decided that we would retrain the guys in a classroom setting on enter and clear room tactics, and then we would walk through some scenarios out in front of the hooch, set up some tape drill scenarios, and then end the training day with team litter drill contests to see who could assess and load a patient the fastest. After going over the basics of clearing a room on the whiteboard in our hooch, we all went over to the ready room to grab our weapons and mission- essential equipment. When we trained we wore everything we would wear on a mission to build proper muscle memory and avoid developing bad habits. Escobar and I individually inspected each of the weapons in our team to double and triple check that they were clear before we started to train. The idea of glass-house training is to be able to see what each individual is doing. The purpose of glass-house training is to practice gaining entry through breach points and training our guys to clear their primary, secondary, and tertiary sectors of fire while simultaneously walking to their points of domination. As a team we could only work as efficiently as the weakest link, and as a team leader it was me and Escobar's job to get us all on the same page and then excel and improve as a team. After laying out a frame with glint tape, creating a makeshift house with three rooms and a total of three breach points, I grabbed my team, consisting of Wright and Sesh, and prepared to enter and clear the rooms. While we were conducting our team SOPs, Escobar and his team, consisting of Gronbeck and Blaise, each stood in the center of one of the rooms and watched closely as we went through their specific rooms and the house as a whole. They were looking at us to make sure we individually cleared our sectors of fire and walked to our points of domination, which are individual tasks when done with precision and speed. It is said in this specific battle drill that slow is smooth and smooth is fast. It is imperative to not go too fast and to make sure all corners and hidden areas are clear. Violence of action is brought with the squeeze of your trigger finger, and if you are moving too fast to accurately shoot for your skill level, then you need to slow down or you will not be effective. Drills like these help you become faster at the basic fundamentals of Ranger tactics. As we drilled this over and over it was good for the guys in bravo team to see how it looks from an outside perspective and it was very beneficial to get involved with a quick AAR after each run through the glass house as a squad. Once we were done, it was bravo team's turn and they followed suit as my team watched closely. These drills are basic, but in combat mastering the basics and becoming proficient at them ultimately reduces the time it takes to clear a building, alleviating the time it takes for an enemy combatant to get to a gun to defend him or herself, or even worse, blow a suicide vest that could take out an entire assault force.

In Two Charlie we train like we fight, we train to the standard
and we don't settle for anything less. If it took us six hours to
get a task done correctly and to the standard where we were all
on the same page, then by God we trained for six hours. If it
took us two hours then we spent the remaining four hours we
had allotted at getting better on our identified shortcomings and
weaknesses. Second squad was a great squad and we took pride
in our job and we were self-motivated. Not one of us needed to
be told or asked to do something twice. We loved our job and
we trained for each other so that in an event that we were tried
we would prove ourselves. We relied on each other and knew
that each and every one of us gave it one hundred percent every
day to be the best, because our lives depended on our Ranger
buddy having our backs. There was a chemistry in second squad
and in second platoon that can't be explained unless you served
in a special ops unit. If you messed up, you better be ready to be
told to your face by your peers that you messed up and to retrain
yourself and get it right. It was a job where you have to have
thick skin, because it is not like the civilian world where if a deal
goes wrong you lose money. In this line of work, if you don't do
your job you could die, or worse, your Ranger buddy could be
killed. As a Ranger who took my job seriously and passionately
throughout my career, at random times I would have dreams in
which I would try and shoot my M4 and my gun would jam or
for some other weird reason I was unable to kill the combatant.
It was so vivid that I would wake up clenching onto something
and would be so tensed up.

Once we trained to the standard on the tape drills, we cleaned up the glint tape used to make the glass house and met in the hallway outside our hooch in the Two Charlie house where first and second squad lived. Escobar had already brought over the squad litter and we went straight into the next training event: assess and package a casualty. My team and I went first and Escobar provided his newest guy on the team, Blaise, as a wounded Ranger for the event for us to treat and package. Our patient for this specific training event suffered a gunshot wound to the chest and arm. As my team assessed him, we immediately took off all his gear, identified his wounds, and determined upon visual inspection that he was only responsive to pain. After treating the chest gunshot wound with a chest seal and verbally going over how to needle decompress his chest, we applied a tourniquet to the wounded arm and dressed it. I maintained control of the patient's head and then Wright and Sesh began the timed portion of getting the litter unpackaged, loading the patient, and securing the patient to be moved out of the CCP (casualty collection point). When we trained a medical scenario, we went over each wound, going through the motions on what we do to treat the wound, and we verbally talked through the process out loud for others to hear exactly what it was that we were doing. When we finished, Wright and Sesh's time was great. Wright was not scared to be an authoritative leader. I remember specifically watching him teach the newer privates during the training cycle about the remedial actions they should perform when a SAW malfunctions. Wright always spoke loud and clear, and as Escobar and I stood on the berm of the range overseeing the training, Wright told this young private who was holding a lightweight, fully automatic machine gun to grab it and handle it like a man. He then said, "I promise, you won't break it. If you do, so what? The army will buy you a new one." As I listened to Wright talk to this new guy in the platoon, I knew I was witnessing a confident Ranger who was a fighter and it put a smile on my face to have him in my team. Throughout training we talked about ways to be faster and how to communicate more efficiently to get the patient packaged in the litter to exceed the standard and be as fast as possible. Escobar, Gronbeck, and Blaise stepped to the plate next and this time Sesh was the patient. I do not remember who had the faster time, but I know that both teams' cohesiveness and chemistry made for an outcome that could have rivaled any team in the Ranger Regiment.

After a few hours passed and we finished up training, we packaged the litter back up and walked our gear and weapons back over to the ready room. Once I hung my weapon back up on the nail inside my wooden locker, I arranged everything in my locker, dusted off my night vision goggles, and checked my mags and demolition charges and initiators (a device used to make my demolitions go boom). Once I was satisfied with the appearance of my kit and locker, I stopped in the TOC to let Staff Sergeant Rooster know that we were done with the daily training and to see if we were looking at any potential upcoming missions. Rooster informed me that there was nothing in the works, but the PL is still looking into the potential mission in the Pech Valley. With that said, I went back to the hooch and told the guys that we have something in the works for the Pech Valley in the upcoming days. They all just nodded their heads and Escobar pulled out his board game "Risk."

Being that we had a little down time, we decided to take advantage and drink coffee, dip Copenhagen, and play a little "Risk" before we went to the gym. During the game we talked about college football and who we thought were the teams to look out for this year. Escobar spent some time going to school and playing college volleyball at the University of Central Florida in Orlando and was talking about how they were the up and coming team to look out for. Escobar was so tall that the top of my head barely reached his shoulders and he loved all sports. He was as competitive with his board games as he was on the court in basketball and volleyball.

A few days had past and the talk about a mission in the Pech Valley turned from "are we going?" to "when are we going?" Our PL and platoon sergeant along with the platoon senior medic and platoon FSO (fire support officer) flew out to check out our staging area for the upcoming mission to see if there was enough space to facilitate the task force that we would be taking. Upon their return we were informed that this was going to be the mission of all missions. When our PL got back he pitched his plan to the commander, and after long discussions we got the green light. Operation Wolverine was a GO! The last time SEALs went into this area they experienced catastrophic losses and the mission, Operation Redwing, has since been the most talked about mission in the Global War on Terrorism. Taking this with complete seriousness, respect, and understanding of what we would be going up against, I also realized that this could be the super bowl of my Ranger career. Once our

PL got back, the squad leaders going—Rooster, Wyatt, and Moose—put together a plan for the upcoming brief to target four compounds, which would occur prior to us flying out to stage at a place called COP Michigan. It was briefed by the PL that one of the insurgents, Sayed Shah, who we were going after was a wanted target in Afghanistan. It is not often that you get a mission like this, but when you do there is a different feeling that sets in because you know all eyes are on you and your platoon. After the PL's brief we broke off into our respective squads and went over the plan and talked about any and every possible scenario. To get a better understanding on the area, we even read Marcus Lutrell's AAR on Operation Redwing. That night I took the entire mission package that Rooster had printed out and studied the infiltration route that we would walk, the entire village, and then read each of the four target's bios to get an understanding of who each of the guys we were after was, what they had done, what they were planning on doing in the future, as well as their appearance. All four of these guys were fighters and from the research we had done, these guys were not afraid of us. They, like most radical Muslim terrorists that I had encountered during missions, did not value life and were not afraid to die. From my experience, Eastern culture does not value life like we do in America, because they have nothing to live for. They do not even fight for each other.

OPERATION WOLVERINE
<u>AUGUST 18, 2010</u>

"Of every one hundred men,
Ten shouldn't even be here,
Eighty are nothing but targets,
Nine are real fighters, and
We are lucky to have them,
for they the battle make.
Ah, but the one, one is a Warrior
and he will bring the others back."

- Heraclitus, 500 years BC

Just six days after Objective Lexus, under the cover and concealment of darkness on the night of August 17, 2010, second platoon loaded up into one Chinook helicopter and flew seventy-three kilometers from Jalalabad, Afghanistan, to COP Michigan, located in the Pech Valley, Kunar province—also known as the "most dangerous terrain for U.S. forces anywhere in the world[1]". In 2011 it was said over one hundred soldiers would pay the ultimate sacrifice fighting in the Pech Vally also known as the "Valley of Death" during Operation Enduring Freedom. Our platoon always operated at night, but everyone's mood aboard this flight was particularly edgy. The cause of our apprehension was not that we were on our way to kill the leaders of a terror network that had launched a series of successful attacks on American soldiers, but that we were going to the center of the Kunar province hornets' nest. Specifically, we were tasked to eliminate the Salafist network operating as a Taliban subgroup, called Jamaat ul Dawa al Quran (JDQ). Almost all of the local residents of the Pech Valley affiliated with the Islamic Salafist tribe were represented by Sahib Rohulla Walkil. Besides being the political leader of the area, Walkil also had the distinction of serving as an inmate in Guantanamo Bay for suspected terrorism ties.

COP Michigan sits in the Pech Valley surrounded by Taliban-filled mountains on the Pakistan border in the Kunar province, where the surrounding mountain peaks push ten thousand feet. The Salafist group we had been tasked to engage operated in the village of Shamun as close as five kilometers away from COP Michigan. The soldiers in Charlie Company of the 101st Airborne Division's 1st Battalion, 327th Infantry Regiment,

1 Tim Hetherington, "The Fight for Korengal," Vanity Fair December 3, 2007

had been defending COP Michigan for almost a year, and the close proximity to the enemy was readily apparent. Their gym was tattered with bullet holes and was called the "World's Most Dangerous Gym" in the August 2010 issue of Men's Fitness magazine. The shower trailer stalls were shot out with recoilless rifles and everyone had to travel through underground tunnels to get around. The tunnels were built with HESCO barriers (four feet by four feet cement walls filled with dirt) and sandbags surrounded the tactical operating center and other areas of high traffic to reduce the chances of anyone being shot by a sniper set in the surrounding mountains. The chow hall looked more like a place for flies to fester. Lights were not allowed to be turned on at night and there was a constant head count to make sure everyone was accounted for. The place was generally so bad that no one of high rank had visited COP Michigan in years.

In February 2010, U.S. forces pulled out of the Korengal Valley, also located in the Kunar province adjacent to the Pech Valley. The void allowed the Taliban to take control of the Korengal Valley, including their command and control base which the coalition forces had abandoned. The Kunar province is known for its warrior and isolationist culture. The Tantil, Shamun, and Sundray villages in the Pech River Valley hardly communicate, but they will share the same fight against any outsider. The Kunar province has been coined "Afghanistan's Heart of Darkness" by the soldiers who have fought there. The designation can be dated all the way back to Alexander the Great when he saw the importance of the Kunar province in the fourth century BC and invaded it to establish a stronghold for his conquest of the East. The local tribes burned their own homes and villages and fought Alexander's army using guerilla tactics that they have passed on and still used today. This kind of fighting was also used to start the Mujahidin resistance when local fighters in the Kunar province started attacking communist police outposts. It was so effective that the fighters in the Kunar province defeated an entire Soviet division in the early 1980s. Following in that tradition, some of the deadliest battles of Operation Enduring Freedom have been fought in the Kunar province, including Operation Red Wing, the setting for the operation where the book-turned-movie Lone Survivor occurred.

Our mission, Operation Wolverine, was to capture/kill high value targets of the Salafist network located in the Shamun Village of the Pech Valley in the Kunar province. The targets were Sayed Shah, Arghwan, Gul Jan, and Amin Khan. They were responsible for two U.S. troops killed in action (KIA) and eleven U.S. wounded in action (WIA) as well as numerous SAF and RPG attacks on the U.S. military-named road MSR Rhode Island, which passes by COP Michigan and runs parallel to the Pech River. The U.S. gathered intelligence that put these guys on the map and narrowed the search to pinpoint them earlier in the year. On May 11, 2010, Sayed Shah met with Salafist and Taliban commanders Arghwan, Gul Jan, and Dowron. They agreed to conduct attacks on COP Michigan, COP Blessing, and COP Able Main, all located in the Kunar province. On May 19, 2010, U.S. forces identified and monitored radio chatter from Sayed Shah and Ataulla leading thirty fighters positioned in the Tantil Village ready to attack coalition forces convoys of convenience. It was also reported that they were helped by Khalid, son of Dowron, who helped communicate over radio where the convoy was and when it will get to their location.

Sayed Shah was the Salafist commander and leader of the Nuristan fighters, who were directly linked to one U.S. KIA and ten U.S. WIAs in an RPG attack on September 5, 2009. He was responsible for attack planning, propaganda, SAF, and RPG attacks against coalition forces. He was considered excellent in understanding the TTPs of special operations forces. He also knew the weak points in MRAPs and how to effectively utilize RPGs against them. Sayed Shah and his network of fighters were so effective that the 101st was almost inoperable. Sayed Shah knew that his day would come when he would have to pay a price for his actions and so he always traveled with a personal security detachment (PSD) team of two to three armed men.

Arghwan was a sub-commander to his uncle Dowron (who was already actioned upon in Objective Celtic, but Dowron was not captured or killed) and was also directly linked to one U.S. KIA and one U.S. WIA in an RPG attack on December 1, 2009. He was thirty-five years of age, sixty-four to sixty-eight inches tall, medium build, black eyes, black hair, and had a black beard. It was also reported that he had a speech impediment. Like Sayed Shah, Arghwan was also involved with attack planning, propaganda, SAF, and RPG attacks against coalition forces. He took command when Dowron was incapacitated. Amin was also a sub-commander to Dowron and is responsible for facilitating weapons and funds.

Gul Jan was a sub-commander for Maulawi Abdul Rahmin, who commands about twenty-five fighters and conducts attacks in Tantil in the Pech district. He is a senior Salafist commander operating in the Pech district and is involved in attacks, attack planning, and propaganda. He also has ties to Dowron and the Kunar shadow governor Rahim and Korengal senior TB Commander Nasarullah.

In addition, the Shamun, Tantil, and Sundray villages had an early warning network system in place at the mouth of the Lagham Valley, across the Pech River from COP Michigan and just before the Shamun Village. The early warning system was headed by a man named Habir, who would call the commanders of the Salafist network to warn them of any coalition patrols entering the valley. Habir lived in an unidentified house. Any infiltration made by our team would require walking past Habir's location to get close to Shamun Village.

The intelligence value of capturing Sayed Shah would degrade JDQ (Jamaat ul Dawa al Quran) and TB operational capabilities in the Korengal and Pech valleys of the Kunar province. Sayed Shah's elimination would cease the collaboration between JDQ and TB networks throughout the Kunar province. Sayed Shah's capture would lead to actionable intelligence on a number of Al-Qaeda (AQ), JDQ, and TB commanders, facilitators, and trainers in Afghanistan and Pakistan to include AQ/ TB commander Dowron, Kunar Taliban shadow governor Rahim, and senior AQ Commander Abu Ikhlas al-Masri.

Prior to flying out to COP Michigan, we planned everything from our TOC in Jalalabad for the upcoming mission with ground reference graphics of the Shamun Village and close-up pictures provided by satellite imagery of the compounds/houses that the Salafist commanders lived in. The mission statement was as follows:

- ***Conduct raid for the following targets:***
  Objectives Nuclear, Yamaha, Bay Street, and City Market
  in order to disrupt the Pech RPG network.

  - <u>Objective Nuclear</u> – also referenced as known
    area of insurgent Rally Point-1 was to capture or
    kill Amin Khan, the Salafist sub-commander

  - <u>Objective Yamaha</u> – also referenced as Rally
    Point-2 was to capture or kill Gul Jan, the
    Salafist sub-commander

  - <u>Objective Bay Street</u> – also referenced as Rally
    Point-3 was to capture or kill Arghwan, the
    Salafist sub-commander

  - <u>Objective City Market</u> – also referenced as Rally
    Point-4 was to capture or kill Sayed Shah

We went over the plan so many times that I had the infil route
memorized like the roads to my house. For every mission
we were provided GRG of the target and the area within the
vicinity of the target area. Rangers even wore these GRGs in a
wrist sleeve like a quarterback wears his play calls in the NFL.
Having comprehensive situational awareness of the target
vicinity is imperative for mission success. The more you knew,
the faster you could respond. The faster you could respond to
senior leadership as a team leader and disseminate the same
information to your team, the less time that the insurgent has to
get to his AK-47. Like all missions, I knew every detail about the
Shamun Village.

The method of travel/transportation to get to each of these rally points was by foot. The plan was to open the gates of COP Michigan and walk out onto MSR Rhode Island and head straight to each of the rally points and assault each of them one at a time. Once each rally point had been actioned, the plan was to walk back to COP Michigan. In total we would be covering approximately ten kilometers carrying about sixty pounds of equipment on our backs. As they say in Ranger Battalion, "You gotta live hard to be hard."

When we landed at COP Michigan on the night of the 17th, we were greeted by Staff Sergeant Cameron Boe from the 101st Airborne Division in a covered tunnel. Cameron Boe was a hometown best friend of Rooster and a friend of Wright. Wright and Boe even went to Sniper School together. After the friends were caught up, Boe showed us where we would all be sleeping. The 101st slept at night and operated in daylight. As the sun crested the mountains in the early morning of August 18, Rooster and I got a quick workout in in the "World's Most Dangerous Gym" and then took a shower. Taking turns in the only working shower stall that was not shot out by sniper fire was not what we were accustomed to in Jalalabad. At COP Michigan you were only allowed to turn the water on to wet your body. After you got wet you immediately turned the water off and soaped up and then took the least amount of water you needed to rinse the soap off. After showering, I tried to get comfortable in my sleeping bag on a wooden piece of plywood that rested on the top of six-foot tall two by fours to make up the roof/top bunk of a squad leader's bed in the 101st. My place to lay down and get some rack was designed to store gear, it was

not a place to sleep, but we had to make due. These guys were
nice, very hospitable, and glad to have us there.

As I finally started to drift off, I was awoken by a tremendous
overpressure from a mortar round fired right outside of the
hooch. This was repeated again and again to the point that I was
not able to sleep. Once this started the squad leaders from the
101st Airborne Division started to run in and out of the hooch
with their radios giving situational reports to their commander
in the TOC. All of this activity interrupted the rest that
would be critical for a successful mission, because our planned
mission was to hit four compounds that night and we would
be walking around ten kilometers. Another factor on the minds
of the Rangers in the platoon was hunger. We were already
malnourished, partially due to the fact that the chow hall was
so terrible, so we filled our hunger void with Cliff Bars. These
factors against us started to add up as I lay awake staring at the
ceiling of the wooden hooch. With all the mortar rounds firing
off, I decided to get up and walk around through the tunnels.
As I was watched the 101st mortar guys send out mortars into
the mountains, I ran into one of the SEALs, who we picked up
the night before, sitting on a chair in front of his hooch. He also
could not sleep and was cleaning his M4 and going over the plan
via a rock drill. After looking at him for a second, I recognized
him from Emergency Medical Services (EMS) school in
Savannah, which we both attended prior to this deployment. He
was going through paramedic school while a corporal. Escobar
and I were attending EMT-I school. I had been this SEAL's
patient during the practical exam of the Paramedic National
Registry course while he was evaluated for care of a critically

wounded patient. I never forget a face, so I re-introduced myself and then I went and found Specialist Gronbeck, who was staying in the same hooch as the SEAL from EMS school and the two other SEALs going on the mission.

After getting an update on the guys from Gronbeck, I stopped in the morale and welfare room, and to my surprise, almost the entire platoon, including Corporal Escobar and the platoon leader, were there as well. The chances of getting into a fight tonight were pretty high, so I wanted to send out an e-mail to my family back home. I took this time to check in and let them know I was doing great and that everything was okay.

After sending out my e-mail, I went back to the hooch to try and fall asleep for a second time. After laying down for a few hours, I woke up and got out of the black PT shorts and tan shirt that I was sleeping in and started to suit up in my multi-camouflaged Crye Precision mission uniform for the night. It was getting close to 1400 hours zulu time and 1700 was the designated start point (SP) of the mission. Prior to SP of the mission, there was a planned FRAGO in the 101st TOC at 1500 to discuss the mission and any changes that need to happen. During the FRAGO we would also discuss what needs to be done to make the changes happen. It was imperative to hash out all details before we opened the gates of the COP and went into "Indian country."

I took the extra time I had before the 1500 FRAGO to PCI my kit, including my weapon and mission-essential equipment. I double checked all my magazines and made sure the rounds were seated right, topped off my CamelBak with water, and made sure my two M67 fragmentation grenades, one concussion grenade (flash bang), and white smoke grenade were set to SOP. Last, I checked all of the batteries in my NODS, lasers, lights, wrist Garmin, and EOTech. In addition to my load of nine mags, I also was carrying two breaching charges. As the alpha team leader of the primary assault squad, these breaching charges were imperative to facilitate my job of gaining entry into each of the buildings for the platoon. Once I breached the door, I had to control the flow of my team during the assault/raid of the mission to capture or kill Sayed Shah, Arghwan, Gul Jan, and Amin.

Once I checked over all my stuff, I went over to the TOC with the squad leaders to receive the brief. We discussed the plan with the SEALs and everyone brought up some key points and ideas for the mission. As a group we decided to change the plan and condense it down to three from the original four rally points that we had initially planned to target. We did not know exactly where Sayed Shah was, and we did not want to tip him off that we were in the Shamun Village before we got to his house so we kanked (canceled) Objective Nuclear, Rally Point-1, for Amin to reduce time before TOT at Rally Point-4, where we believed him to be. This mission was planned on intelligence gathered over time. We were only able to go off of what we knew through past human gathered intelligence and signal intelligence. With no positive location of where our targets were at the moment, we planned to assault the historical place of bed down for Sayed Shah, Arghwan, and Gul Jan. The new plan was to walk straight to Rally Point-2 and assault Gul Jan's house. From there, we planned to flex over without making a noise and action Rally

Point-3 where Arghwan lives. Lastly, we planned to raid Rally Point-4, Sayed Shah's position. If executed properly, we would have three rounds in Sayed Shah or his hands bounded in zip ties before Shah knew we were in his village.

Overall, the FRAGO brief reinforced the basic concept of the operation to capture/kill Gul Jan, Arghwan, and Sayed Shah. The purpose was to disrupt the RPG network in the Pech Valley and the decisive point to this operation was the containment of the target area without compromise. This is decisive because it will prevent escape of personnel and will allow for follow-on missions (FOM) in the village for the assault force. The primary plan of action was a silent clear of all areas and target compounds. The alternate plan of action was a callout with escalation of force.

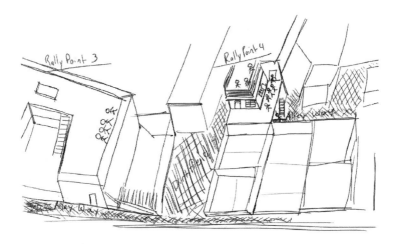

The operation was to occur in five phases:

- Phase 1: infiltration. During infil we planned a squirter

(fighter fleeing target building) control contingency plan, set rally point, and target update as well as asset posture.

- Phase 2 and Phase 3: establish isolation and conduct assault on Rally Point-2, Rally Point-3, and Rally Point-4.

- Phase 4: exploitation of each rally point. During phase 4 we will conduct battle interrogation and exploit the mission while conducting sensitive site exploitation (SSE) including detainee ops. The dog team handler, Sergeant Tango, will facilitate the SSE piece with his K9, Bruno. Bruno will sniff throughout the house for anything that could be detrimental to the task force. When phase 4 is complete we will collapse, cordon, and prep for exfiltration back to COP Michigan.

- Phase 5: exfil back to COP Michigan.

Specific jobs during the mission for each element are as follows:

- Sniper team: Sergeant Baumeister serves as the Ranger sniper team leader and spotter for shooter Specialist Devon Swanson. The sniper team's mission is to provide overwatch of the target area and allow weapons squad to set in a support by fire (SBF).

- Support by fire: Weapons squad, led by Staff Sergeant Moose with his medium-weight machine gunner Corporal Smitty

- Primary assault: Second squad, consisting of Staff
  Sergeant Rooster; myself, Sergeant McGarry; Corporal
  Escobar; Specialist Gronbeck; Specialist Wright; and
  Private First Class Blaise. Our mission is to clear through
  the objectives and capture or kill Gul Jan, Arghwan, and
  Sayed Shah. As a last resort, we will react to contact if
  the situation presents itself.

- Secondary assault: First squad, consisting of Staff
  Sergeant Wyatt, Sergeant Plagge, Corporal Jenkins,
  Specialist Hanley, and Private First Class Lowry, is
  responsible for walking point and navigating to the
  target buildings as well as assisting in the assault of the
  rally points to capture and or kill Gul Jan, Arghwan, and
  Sayed Shah.

- Security: The Navy SEAL element is responsible for
  providing isolation of the known area of insurgents. It is
  their job to prevent enemy movement to and from rally
  points in the village.

Once everyone was good to go with the plan, I went back to
my hooch with Staff Sergeant Rooster and Wyatt. We all talked
about the mission while we were doing last minute preparations.
I put my gear on as we listened to "Rooster" by Alice in
Chains. While singing to the song, I undid the Velcro strap/
cummerbund on my kit and slid into my shoulder straps like I
had done over a thousand times before. As I donned my kit, the
Saint Christopher medallion that my grandma gave me before I
went to basic training broke off my dog tag chain. I immediately
started looking for it and couldn't find it. I asked Wyatt to

look on the ground by him, but he didn't see it either. I took a minute to look for it and couldn't find it. It pissed me off that I did not feel it pressing down on my chest from the weight of my kit. It was a sensation that gave me comfort. I took a seat to finish strapping my helmet down, and when I stood back up my Saint Christopher medallion fell out of the bottom of my right pant leg and rolled on the ground. With a sigh of relief, I looked over to Wyatt and said, "Looks like I will make it out of this one." Wyatt laughed and went back to putting his kit together. I quickly put the medallion back on my dog tag chain with my multi-tool/Gerber and then grabbed my rifle and walked out of the hooch. As I stepped out of the hooch into the darkness, I saw Wright sitting in a chair next to the hooch door with a huge dip in his mouth. He looked up at me and said, "Hey Sergeant." I just gave him a head nod back and asked him where the rest of the guys were. Before he could respond, I saw them all over to the side talking and asking last minute questions.

It was time to go over the mission and rehearse TTPs. Corporal Escobar, the bravo team leader, was carrying seven mags, totaling 210 rounds, which is considered a combat load; two M67 fragmentation grenades; a concussion grenade; and a Hooligan breaching tool. Gronbeck, the SAW gunner, was carrying a lightweight, fully automatic machine gun that fires from the open bolt position. He was carrying five hundred rounds of linked 5.56 on his kit and had one hundred rounds attached to the bottom of the gun. I checked and he had all the rounds seated in his links perfectly and he already had them fed and laid on the feed tray closed and covered by the feed tray cover with the bolt closed. Next, I checked Wright. He was carrying a load out of nine mags and twelve M203 40-mm HEDP grenades. Wright was also carrying a ladder and sledge hammer on his back for breaching. Last, I checked on Private First Class Blaise. At only eighteen years old, this would be Blaise's first mission. He was carrying a combat load of seven mags for his M4, and like Wright, he was carrying twelve rounds of 40-mm HEDP fragmentation grenades for his M203, which was attached to his M4, and a fifteen-foot carbon breaching/assault ladder. As I was checking the guys, Corporal Escobar followed behind me checking Wright, Gronbeck, and Blaise one at a time to double check their mission-essential equipment. Pre-combat inspections are taken seriously; Escobar and I paid attention to every detail, and working together, we never missed anything.

Next Escobar, Wright, and I went over and rehearsed a ladder drill with Blaise on the HESCO barrier next to the hooch. The five of us, including Gronbeck, then practiced and talked about routine drills when clearing rooms and entering breach points. We also talked about the importance of paying attention to every step when approaching a target building and walking through streets. These were basic concepts to the seasoned veteran, but this was Blaise's first mission and we wanted to make sure he was good to go on everything. It was imperative to stay as stealth as possible and not step on anything or kick anything that would make a loud noise when approaching a target building. Silent entry was a key element to maintaining the element of surprise, because this could make the difference between life and death. A mission accomplished with no shots fired and moving in and out of a village like a ninja in the shadows of darkness and taking home with us bad guys cuffed, masked, and bagged, without anyone knowing someone was missing till the next morning was perfection.

Corporal Escobar brought a very important piece to the fight tonight; he was the designated squad EMT and was responsible for setting up casualty collection points (CCP) in the chance we have a casualty. We trained this scenario throughout the training cycle and we had it down to the point that we didn't even have to talk. While Escobar's job is to set up the CCP and provide first responder care on the battlefield, it was my job to set up a perimeter around the CCP and take charge of the security element for the squad until care and package of the wounded onto a litter is provided.

Tonight we were primary assault on a capture or kill direct action raid mission on target Salafist commanders Sayed Shah, Arghwan, and Gul Jan. This is what we trained for. Collectively our squad had over twenty years of experience between the six of us. We were tried, tested, and proven Army Rangers and after last week's mission, Objective Lexus, we felt invincible.

As we finished going over the mission, Staff Sergeant Rooster showed up with all his mission-essential equipment on and ready to go. He asked me a few questions about the target and quizzed me on certain details to make sure my head was right. Once our squad leader gave us a double and triple check, we linked in with the rest of the platoon next to the only gate/entrance into the COP. We were taking two 101st soldiers who were already familiar with the village to help us navigate right to the three target compounds. Prior to stepping off for infil, we had a radio check over the assault channel on our MBITR. After the radio check our PL came over the radio and said, "Ten minutes till ISR comes on station." With that call we took a knee for what seemed to be a second, and then we all flipped our NODs down and viewed the world through a green tint.

Before flying out to COP Michigan, our platoon forward observer (FO) Sergeant McCabe worked hard to reserve us an ISR platform and three F-16s for this mission without the help of our PL who didn't think we would need air assets. McCabe reserved the assets for five days. He had to go about doing this behind our PL's back. Our PL did not see the importance of having ISR and assets overhead. When ten minutes were up we still did not have ISR, but we stepped out of COP Michigan anyway. Our PL decided that we could move out the gate and into the Pech Valley without any overwatch, and he did not disseminate this information to the assault force. When the ISR platform arrived and came on station, the pilot informed our FO of incoming weather. Sergeant McCabe told our PL of the incoming weather and suggested to him that we roll the mission to another night when the conditions were more favorable for us to use the assets. Our PL responded to the FO telling him to inform the TOC that we will accomplish this mission tonight— no matter what.

As we walked out the gate in platoon file formation, I stepped over a metal rickety bar, which was the bottom of the door frame for the gate of COP Michigan, and stepped out onto MSR Rhode Island heading toward Shamun Village. Once I got out on the road I created my separation with the Rangers in front of and behind me, at the same time looking back to make sure everyone in my team was following suit. We kept a fifteen meter separation between each Ranger in front and behind with no Ranger to your left or right. We staggered and separated at distances like this to reduce the number of potential casualties if a Ranger were to step on an IED.

Sergeant Plagge, first squad's alpha team leader under Staff Sergeant Wyatt, was leading the way to Shamun Village and the target buildings plotted for attack via the infiltration route he had planned and loaded into his handheld GPS. Plagge loved to lead out and wanted to show off his ability to move out, and in true Ranger team leader fashion, he did so with his hair on fire and with a motto of "follow me." Plagge stepped off with the determination and the intestinal fortitude to get us to the Shamun Village at a pace that was not for the weak hearted. The infil was moving along as planned with no issues. As we passed through the shadows of the Tantil Village to the right and the Lagham Valley to our left, each Ranger was scanning through NODS the surrounding village homes with their infrared flood lights and infrared laser center points zeroed in at two hundred meters and searching for enemy combatants. Our first stop was Gul Jan's house (Rally Point-2), but prior to getting to Shamun Village, we had to cross a wooden drawbridge over the Pech River.

Once Plagge got up to a close but safe distance, keeping out of blast range distance in the event of a potential roadside bomb, he called for the platoon to halt. As Two Charlie took a knee and pulled security, our Ranger dog team led by Sergeant Tango with his K9 Bruno, who was always by his side, made their way to the bridge. Bruno started to get excited and jumped up and down knowing that he was about to get to do some work. Once Tango calmed Bruno, they went into action. In a matter of minutes Tango and Bruno checked every inch of the bridge and cleared the entire bridge for potential IEDs. Immediately following the all-clear from Tango, Plagge stood back up and once again lead out. Two Charlie followed him in a Ranger platoon file heading into Shamun. Plagge continued to hold a steady pace of 5.2 kilometers per hour, which is what we call "moving out." Being that the infil was about five clicks, we ended up getting to the bridge in a little less than an hour.

As I walked over the river on the surprisingly sturdy wooden bridge that made a few rickety noises, I could hear the rushing water underneath me churn through the Afghanistan rocks. The noise was so loud and powerful that I thought for a second about the dangerous possibilities of the ruthless terrain in the Pech Valley and couldn't help but respect it. I took a quick glance at the water, and through my NODs I could see the splashing water and white-capped waves crashing into the rocks; I considered how terrible it would be to fall victim to that river.

After walking over the Pech River and through the alleyways and side streets of the Shamun Village, Two Charlie continued to silently and stealthily walk but at a way slower pace as the target building came into view. First squad moved around to the backside of the house and postured themselves at a breach point on the third floor, which was only accessible by the climbing ladders they propped up on the house. The steep terrain made it more accessible for us, and as we walked up I gazed at the target building sitting high up on a hill, and I took in the big picture to get my bearings. In the best case scenario, we would capture Gul Jan to get the intel needed to find Sayed Shah. With his capture and anyone else in his family, we would also be able to get a follow- on mission that would hopefully take us directly to Sayed Shah and Arghwan. Worst case scenario would be for us to tip the entire village of our presence. The last thing we want to do now is to let Sayed Shah and his PSD know that we were here to get him.

As I approached the building with my team and squad in trail, Rooster lasered a stairwell with the infrared laser attached to his M4, which was only visible through NODS. The stairwell lead straight up to the breach point on the second floor. I responded with a head nod, confirming to him that I got it and I understood what he wanted. I climbed the squad up the narrow stairwell that was carved out of the rocky terrain provided by the mountains bordering the village, and I carefully planted my heal, rolling to my toes one step at a time and trying not to make a noise. As I approached the doorway of Rally Point-2, I aimed my M4 directly at the door. Behind me were Escobar and Rooster along with the rest of the guys pulling security on windows and rooftops on the second and third floors. Before I even got up to the breach, I located the hinges on the wooden door, which was always my first assessment of the breach, to determine if it was an inward or outward swinging door. Being that the hinges were on the outside of the rickety wooden door, I knew that this was an outward opening door. After scanning the door for any wires or anything that looked out of the ordinary, I tried to open the door slowly and silently. I was stopped by a rusty chain on the inside of the house. The chain was long enough that I was able to pry my fingers around the backside of the door. My plan was to pull the door open and rip the chain right out of the mud wall that it was secured on.

First squad was positioned to action Rally Point-2 and the conditions were set. The sniper team was providing overwatch and weapons squad and the Navy SEAL element was postured, providing security and overwatch on the village and target building. Everyone was ready; I gave a head nod to my squad leader, letting him know we were good to go as well. Once I did this Rooster made a radio call to our PSG to relay that second squad was good to go. Then, the PSG came over the radio and cleared the channel so no one else would interrupt the upcoming radio call that he was about to make. Our platoon sergeant followed up, and to make for a simultaneous breach into Rally Point-2, he counted down from three.

As I patiently waited as best I could for the call of "one," my nerves and adrenaline began to rise. I was so amped that when I heard one through my headphones, I ripped the door right off the hinges. To my surprise the structure of the door was a lot weaker than I expected, and with the momentum I had created I started to stumble back toward the edge of the porch/ stoop of the house. Before I almost fell off the twenty-foot porch onto the alleyway rock and stone, Escobar reached out his long arm, grabbed my carrying handle on the back of my kit, and pushed me right back toward the breach. My momentum abruptly changed and I grabbed my rifle and went straight in the breach and into the house. I was the first one in the second floor and immediately cleared the main foyer. There was no one in the room, but I noticed quickly that there were two stairwells leading downstairs and upstairs and two closed doors in front of me. With a split second to make a decision, I went straight to the closest door. I tried to open it but it was locked. Just like before, I looked for hinges and didn't see any, so I knew this was an inward swinging door. So I did what most Rangers do and used my boot to try and kick it in. The door didn't budge. I looked at Wright behind me and said, "Sledge." Without blinking an eye, he turned around so I could grab the sledge off of his back. As I was getting the sledge, Private Lowry showed up from first squad and secured the door with his M4 aimed at the locking mechanism, waiting and itching for someone to open the door. Once I got the sledge off of Wright's back, I positioned my body offset from the door to keep out of the fatal funnel and to utilize my core strength to knock the door down. I also flipped my NODS up because there were lights on in the house. I hit the door once and it only budged, so I reared back again with all I had and hit the door so hard that it flung around and smacked the wall on the inside of the room, leaving a cloud of dust from the force. I immediately stepped out of the way, dropped the sledge, and let Wright and Lowry enter and clear the room. Before I was even able to breach the doorway, they had the room cleared. There was no one in the room and there were no doors or windows leading to another room. After a visual clear of the room with my eyes and confirmation that it was cleared by Wright, I turned around and saw Wyatt and Plagge headed for the stairwell leading to the bottom floor.

Being that this room was cleared, I linked in with Wyatt and

Plagge and went down the stairs after them. As we entered into the dark bottom floor foyer, we used the flashlights attached to our M4s to clear the first room. Once it was cleared we moved to the next room, and just like the two previous rooms, there was no one there but we still scanned the primary, secondary, and tertiary sectors of fire with our rifles. After the bottom floor was cleared, I sent a situational report (SITREP) to my squad leader via my MBITR to let him know the second floor and bottom floor was cleared.

The PL and PSG were busy using the interpreter to interrogate the one fighting-aged male captured on the third floor. While this was going on I began a sensitive site exploitation of the house. I began to mark the rooms and take pictures for documentation. Escobar followed up behind me drawing a sketch of the house on a three-by-five card documenting what was in each room. As we did this Gronbeck, Wright, and Blaise collected anything that looked worth bringing back for intelligence gathering purposes to help action future targets. Once these items were compiled, they were then labeled and put in a nylon parachute bag. The PSG, weapons squad leader, and PL were still interrogating the captured male, so I set my guys in windows facing out in the village to pull security after the SSE was complete. I then linked in with Wyatt and Plagge on the bottom floor to see how their breach and clear of the third floor went. We talked for a second and waited for a radio call from the PL. It was okay to take a little bit of time, because we had a stronghold in Rally Point-2 and we maintained the element of surprise by not making any abnormally loud noises.

A few minutes went by and our platoon sergeant came over the radio and announced the FOM. The follow-on mission was Gul Jan's guest house located next door to Rally Point-2. Staff Sergeant Rooster, Corporal Escobar, Staff Sergeant Wyatt, Sergeant Plagge, and I were going on this mission. The rest of the task force was staying behind, so I made sure to let Gronbeck, Wright, and Blaise know. To facilitate the FOM we brought along the detainee and our interpreter from Rally Point-2. Our detainee seemed a little flustered, but that was expected from someone who was just captured in the middle of the night. He said that he knew that Gul Jan had been at the house he was taking us to in the past. As we approached the door of the target, Rooster and I assessed the door. The breach was locked so Wyatt told the interpreter to have the detainee knock on the door. Once someone opened the door, we would rush the door and assault the building. No one came to the door. Rooster used a breaching sledge off of Plagge's back, and then he began to try and knock the door in. The noises from trying to breach the door with a sledge hammer woke a sleeping male, and he opened the door to see what was going on outside his house.

As soon as he did so, Wyatt and I immediately rushed the unarmed man and detained him. We threw him on the ground and cuffed him with heavy duty plastic zip ties in a side room off of the stairwell. While we were detaining this MAM, I saw out of my peripheral vision the rest of the assault force charging up the stairs to the main floor. Once we had the detainee contained, I left him lying on the ground in the fetal position and ran up the stairs to assist the rest of the assault and clear the building.

I crested the stairs and entered into an open courtyard. To my left I saw Escobar fighting a male and trying to keep the others in the room at bay; he called for my help, but I had to run past him as there were more rooms to clear and women were walking out of a room directly across from the stairwell. I ran toward the three older-aged females who were running back into the room that I was headed for. As I crested the breach into a long prayer room, I cleared the room by myself, which is against our TTPs, but I had no one else so I had to do what I had to do. I came back out of the room, and I noticed that there were twelve to fifteen people in the courtyard sleeping under blankets on cots. Not one of them even knew we were there as they were all asleep. Because there was no air conditioning, it was custom for families to sleep outside on rooftops and courtyards for a cooler, more relaxing temperature. Once we had everyone detained, we started the battle interrogation piece with the two military-aged males to see if they were Gul Jan or if they knew where Sayed Shah or Arghwan were. Neither of the two detainees were anyone worth a crap and they did not know any details pertinent to facilitating our mission.

We took a tactical pause and our platoon sergeant made a radio call to the PL back at Rally Point-2 to let him know we had the follow- on target building clear. During this time, Rooster, Sergeant Plagge, Corporal Escobar, and I all took a seat on a stoop in the courtyard. We were taking a breather and catching our breath; we were all exhausted from the adrenaline and amount of energy that we had exerted from the infil pace and the clearing of the two buildings. Being that we had already made a lot of noise and were fatigued, I mentioned to our platoon sergeant in group conversation that we might want to take it back to COP Michigan. It was not his call to make and it was not becoming of a Ranger to head back without the mission accomplished. The Ranger Creed states: "Readily will I display the intestinal fortitude to fight on to the Ranger objective and complete the mission, though I be the lone survivor."

As we got our legs back under us and our breath back, the PL came over the assault radio and informed us to prepare to move out to Rally Point-3. Immediately, I ate a few Sports Beans for electrolytes and took a swig of water from my CamelBak and was ready to rock. It also states in the Ranger Creed: "Energetically will I meet the enemies of my country," and this is exactly what we were getting ready to do again at Rally Point-3, because we were "mentally alert, physically strong, and morally straight," and through the years we were sculpted into hardened machines from rigorous and tough training.

We took the two fighting-age male detainees with us and went back down to the alley and over to the entrance of Rally Point-2 to link up with the assault force. Being that we were primary assault, we passed the detainees off to the enablers. First squad linked back in with the 101st guys, and with their help first squad led the way through the Shamun Village back roads and alleyways right up to the east side of Arghwan's two-story house (Rally Point-3). As we approached the house, I picked up speed and bypassed first squad so that second squad as a whole could take primary assault on Rally Point-3. While we were doing this, weapons squad and the sniper team simultaneously set in security using a rock wall that overlooks an empty grass lot between them and Rally Point-3 as cover. The conditions for assault on Rally Point-3 were set. The only visible way into Rally Point-3 was through a door on an elevated patio. Leading up to the patio was a wooden step ladder and a wooden gate latched by a chain to keep intruders out. I lasered the wooden ladder with my infrared laser, indicating to Rooster that I was going to lead the way up the ladder. He also lased the stairwell to confirm that he understood. I climbed the ladder stealthily and silently like a ninja trying not to make a noise, while my squad and the Navy SEAL element were postured below, waiting for me to unlock the gate and make entry on the patio. At this time, first squad maneuvered to a breach point on the first floor. While I was working as silently as possible to move the chain off of the Afghanistan-engineered latch, my squad was scanning the house with their infrared lasers and providing security for me.

As I unlatched the chain and started to open the gate, a fighting-aged unarmed male sat up on the cot that he was sleeping on by the door, which was about ten feet away from me on the patio. Without hesitating, I climbed the last rung of the ladder, went through the gate, and ran straight to the Afghan in a white dishdash with my M4 pointed right at him. As I closed the distance between us, I moved my safety selector switch from safe to semi hoping he would give me an opportunity to put two rounds in his chest and one in his head. Being that he was surprised that I was there, he was so frightened that all he did was freeze and put his hands in the air. I moved my selector switch back to safe and ran at him full speed and then gave him a leaping boot to the chest with my right leg. With the adrenaline and force of the kick, the male went straight to the ground. As I started to turn him over, I saw out of my peripheral vision Rooster, Corporal Escobar, Specialist Gronbeck, Specialist Wright, and the Navy SEAL element run by and enter the doorway leading into Rally Point-3. To get back in the mix I yelled at Private Blaise as he was running by. I told him to flex tie this guy with his zip ties and pull security on him. Private First Class Blaise responded with "Roger that." Once Blaise had this guy under control, I ran into the breach and into the house.

The second floor had a wraparound hallway with a banister lining the open and roofless area inside the compound. The hallway was in the shape of a horseshoe with doors on the left side of the entire hallway. I ran straight down the hall and ran up behind Wright. As he was about to enter a room he said, "Give me one." Wright wanted to confirm he had a second guy to clear the room with him. I responded, "Take it." (This was me saying I got your back.) Wright hesitated for a second, because he didn't hear me so I put my left hand on his back, keeping muzzle control of my M4 with my right hand on my pistol grip, and gave him a nudge forward to reassure him that I was there. Wright crested through the doorway and tripped on a metal one-inch rail in the door frame that he did not see. He fell into the room so I stepped over him, covering his body, and cleared the room with no one or anything in it. Wright looked up at me and he and I made eye-to-eye contact. For a second I felt frustrated with him for tripping, but it was just an unpredictable error that has happened to everyone in this line of work. I immediately ran back out into the hallway and ran down the hall toward a closed door at the right angle of the hallway. As I sprinted toward the door, I looked to my right through the open courtyard of the compound and saw Rooster making his way to the same door from the perpendicular hallway. Without saying anything I knew he was going to be right behind me into the room. I leaped and gave a swift kick to the door with my boot. The door swung open and we cleared the room. As we exited out of the room I marked the room clear for the rest of the assault force. Wright linked in with Rooster and me and the three of us started making our way over to the stairwell leading to the rooftop of Rally Point-3. We climbed the stairwell fast   and efficiently. We cleared the roof and found one unarmed male covered in a blanket and sleeping on a cot. As the three of us simultaneously moved toward the sleeping male, Specialist Hanley and another Ranger from first squad made their way to the rooftop.

Hanley and Lowry ran up to the sleeping male as Rooster, Wright, and I pulled security for them, aiming our muzzles at the sleeping male. Hanley ripped the blanket off of the man and then immediately backed up. We scanned the cot through our NODS with our infrared lasers and did not identify a weapon. He was unarmed and he appeared older than fighting age. He began to stand up and with this action I moved my selector switch from safe to semi as a safety precaution till I could determine that what he was doing was not a threat. As he stood up it appeared as though he was either high on drugs or mentally challenged. Without wasting any more time Specialist Hanley moved forward and detained him. The initial clear of the building was complete.

As we were about to go down the stairs, a siren started to go off in the Shamun Village on a loud speaker. I had heard similar

sirens before in Iraq and Afghanistan, but never at this time of
night. These sirens usually indicated prayer, but most of the time
prayer took place at sunrise. I stopped and looked off into the
village through my NODs from the rooftop of Rally Point-3 to
see if there was anything going on in the village. There was no
sign of any life or movement in the surrounding compounds/
homes.

Rooster, Wright, and I started to head back down the stairs
while the siren was still going off on a loud speaker throughout
Shamun Village. When I was only a few steps down the narrow
rickety wooden stairs, the PL came over the radio and told us to
go hit (military slang for assault/raid) Rally Point-4. We had not
finished the clear of Rally Point-3, and I was pissed, thinking to
myself— we have to finish clearing this building! Nonetheless,
I quickly changed gears and started to make our way to the
bottom floor, because we were going whether I liked it or not.
On the way down Rooster told me to get all the guys in front of
Rally Point-3 and have them ready to go over to Rally Point-4.
I made a quick radio call to Escobar and he was already ready to
go. Escobar, Gronbeck, and Blaise had cleared the second floor
and beat us down to the bottom floor and were waiting on us. I
relayed this information to Rooster, and when he heard this we
picked the pace up.

Once Wright and I got to the bottom floor, Rooster went and
discussed the plan with the platoon sergeant and the platoon
leader. Our PL did not tell our squad leaders that the ISR
platform could not see Shamun Village anymore due to cloud
coverage. When the pilot aimed his ISR capability at Rally

Point-4, he could not see the rooftop through the layer of clouds. The cloud deck was also too low for the pilot to get under; if he were to have flown below the cloud level, the noise of his aircraft would have woken the town, alarming Sayed Shah and his PSD team in Rally Point-4.

I linked up with Escobar; he brought Gronbeck and Blaise with him. Once I had all the guys with me, we walked out into the alleyway that led toward Rally Point-4. As we got to the end of the alley, we linked up with first squad. Plagge had his GRG out and was looking for Rally Point-4 on his wrist Garmin. I knew exactly where Rally Point-4 was and made a call over the radio that I would lead out. Rally Point-4 was just twenty-five meters away and was accessible through an open lot in the middle of Shamun Village. I started to lead out and lased the target building with my infrared laser for the rest of the assault force to see. I started to assess the building to get an idea of how we were going to assault and conduct a simultaneous breach with first squad. While we were approaching Rally Point-4, the sniper team was getting set in to provide overwatch on Rally Point-4 with the Navy SEAL element and our weapons squad leader, creating a SBF position on an adjacent rooftop to building Rally Point-4.

As I stealthily approached the north side of the first floor entrance, I walked underneath a covered concrete slab that created a roof over the alleyway. The roof also covered the double door main entrance into Rally Point-4. This double door was locked by a thick chain and pad lock. I scanned the door through my NODS, illuminating it with my infrared laser, walked past it, and headed toward the west side of the house.

As I turned the northwest corner and walked down the west side of the house, I saw a wooden ladder that led to the rooftop/ patio of the second floor of Rally Point-4. Rooster and Corporal Escobar were right behind me and saw the same thing. Without saying a word I climbed up, moving smooth and fast, with my left hand grabbing each rung and my right hand on my pistol grip with my M4 canted up and aimed toward the rooftop. Once I got to the top of the ladder, I exposed the upper half of my body and quickly scanned the rooftop through my NODs. After having given the roof a visual clear, I immediately identified two closed wooden doors and a window in the "L"- shaped seven-foot concrete wall in front of me. I could not see through the window because of a sheet or curtain covering it. One of the two doors was to the right of the window on the same wall. The other door was in the concrete wall perpendicular to the wall with the window and other door. Between me and the wall was a six-foot concrete slab patio/rooftop that wrapped around to the north side of the building. The north side of the patio/rooftop was the same roof that covered the chained double doors. On the roof of the room in front of me was an old wooden wall made up of what looked to be four two-by-twelve inch pieces of wood with small holes and cracks throughout the planks of wood that made up the wall. Between the concrete wall and wooden wall was the roof of the room and the roof had a one-foot ledge that stuck out over the patio and created cover for the windows and doors.

Due to the crummy architecture in Afghanistan, it did not

stick out as something out of the ordinary at the time, but looking back on it, I had never seen this type of structure before. Having not seen or heard anyone, I stepped onto the rooftop and Escobar, Rooster, Gronbeck, and Wright followed suit. As we were all climbing the ladder, Wright looked back at Blaise and told him to not come up on the rooftop with us. Wright told Blaise to stay right there at the base of the ladder and pull security. Blaise listened to Wright and pulled security at that same spot throughout the rest of the mission just like he was told to do.

As I walked onto the patio/rooftop, I went straight for the window in front of me and tried to look inside through the crack with my NODs and with the help of the illumination from my infrared laser, but I couldn't see anything. Next, I went to the closed wooden door just a foot to the right of the window. I checked to see if it was unlocked. The door was locked. I kept working my way to the right and moved toward the other closed wooden door. This door was located in the perpendicular wall that intersected with the wall for the room with the window. I tried to silently open this door as well but it was also locked.

At this time I looked behind me and saw Wright pulling security for me on the window and Gronbeck was to his left pulling high security on the rooftop. Before I was able to make a radio call and give a SITREP, Rooster called me over to the north side of the patio/ rooftop via MBITR where he and Escobar were. First squad at this time was getting postured at a breach point on the bottom floor and was ready to make entry on the first floor for another simultaneous breach to enter, clear, and assault Rally

Point-4. Time was of the essence and we needed to clear Rally Point-4; the random siren that went off in the village intensified our sense of suspense and suspicion. The assault force and security element were postured and it was go time. We, second platoon, needed to get to Sayed Shah and fulfill the mission to capture or kill him before he knew we were in his house. Once I got over to the north side patio, Staff Sergeant Rooster told me over MBITR that we were going to enter through the door that Escobar had locked down (security). As Rooster said this I looked over and saw Escobar assessing the breach; he was postured and ready to make entry. The door was a normal looking wooden door, but like the others on the second floor, it was locked. When Rooster let our platoon sergeant know we were ready to go, he started the countdown. I flipped my NODs up, since we were planning to clear this room with white lights (meaning we were using the tactical flashlights attached to our M4s to illuminate the room instead of clearing with our NODs). When he said "one" Escobar kicked the door in with his boot and then stepped off to the side. Rooster was as amped as a fighter getting ready to get in the ring; he bolted right through the door with his M4 leading the way and I followed suit with my gun at the high ready. I button hooked and went the opposite way he did to clear and cover his six. Behind me in order were Wright and Gronbeck. The two of them entered the prayer room and moved out of the fatal funnel locking down the eleven to one o'clock sector of the room and clearing their primary, secondary, and tertiary sectors of fire. Before Escobar even made it into the small ten-by-ten foot prayer room, we had it cleared. Just to make sure no one was behind the curtain,

Rooster ripped it off the wall. As he ripped the curtain off the wall, I inspected a mattress and tossed it up in the air with my non-firing hand (left hand) to visually inspect that there was nothing underneath. I was looking to see if there were any weapons or munitions. There was nothing; the room was clear and without yelling we told Escobar that it's a clear.

When you hear the words "clear" muscle memory takes over and you move out to find a new room to clear. When clearing a building you must always do the basics … doing the basics fast and to the standard is what saves lives. When Escobar heard "clear" he took off at a fast but controlled sprint toward the west side of the patio/ rooftop to gain entry into the door that I assessed earlier. When he turned the northwest corner, he went straight down the six-by-twelve foot concrete slab for the closed wooden door on the perpendicular wall. To catch up with Escobar, we exited the room in the reverse order of how we entered the room. Gronbeck was the first out with Wright behind him and me behind Wright. Rooster was the last one out, because he was the first in the room.

We quickly sprinted to catch up to Escobar. I turned the northwest corner a foot or so behind Wright. While we were hurrying to close the gap between Escobar, I headed to the left of Wright towards a breach point to make entry into a closed door that Escobar by passed. At this point I was almost to the door and was under the rooftop ledge and saw a small black object out of the corner of my eye that looked like a rock falling out of the sky. A sequence of events followed the split second after I saw the black object falling out of the sky in front of me. First, I heard Escobar kick in the door with his boot, and then the loudest noise I have ever heard went off in my face. Two fragmentation grenades blew up on the patio/ rooftop in the middle of our squad, creating a blast of shrapnel that went everywhere. Simultaneously a barrage of AK-47 fire was pouring down on us from above, impacting into the concrete slab and kicking concrete all around and in between us. As the rounds were ripping past our heads, body, and feet, I could see shrapnel and flashes of light spraying everywhere. The volume of fire was earth shattering, and directly in front of me I saw Wright get knocked onto the ground like he was hit by something with incredible force. Wright screamed out as he lay on his back, "I'm hit! I'm hit!" I immediately stopped in my tracks and jumped back. My eyes went straight to the rooftop, and I could see Gronbeck in the center of grenade shrapnel. He was barely visible due to all the flashes that surrounded him. I did not have my NODs down but I was able to see the head of the combatant peering down on us as he sporadically shot his AK-47, sending rounds all around us and in-between us. He was just a few feet in front of me and literally it seemed as though he was on top of us posted up close to the corner of the wall. His AK-47 was pointed straight down, and beside his head, the only thing visible were his arms hanging over the wall to get his AK-47 as close to us as he could. He continued to shoot sporadically for what seemed to be an eternity and as he engaged there was a fire-flame pouring out of the end of his barrel that resembled a flame thrower. It was obvious that he was not aiming, but instead spraying 7.62 all around us; he had taken us by surprise. Through the fog of war I could hear Wright screaming, "Up high, up high!" Wright was hit but he was not going to succumb to his wounds. He was staying in the fight with us. Rooster recalls hearing me scream, "Mother fucker!" as I quickly raised my weapon from the high ready position, I turned on my white light out of muscle memory, illuminating the combatant, and as I brought my weapon up to my right cheek, I simultaneously acquired the combatant with both eyes wide open through my EOTech and, along with Rooster and Escobar who went through the same immediate actions at the same exact moment we unleashed hell from our M4s, shooting him in the face. We sent a volley of fire back at the combatant that was so effective that Wyatt later told me, "It was so loud that it sounded like World War II up there." After we shot the first Salafist fighter in the face, I continued to shoot and adjusted my fires to the left to shoot into the wooden wall above us, laying suppressive fire into the fighting position and trying to gain fire superiority and an understanding of what was happening. I could hear Rooster and Escobar shooting as well, and as a squad/ team, we regained fire superiority. While we were all continuing to suppress the wooden wall, I could still hear gun shots on the other side of the wall above us from combatants at a cyclic rate and could also hear grenades going off from what sounded like behind the wall in front of us inside the house. The gunfire was not directed toward us and there was no one else on the rooftop at that moment. Second squad was experiencing what one might call a lull in fire. After the dust of the initial ambush settled, I ceased fire and continued to scan the rooftop and wooden wall with my white light and with my M4 pointed at the top of the wooden wall ready for heads and targets of opportunity. As this was going on I could see Gronbeck out of the corner of my right eye holding his SAW barrel in his left hand with his buttstock on the ground. I then saw Gronbeck jump up in the air and use his body weight to try and charge his SAW by mashing down the charging handle with his boot.

Throughout I could hear Wright screaming in pain, and with still no visible targets to acquire, I ran to Wright and found him lying on his left side with his legs tucked up. As I rolled him over onto his back, we made eye contact and I could see the pain he was enduring through the look of his blank stare. I grabbed the right shoulder strap of his kit with my right hand and began to drag him back to the north side of the patio/rooftop of the house. I quickly realized that I would need to use both hands and more strength to move him, so I threw my M4 to the side, anchored down, and started to drag Wright. Wright was acting tough as nails, but I could tell he was in a lot of pain—more pain than any human should ever have to endure. As soon as I started to get a little momentum, Escobar and Gronbeck ran up to Wright as well. Escobar immediately grabbed his shoulder strap and started to pull with me. There was a second that we were unorganized and not getting anywhere fast. Our adrenaline was spiked; we were reacting on our own accord the best we could to help our buddy and get him to safety. It was as simple as we were fighting for each other and working together in an attempt to save one another. To increase our efforts to get Wright out of the "kill zone," I let go of his shoulder strap and grabbed his legs to try and pick up some of the weight as Escobar pulled. As I did this, I told Gronbeck to grab a leg and together we both had a leg suspended while Escobar was pulling and dragging

Wright's shoulder straps. While we were getting Wright to safety, Rooster positioned himself out in the open at the northwest corner to cover our movement. Rooster was still scanning the wooden wall for targets with his white light to provide cover for his squad, suppressing the wooden wall with a rapid rate of fire to maintain fire superiority and keep the insurgents' heads down.

As we turned the northwest corner, we were under the one foot ledge/overhang of the roof. It was providing us cover from the fortified fighting position directly above us. Once we all made it onto the north side of the patio, I started to see rounds impacting at my feet from above and concrete was kicking up and hitting my feet and calves. We were getting shot at and to this day I do not know why I had to ask, but I asked Escobar a rhetorical question: "Fuck, are we getting shot at again?" He responded with a sharp, "Yes." After Escobar gave me this affirmative, I told Gronbeck, "Take Wright's legs and help Escobar get him in the room." As I passed Chris's leg off to Gronbeck, I shouted, "Let's go! Let's go! Get him in the room!"

Without saying anything, Gronbeck grabbed both of Wright's legs and they continued to drag Wright toward the room that we had already cleared. Quickly, I got out from under the ledge that provided cover to get back in the fight. I knew my best friend, who was standing alone, needed my help and I wanted a piece of the fight too. I stepped out with my left foot, pivoted off of that same foot, and spun around, raising my M4 into a muzzle flash from an AK-47 that was so close I could have reached up and grabbed it. The rounds were so close to my face I could feel that heat of each round as it passed by. I immediately started to shoot right back into the muzzle flash. As I shot out of reaction, muzzle flash rounds from the AK-47 were ripping over my head at point blank towards me and Rooster.

The noise from the AK-47 was so loud that words can't describe. As I continued to shoot into the muzzle flash, I walked my fires to the face of the combatant in a zipper effect, shooting him through the wooden wall as I made a complete turn to face the combatant.

Simultaneously, Rooster, who had rounds impacting at his feet, which was kicking concrete into his pants legs and tearing away one of his ankle cargo pockets, remained in the open. Rooster stood only a few feet behind me on the open rooftop with his white light on trying to attract fires in his direction. He was also shooting his M4 at a cyclic rate of fire a foot over my head and directly into the combatant through the wooden wall. Together we eliminated the Salafist fighter. Once the fires from the Salafist fighter using the gun porthole in the wooden wall was eliminated, I continued to shoot until I went "cold" (out of ammo in my current mag). In total, I shot about ten effective rounds in a matter of a few seconds. Immediately after going cold, I ran back under the ledge to conduct a mag change.

My ears were ringing because the earbuds I wore for the first time instead of my peltors were somehow knocked out of my ears. I knew that there could still be a threat in the elevated wooden barricaded fighting position. Utilizing the cover of the lip of the rooftop, I pressed my mag release button, dropping my empty mag onto the concrete slab. I did not bother to recover that empty mag and left it there, and to this day I wonder where that mag could be. Time was of the essence and I had to get back into the fight and could have cared less about reaching down to get that mag or putting it into a cargo pocket. It was fight or flight time and I needed to get my gun up and get back in the fight. I went straight for a fully loaded thirty-round mag of 5.56 lodged in the mag pouch that was attached to the front of my kit covering my abdomen. As I pulled a "fresh mag" out from my mag pouch on the left front side of my kit, I started to feel the complications of an adrenaline dump. I pulled the magazine out of my mag pouch and quickly brought it toward the "mag well" of my M4 just as I had done over a thousand times before. With all the adrenaline dumping I began to find that my fine motor skills and ability to accomplish detailed tasks was faltering. As I began to load my new, fully loaded magazine of thirty rounds into my mag well, I caught the fresh mag on the lip/ exterior of my mag well. I had done exactly what I was trained not to do; I missed the mag well on my first attempt. However, I did not blink an eye and reinserted the fresh mag on my second mag change attempt. As I slammed the fresh mag into my mag well, I felt the ever so reassuring sensation of inserting the mag properly. Looking back on it, the feeling was climactic. In sequence and without missing a beat, I pressed the bolt catch/release button, releasing my bolt, charging my M4, and chambering a 5.56 round.

I was back in the fight and had a fresh mag and a 5.56 round loaded securely into my M4. I stepped back out from under the ledge of the roof and jumped up, grabbing the roof/ledge with my left hand and placing my M4 onto the roof. With my right hand holding the pistol grip of my M4, I pulled the trigger and began to lay "waste" (expending rounds as fast as I could) right into a gun porthole of the fortified fighting position. I continued to push my muzzle all the way up until my arm couldn't reach any further. While I hung from the ledge I expended almost an entire mag of 5.56 before my grip began to weaken. Once I could no longer hang on to the ledge with my left hand I let go of the trigger with my right index finger and dropped back to the ground. Without skipping a beat I ran straight to the open door of the CCP, where I could see the lower half of Wright's legs coming out of the doorway of the room onto the rooftop.

Earlier, during the lull of fires that we (second squad) experienced after the initial ambush on the west side of the rooftop, Staff Sergeant Wyatt and Sergeant Plagge from first squad were wounded in an attempt to make their way into the fight through the inside of the house. Wyatt and Plagge ran up the stairwell inside the house to the second floor when the thunderous gunfire erupted. They then pushed up the stairwell, working their way to the fight. Once they crested the stairs to the second floor, first squad had used white lights to clear the only room on the second floor. Just before they worked their way toward the gunfight on the third floor, with Wyatt leading the way, Plagge told him, "I got you." With that the two made their way to the third floor, and as Wyatt shined his white light in the stairwell toward the rooftop/third floor, they were ambushed by a barrage of AK-47 fire bouncing all over the place in the stairwell. Wyatt was immediately hit in the left forearm and lost his ability to hold up his M4. As Wyatt pulled back, trying to gather his arm and perform self-aid, a fragmentation grenade came rolling down the stairs and exploded in their faces. Plagge took shrapnel all over his body, and later he could only describe the initial blast as a force equivalent to being hit in the face by a baseball bat. As the hot metal shrapnel entered and pierced his skin, Wyatt screamed out, "Are you okay?" Plagge, unable to answer back due to the blunt force that had him momentarily disoriented, couldn't move, and to his surprise two more grenades blew up in his face a moment later. After charging through the ambush of a wall of AK-47 fire and three grenades, Wyatt and Plagge moved back to a room on the second floor next to the CCP room that second squad was in; they were separated from us by only a wall. With complete disregard for their safety, they continued to wait for the rest of first squad and our platoon sergeant. While in the room they performed self-aid and took a tactical pause to assess the situation and to decide what to do next. They realized that they were pinned down and that it would be suicide if they were to try and go to the third floor without back-up. Although they were still taking suppressive fire from the combatant shooting from the fortified fighting position, Plagge then woke up and said, "We got to get the fuck out of here!" However, Wyatt's left arm was nearly shot off and was only hanging on by a tendon at the elbow. Sergeant Plagge was still disoriented and he was covered in shrapnel from head to toe. Wyatt only had one good arm so he drew his pistol and aimed it toward the top of the stairwell with his right hand to provide cover and overwatch for him and Plagge. After he drew his pistol, still not knowing what else to do, an opportunity presented itself and they acted. Once Wyatt drew his pistol to lay suppressive fires, he and Plagge experienced a lull in fires as the combatant left to suppress us (second squad) on the rooftop while we were dragging Wright and making it back under cover and into the CCP. As soon as Wyatt and Plagge experienced the lull, Wyatt said to Plagge, "Let's go!" The two wounded Rangers ran toward the stairwell to get back down to the bottom floor. As they maneuvered to the stairwell, Wyatt continued to cover the both of them with his pistol in his right hand and his eyes on the top of the stairwell. This was their only way out alive.

Once Plagge and Wyatt reached the bottom floor, they ran out of the house and sat down under the cover provided by the north side patio/ rooftop that second squad was on top of and in the midst of battle.

Meanwhile, Corporal Jenkins was finishing the clearing of an initial block of rooms and courtyards on the first floor with his SAW gunner, Specialist Hanley, in trail. After clearing four rooms, Jenkins heard the gun shots and frags and ran straight to where the noise was originating from. Jenkins was ttempting to take himself and Hanley to the fight to link in with Wyatt and Plagge, but he was held up by our platoon sergeant; Jenkins recalls that he was like a pit bull trying to get into a fight, but was ordered by our platoon sergeant to stay put.

Once Wyatt sat down under the cover of the north side rooftop, he began to start first aid on himself. At the hasty CCP he had established, Wyatt began to look at his left arm, but he saw nothing there. He had no feeling in it and the loss of blood was starting to take effect. He immediately jumped up and ran to the stairwell to go look for his arm, which he thought was still in the room that he had just ran out of on the second floor. Once Wyatt stood up and started running, his arm flapped around and hit him in the leg. He looked down and saw that he still had his arm, and with a sigh of relief and amazement, Wyatt realized that he must have been sitting on it. Seeing that his arm was hanging onto his body by just a ligament or tendon, Wyatt sat back down and began directing Jenkins and Hanley. Hanley was looking at the bullet hole in Wyatt's arm in amazement and saw out of the corner of his eye that Blaise was still pulling security in the same walkway under the cover of the patio/rooftop on the northwest corner (where Specialist Wright had ordered him to stay prior to climbing onto the rooftop). Wyatt looked at Hanley and said, "Stop looking at me and pull security!" Jenkins started to bandage up Wyatt's arm and get it ready to be put in a sling for the upcoming walk out of Shamun Village. Plagge was also in the hasty CCP and was still disoriented from the overpressure of the grenades, but he was becoming more alert and began yelling at Jenkins, "Where were you?" Plagge's entire body was covered head to toe in shrapnel, including those places and parts that only men have.

Wyatt and Plagge's attempt to assist second squad saved our lives and allowed us to maneuver to get Wright out of the kill zone and regain fire superiority. If it were not for Wyatt and Plagge's complete disregard for their own safety more men would have died that night. Their heroic actions saved the lives of their Ranger buddies. Even while wounded, Wyatt had complete control of his squad and was continuing to order his Rangers on what he wanted done and carried out.

From their cover position, Hanley, who was pulling security as directed by Wyatt, was able to see the northeast corner of the fortified fighting position and began to hear the last volley of fire that second squad was giving and receiving. Hanley raised his SAW and scanned the east side of the building, and to his surprise, he saw an AK-47 barrel stick out of a gun porthole from the wooden wall that made up the fortified fighting position three floors up. Because he did not know where we were, he did not fire, but instead he continued to scan the rooftop. He saw the barrel poke out and pop off a few more rounds. Without being able to see anyone and without knowing where second squad was, he maneuvered to a new spot on the east side of the building where he could effectively lay a suppressive burst. Hanley ran as fast as he could with his lightweight machine gun to a new spot and laid a quick burst into the wooden wall in an attempt to protect the CCP and keep the combatant from firing in their direction again. Hanley continued to pull security for first squad's hasty CCP from that same spot for the rest of the mission and never saw a muzzle again.

As I crested through the doorway, I stepped over Wright's lower half to get through the small entrance and saw Escobar with Wright's head lying in his lap. Escobar already had Wright's kit off and was now taking his shirt off. Escobar and I made eye-to-eye contact as he screamed at the top of his lungs, "Rooster, urgent surgical!" As Escobar was shouting, I saw an exit wound in Wright's right armpit from an AK-47 round and knew exactly why the tone of Escobar's voice was so demanding. The mission just changed; we lost the initiative. We were no longer here in the Shamun Village to capture or kill insurgents. Our new mission was to get Wright out of the Shamun Village alive and get him to a casualty evacuation bird ASAP before he bled out. Time was our new enemy.

STAYING IN THE FIGHT

"Above all, we must realize that no arsenal or no weapon in the arsenals of the world is so formidable as the will and moral courage of free men and women. It is a weapon our adversaries in today's world do not have. It is a weapon that we as Americans do have. Let that be understood by those who practice terrorism and prey upon their neighbors."

- Ronald Reagan, 40th President of the United States of America

Staff Sergeant Rooster heard Escobar and ran into the second floor CCP right behind me, took a knee in the doorway of the room, and started screaming into his MBITR for first squad. Rooster was trying to contact Wyatt to see where he and his squad were. Wyatt only had one hand and was not able to make a radio call, and it was later discovered that in the CCP on the first floor of Rally Point-4 his radio cord connecting to his ear buds was cut in the process of getting his gear off to assess his wounds. Wyatt heard a few radio calls but once his radio went dead his ability to hear and make a call was over. With no response from first squad, Staff Sergeant Rooster continued to kneel in the doorway looking out toward Rally Point-3 and scream into his MBITR boom mike to get a SITREP from someone, but no one responded. It was a very lonely feeling and Escobar was also still screaming, "Rooster, urgent surgical! We need a casevac (casualty evacuation) now!"

While this was going on I went over and checked Gronbeck for wounds. I felt Gronbeck's neck, back, legs, arms, shoulders—front and back—looking for blood, dragging my fingers along his exposed areas, and feeling for bullet holes or wounds. Adrenaline will allow you to fight through combat wounds, and unless identified you may not know you have even been shot or wounded until someone else discovers it. This is a perfect example because when I checked over Gronbeck, I missed small shrapnel wounds that were cauterized and not bleeding in his left knee and calf. Gronbeck did not even know he was wounded until he took his pants off when we got back from the mission. As I was checking him, Gronbeck looked at me and said, "My gun is jammed, sergeant." He then jumped up and tried to kick start his SAW by jumping down on the charging handle with the insole of his boot again and again. On his last attempt to charge his SAW Gronbeck almost broke his foot, ripping a hole in the insole of his right leather mission boot. This repetitive action to get his weapon in the fight resulted in a bruise that would later cover the entire bottom side of his foot. While Gronbeck was continuing to try and charge his machine gun, I ran over to Wright and Escobar and grabbed Wright's M4. I undid the shoulder strap to get it out from under Wright's equipment and brought it over to Gronbeck. I handed Gronbeck the M4 with the grenade launcher attached to the bottom and started to assess the situation again. I did not know exactly why Gronbeck's SAW was jammed and at the moment I did not care. We later found out that Gronbeck's SAW was shot with a 7.62 round from the AK-47 in the initial ambush. The 7.62 round shot and pinched the gas tube of his machine gun and compressed it, dead-lining the gun even before Gronbeck could shoot it. When Gronbeck pulled the trigger to engage the combatant shooting down on us from above, his operating rod attached to the bolt of his gun got stuck where the 7.62 round pinched the gas tube of the SAW, which fires from the open bolt position. This, unfortunately, took our most effective and powerful gun out of the fight.

Gronbeck positioned himself at a vantage spot to provide security from inside the CCP, taking the initiative to post on the corner of the window to conceal his body, but where he could also have a good view on the west side of the patio. Gronbeck then crested around the wall, leading with Wright's M4 aimed directly at the open door (the one Escobar kicked in) in front of

him. I then said, "If anyone comes out that door light 'em up."
Gronbeck shouted back, "Roger that." At that same moment,
as we were scanning out to the west in the village, we saw a
red flare coming straight for our window. Luckily, the red flare
missed the window and hit the wall of the house and bounced
around on the ground until the red fire flame burned out.

After setting up Gronbeck to pull security for the CCP, I went
back to the door where Staff Sergeant Rooster was looking out to
the north and screaming in his radio for someone to answer him.
I ran up and took a knee beside Rooster; he shouted that he was
throwing a frag (M67 fragmentation grenade) on the rooftop
(directly) above us. With his right hand holding the frag and his
left index finger starting to pull the pin, I shouted at him, "Do
you know where first squad is?" Rooster said, "No. Nobody from
first squad is responding." I immediately thought that we need
to find out where they are at before we throw that frag. I also
thought that there is no way this roof above us will hold up if he
puts that frag on the roof directly on top of us. Lastly, I thought
of an even worse case scenario: what if he misses and the frag
doesn't get over the wooden wall and it falls back down on the
rooftop/patio just outside our room that was barely larger than
a master bedroom closet. We had already been in the middle of
two grenades that were not nearly as powerful as the M67 frag
that Staff Sergeant Rooster was prepping to throw. With all this
said, Rooster continued to scream into his MBITR, but this
time he made a radio call to the weapons squad leader hoping
for a response, saying "Shoot 'em all!" As Staff Sergeant Rooster
was asking for the SBF position to open up into the wooden
wall with the medium-weight, fully automatic machine gun, I

saw the actual gunner, who was carrying the machine gun, below us at the northeast corner of Rally Point-4 in the vacant lot. I screamed at him, "What are you doing down there? You're gonna get killed. Get the fuck outta here!" With that said, he got up off his knee and ran through the vacant lot back to Rally Point-3 with his medium-weight machine gun, which we needed at the SBF position.

Rooster then came over the radio screaming at anyone located at Rally Point-3 in the SBF overwatch position to shoot into the fortified fighting position. He came off of the radio screaming, "Shoot 'em." Rooster knew that we could not run back out onto the rooftop, because there were still potential combatants that could be up there and they had the advantage with the fortified elevated position, and we were not about to give up our cover. Kneeling in the doorway and keeping his body under the cover of the rooftop ledge, Rooster screamed again, "Shoot 'em." He continued to scream, "Shoot 'em!"

Sniper team leader, Sergeant Baumeister, who was armed with an SR-25 sniper rifle, scanned the entire house looking for targets of opportunity through his night vision capable PVS-22 mounted in front of his scope, and using his infrared laser, was already taking care of it. Baumeister, who continued to scan for targets through his SR-25 sniper rifle from his position at the southwest corner of Rally Point-3—approximately thirty yards away from our position—was soon accompanied by a Navy SEAL and the weapons squad leader. At about the same time, Ranger sniper Specialist Devon Swanson, who was at the northeast corner of Rally Point-3—approximately fifty yards away—heard the call from Rooster, not only over the radio in his ear bud, but he also heard it echoing through the Shamun Village off of the walls of the surrounding buildings. He immediately picked up his sniper rifle and ran to the southwest corner of Rally Point-3, hurdling over the bed that Hanley and Lowry had ripped a man out of earlier with Rooster and me on the initial clear. Swanson arrived to the southwest corner and linked in with Sergeant Baumeister and the Navy SEAL, who also heard the call, and started to get his bearing and situational awareness. As soon as Swanson set in on the ledge of the southwest corner of Rally Point-3 with his team leader, he quickly propped his sniper rifle up on the ledge of the roof. Sergeant Baumeister was scanning for targets. He then identified a lone Salafist fighter who was poking his head over the wooden elevated fortified fighting position. Sergeant Baumeister identified a weapon and then the Salafist male fighter exposed his entire chest over the fighting position. Before the insurgent could make another move, Baumeister zeroed in and shot him square in the chest and continued to put three more rounds into him.

Swanson also zeroed in on the combatant with his infrared laser through his night vision goggles and began ripping off rounds as fast as he could. After shooting the Salafist combatant in the chest, Swanson continued to pull the trigger over and over, shooting eleven more rounds into the fortified fighting position until he was ordered by Baumeister to stop shooting. Swanson's rapid fires landed only a few feet above the room we were in, and we could hear the thunderous noises of each round ripping through the wooden walls just seven to ten feet over our heads.

The noise of the rounds created an elevated emotional feeling in the room, and even though you knew he was trained to take that shot, it made you want to get as small as you could so that you reduced the chances of being shot yourself. After Swanson, who was smiling ear to ear, ceased his fires, he turned his head toward Baumeister expecting an "atta boy" comment, but noticed that Baumeister and the Navy SEAL were still scanning for targets of opportunity through their NODS. Swanson immediately went back to scanning for targets as well, and while he did so, he recapped—play by play—in his head what had just happened.

In a matter of a minute, Swanson sprinted twenty meters, and with an elevated heart rate, he drew down, caught his breath, acquired a target, and helped facilitate his team leader and the Navy SEAL take out a combatant thirty-five yards away just like that. Swanson, Baumeister, and the SEAL were still scanning, and at that time the weapons squad leader made a call that there were no more living armed males on the third floor rooftop and that he was not going to order anyone to shoot unless one is identified. As they continued to scan the rooftop they were all itching to pull the trigger again hoping for an opportunity to kill again. Unfortunately, there were still no identified males—only women—and the weapons squad leader would not allow them to engage. Because there were still AKs and possibly more grenades on that rooftop in the fortified fighting position, they were not against killing the women, but would not do so unless they identified them carrying a weapon. Rooster, however, continued to scream, "Shoot 'em all!" We felt trapped and all we wanted was a response from someone that we were good to go, but Rooster was not getting anything. It was then that the weapons

squad leader finally made a radio call saying, "They are all dead
up there, Rooster, and there is nothing but unarmed women and
children."

Not convinced that all the fighting-aged males were dead at
the time and knowing there were women and children on the
rooftop changed everything. We were still on a knee in the
doorway, not knowing what to do. I said, "Let's just throw a
concussion grenade up there to see if we can stir anything up."
Rooster handed me the frag; I made sure the pin was secured
and put it in my utility pouch. With the weak and terrible
construction of homes in Afghanistan and our already wounded
"urgent surgical" patient, we thought the blast would have
collapsed and brought the roof down on us. I was too worried
this frag could wound or even kill us. As I was placing the
frag into a multi-purpose pouch on my pistol belt, Rooster
got the concussion/nine flash-bang grenade off of my back. In
the background, I could hear Corporal Escobar saying again,
"Wright is urgent surgical. We need to get him out of here
ASAP." We continued to work furiously to secure the CCP so
we could get the medics up here. Rooster made a radio call to
let everyone know what we were doing and then immediately
pulled the pin on the concussion grenade. We ran out onto the
rooftop/patio and he tossed the concussion grenade into the
fortified position above us as I pulled security for him and then
we sprinted back under the cover of the ledge and into the CCP.
Immediately, the nine blasts starting popping off and during
the nine blasts Swanson, Baumeister, and the SEAL scanned
the rooftop searching for more combatants that would get up
and try to run from the nine concussion blasts to shoot and

kill. Once the nine blasts ended, the sniper team and the Navy SEAL element continued to scan the fighting position and the rooftop, but they did not see any fighting-aged male combatants on the rooftop. The next radio call was from the sniper team and the Navy SEAL element saying all is clear on the rooftop. After the concussion grenade, all fires and blasts immediately ceased. There was no more chaotic confusion amongst us in the CCP about whether or not there was anyone else up there with an AK-47.

The medics were already staged and ready to get to work. As soon as the fires and blast ceased, Staff Sergeant Rooster called up the medics, Specialist Joe Vetter and Specialist Swett, over the radio. Rooster told them to get up on the rooftop of Rally Point-4 immediately, because we have an urgent surgical patient. This was the first radio call made to the rest of the task force notifying them that we have an urgent surgical patient. Everyone remembers hearing that radio call and knows exactly where they were when it was made. With complete disregard for their own safety, Specialist Vetter and Specialist Swett ran through the vacant lot from Rally Point-3 toward the north side of Rally Point-4. As they were running through the vacant lot, Rooster and I walked out onto the patio/ rooftop and told them how to get to the ladder. I then ran back into the CCP to tell Gronbeck that the medics were about to come up the ladder and to keep his weapon down until they pass. As I came back into the room, Gronbeck was at Wright's side, and being the longtime friends that they were, I gave him the second that he needed to tell Wright four simple words that only a Ranger would understand, "I love you, brother." From the window of the CCP, I saw the medics run past. I screamed at them: "We are in here! Come around the corner." The warmest and most comforting feeling of that night was when Vetter and Swett ran through that door.

As soon as Vetter entered into the CCP, he took his med bag off of his back, threw it onto the floor of the CCP and immediately took charge and went to work. While he was starting to go to work, Escobar gave Vetter a quick down and dirty overview of Wright's injuries, showing him the two entrance wounds on his right shoulder that were cauterized (due to how close the muzzle was to Wright when he was shot) and the one exit wound under his right armpit. There was no second exit wound from the second 7.62 entrance wound; the round was later found in surgery lodged in his spine. Vetter started to task out jobs to his junior medic, Specialist Swett, while Corporal Escobar, who already had Wright stripped down naked and completely assessed, was ready to go with an IV, nasopharyngeal airway (NPA), and a fourteen-gauge needle prepped and ready to combat the tension pneumothorax that was starting to occur.

It is now 2152 zulu time and Wright is alert with a thready systolic blood pressure of 70. He was so alert that he told Swett that if he steps over him again, he is going to beat his ass. The team of three medics, led by Vetter, established a chest seal, inserted the NPA, and got a saline lock inserted for an IV to push meds through. Wright had bilateral rise and fall of the chest. To combat that Vetter had Escobar perform a needle decompression with the fourteen-gauge five-inch needle between the second and third intercostal space of his ribs and on the mid-clavicular line of his right side. When Escobar inserted the

needle decompression, there was a burst of air that was released
that allowed for unilateral rise and fall of the chest. While
Escobar was re-assessing Wright's chest for unilateral rise and
fall, Vetter pushed one milligram of Dilaudid through the saline
lock to manage Wright's pain. They then gave Wright an eight
hundred microgram Fetanyl oral lozenge to reduce pain as well.

I grabbed a nylon parachute bag and started to compile all of
Wright's gear into the bag to prep for exfil out of the CCP. It was
SOP to make sure we had all sensitive items with serial numbers
accounted for before we left. I could hear Rooster on the radio
coordinating the exfil to get Wright to the casevac bird. Time
was of the essence and we knew it; everyone was performing
flawlessly and as fast as humanly possible. As I continued to
pick up Wright's gear, I consolidated it into the parachute bag
to make sure I had everything. I flipped the mattress that was
on the floor out of the way and bent down to pick up Wright's
combat top and sat directly down on one of the fourteen-gauge
needles used to decompress the tension pneumothorax. The
needle was stuck in the mattress like a pin cushion, and as I sat
down the needle went directly in my left butt cheek sending
chills up my spine. I stood up with a sense of urgency and went
straight back to work. Next, Gronbeck and I got the foxtrot
litter prepped in less than two minutes. Prepping a litter for a
casualty was something we had drilled thousands of times, and
we were able to complete this task wordlessly. Once we finished
laying out the litter, Gronbeck went back to pull security at
the window. He shouted to Wright, "I love you, brother," for a
second time to make sure that Wright knew he was here with
him.

The team of medics was still working hard, completing nine
more needle decompressions to keep unilateral rise and fall of
the chest. Once the medics were ready to load Wright onto the
litter, they rolled him onto his uninjured side and I slid the
foxtrot litter under his back. I looked at Wright and said, "You
are going to be okay." Wright responded with a sharp, "Shut the
fuck up. I am fucking dying." For a second, I thought to myself
how stupid that was of me to say. Truthfully, I didn't know what
to say, so I didn't say anything back. I just shook his hand and
continued to assist loading him onto the litter. That would be
our last conversation.

Once we had Wright loaded up, we picked him up and started
to carry him out onto the rooftop. On the roof with Wright
secured in the litter, Rooster was on the radio and had the Navy
SEAL element bring the ladder that Blaise had humped in on
the mission and cant it at about a forty-five degree angle up onto
the rooftop leading into the vacant lot between Rally Point-3
and Rally Point-4. Vetter, Escobar, Swett, Rooster, Gronbeck,
and I placed Wright down on the concrete slab of the patio/
rooftop and then began to slowly guide him over to the ladder.
As we were doing this Wright shouted at Rooster, "Make sure
you call my mom." We then all prepared to do something we
had never done before, but Rooster thought it up on the fly.
Staff Sergeant Rooster used the nylon tag cord that we had
attached to the head of the litter and hunkered down as an
anchor and everyone else grabbed the side straps to guide him
slowly down the ladder feet first and down to the Navy SEAL
element that was waiting to receive him below. As he was sliding
further down the ladder, I continued to grasp on to the nylon

strap and was to the point that only my pelvis and legs were on the roof. Wright said, "Don't drop me." Staff Sergeant Rooster was still anchored down with his feet planted firmly on the patio/ rooftop and leaning back at a forty-five degree angle as if he were repelling down a mountain face; he carefully lowered Wright down by the tag ever so slowly to the SEALs waiting below. Escobar and I continued to guide Wright down by the straps attached to the side of the litter making sure he did not slide off the side of the ladder and fall. Because he was strapped with no extremities exposed and because of his extensive wounds, it was imperative that we take our time to make sure he did not slide off. If he did, the end result would have been disastrous. If he slid off of the ladder, Wright would have most likely flipped over in midair and landed on his face and front side, worsening the effect his body was enduring from the two gunshot wounds. After nearly dislocating my right arm out of its socket and leaning out as far as I could reach, the SEALs were able to take control of Wright from the ground. In silence but with great immediacy, the SEALs picked him up and took him over to Rally Point-3 to establish a new CCP while the rest of us would make our way down the same ladder from Rally Point-4.

Medics Vetter and Swett assisted us with the lowering of Wright, but there was not enough room for everyone on the small patio/ rooftop. At one point, while we were all trying to help, Vetter almost fell off of the patio. As I was slowly suspending my body off the rooftop to lower Wright, Vetter said, "I am going to fall off the roof!" I shouted back, "Well, let go! I got it!" With that, Vetter and Swett grabbed their med bags, ran back to the ladder on the west side of the roof, and went down the wooden stairs that we had used to climb onto the roof in the beginning. They headed toward Rally Point-3 to prep the new CCP and to link back in with Wright to reassess his wounds and triage two other patients that were patiently awaiting his arrival.

Once Wright was down safely, I ran back to the CCP to pick up the heavy parachute bag with all of Wright's equipment. Escobar came running into the room to help. But before we did anything, he bent down and asked me to check his back and feel for any bullet wounds. He was sweating so bad from the heat, adrenaline, and work that he had done that he thought he was bleeding. This time I took my Petzl flashlight and aimed it down his back, visually inspecting his neck and feeling his shoulders and upper back for bullet holes. I did not see anything and he quickly thanked me. Then, I asked him to check me. I had not even thought for a second that it was possible that I could have also been shot. Escobar quickly gave me a once over as well and he said, "You're good." Without another word, I shouldered all of Wright's gear and followed Escobar to the door leading back onto the patio/rooftop. I was now weighing in over three hundred pounds and had to make my way down this same ladder, which was now warped in the center. I was going to take my chances with a damaged American-made ladder over the skinny, piece of junk wooden ladder made by Afghans with rope and rusty old nails. On my way out of the room, I turned around and gave the room a quick glance; I saw a piece of Wright's combat top on the ground. Due to a sense of urgency to move on and considering how heavy I was, I left it there in the room. I still think that I should have taken the time to grab his top with the glint-taped American flag patch that was Velcroed onto the right shoulder. I turned back around and waddled out the door with Wright's gear on my back and slowly made a step onto the ladder, maintaining three points of contact and continuing to do so as I made my way down the ladder while Escobar braced the bottom rung for me with his foot. Once I finally made it down off the roof and onto the ground, I looked at Escobar and he and I had a moment of silence. Our adrenaline and energy levels were dropping and we knew that we had to move out and we had to move out fast. Time was ticking and our Ranger buddy needed to get into surgery ASAP.

While we took a breather for just a few seconds in the vacant lot between Rally Point-3 and Rally Point-4, it was then that I overheard on my MBITR that Wyatt and Plagge were also wounded. With this news Escobar and I grabbed the ladder and I slung it over my shoulder. The two of us picked up the parachute bag straps that had all of Wright's equipment in it and carried it over to the new CCP inside Rally Point-3. As we approached Rally Point-3, there was a gathering of medics, first responders, and the platoon leadership making radio calls. Vetter was leading the new CCP with Swett and the help of the SEAL that I knew from EMS school in Savannah. Vetter triaged, reassessed, and prepped his patients, Wright, Wyatt, and Plagge. I began to get a headcount of the guys in second squad; Escobar, Gronbeck, and Blaise were all right there ready to go. Rooster was off in the alleyway that we used to approach, access, and assault Rally Point-3. I walked over to him and he and I had a quick talk; he said we were going to lead out to the casevac HLZ and that the Navy SEAL element, along with the PL and his attachments and support group of forward observers were going

to carry Wright and the gear. I said, "Roger that" and pulled up
the casevac HLZ plot in my wrist Garmin. I knew exactly where
we were going, but it is better to be safe with the reassurance
of the Garmin than to be lost. As I got ready, I told the guys in
second squad that we were about to lead out to the casevac HLZ
that was five hundred meters away in a field on the opposite side
of the Pech River between MSR Rhode Island and the river. As
I was talking to Blaise to see how he was doing, the two 101st
soldiers linked in with us to help us lead out through the village
alleyways and roads, which are surrounded by fifteen to twenty
foot walls. The village structure was like one big maze so having
the 101st guys with us was reassuring, because they had walked
these roads during the   day many times before and the last thing
I wanted to do was get the platoon lost. Time was still ticking
and we needed to move out. Being the cohesive, great-working
platoon that we were, everyone was ready to go. Once I got the
radio call to lead out, I stepped off using my Garmin and the
advice from the 101st guys to walk point. Rooster was by my
side and the guys from the 101st and Escobar were right behind
me. My Garmin took us exactly the way the 101st guys would
have gone by memory. After walking through the alleyways for
about five minutes, pulling security on rooftops and windows
through the narrow rocky roads, we had to stop.

Our platoon sergeant came over the radio and commanded us
to halt and pull security for a second. We didn't ask why and
Rooster just replied over the radio with a simple, "Roger." The
element that was carrying Wright and his equipment needed to
readjust the dangling nylon lines on the litter and readjust their
grips. As the tag line and straps were continuing to get stepped

on by the guys carrying Wright, causing them to get tripped up, they had to take the time to get the straps secured or to cut them so that they could move out at a fast pace. We also had to hold up for snipers Baumeister and Swanson as well as Private First Class Lowry who were on the Rally Point-3 rooftop pulling security. In addition to carrying their sniper rifles, Swanson was also carrying a twenty-five pound climbing ladder. Each of them were loaded down and needed time to get off of the rooftop from where they were positioned to provide overwatch for us as we exfiled out of the target compound area.

While all this was going on, I took a knee and grabbed a quick breather. I saw Escobar doing the same. Escobar and I had just worked our tails off carrying and humping everything out of Rally Point-4, and it was not until this moment that I realized how exhausted I was as my adrenaline continued to fall. As we were catching our breaths, one of the 101st soldiers walked up, pulled a Gatorade out of his cargo pocket, and handed it to us; Escobar and I each took a gulp. After a sip of Gatorade and a sense of replenishment, we got a radio call that the litter team was good to go and they were already moving out. Being that this town was one big maze with tall walls, I was not able to see them, but Gronbeck and Blaise, who were in the rear of our squad's formation gave us a head nod, letting us know that they were coming around the corner. When I saw them stand up with a sense of urgency, I knew it was game time. We stood back up and moved out like a marathon runner on the home stretch but with the finish line not yet in sight. I made two more turns and we walked out of the village. I could see the wooden bridge we had crossed over on infil when we entered the Shamun Village.

As I continued to walk closer to the bridge, I saw the 101st QRF element from COP Michigan pulling up around the bend of the ridgeline on the other side of the river in their MRAPs. I continued to press forward and at this point I was moving even faster. When I was halfway across the bridge, I noticed the 101st soldiers getting out of the MRAPs. We continued to close the gap as the QRF element was making their way to us as well. I noticed Wright and Rooster's hometown friend Cameron Boe walk by. He and his squad went straight to the litter to relieve the litter team and give them a breather. As Boe approached the litter, which was behind me, I heard Wright say, "Is that you, Boe?" As Cameron Boe and a few of the fresh 101st soldiers took over and helped carry Wright across the bridge, Wright's voice sparked up in excitement. The MRAPs moved in to create a security buffer for us, and I could hear Wright's voice over the loud diesel engines talking to his buddy Cameron Boe. This was a good sign and it gave me and the rest of the guys a dose of optimism that Wright will be okay.

Once we were over the bridge, I moved out toward the 101st Airborne Division convoy of MRAPs to set in security and took Gronbeck, Blaise, and Corporal Smitty along with me to create a security perimeter around the casevac HLZ. It was now 2245 zulu time and Wright had an improved systolic blood pressure of 80. Within only a minute or so of us arriving to the HLZ, I briefly saw Wyatt with his left arm bandaged in a sling. I tried to see how he and Plagge were doing, but Plagge was so stunned and disoriented from the grenade overpressure that he was not able to communicate that well. Wright, Wyatt, and Plagge were being prepped to be flown out, so I did not waste anyone's time and maintained focus on setting in security. At that moment I heard the inbound, thunderous familiar tone of the MH-60 rotors bounce off of the northern ridgeline. Escobar was still at Wright's side as the bird came in and the two of them were talking and joking. Escobar told Wright not to use this as an excuse to not go to Ranger School when we get back. Wright laughed and Escobar and the team of medics, including Vetter and Swett, carried and placed him on the Black Hawk.

The flight medics on board the Black Hawk took control of Wright, Wyatt, and Plagge. As the 101st loaded up into their MRAPs, we waited for them to turn the vehicles around on MSR Rhode Island to head back to COP Michigan. They did not have enough room for us, so we were going to walk back on foot to COP Michigan with the MRAPs leading the way for us. The sun was getting ready to rise and I wanted to get us into COP Michigan and under the concealment of darkness. I lead out at a pace of 5.5 kilometers per hour. We had 4.5 kilometers to go and we were losing darkness fast. In route to COP Michigan the villagers living off of MSR Rhode Island in the Tantil Village were starting to wake up and come outside. As we walked at a very brisk pace, I called for the interpreter to get up and walk point with me. The interpreter was scared out of his mind. I told him to get on his loud speaker and to tell everyone to get back in their homes or we will kill them. We had our M4s at the ready and we were scanning for targets of opportunity with our selector switches on semi-automatic. There were no armed combatants. Without hesitating, the interpreter started screaming into the microphone. To my surprise, they all went back inside without a fight.

While Two Charlie was walking back to COP Michigan, strung out and tired, Wright was still talking it up with the flight medics. Wyatt, Plagge, and Wright arrived to the casevac site and were greeted by a little less than a dozen nurses. They were immediately triaged once again by the nurses and were all wheeled off in separate directions. The last Plagge saw of Wright, he said Wright was talking a million miles a minute to the nurses as he was being wheeled into surgery. Not knowing that this would be the last time he saw Wright, he and Wyatt made eye contact and Wyatt gave Plagge a thumbs-up saying, "It's going to be okay brother. We made it and we are all okay."

We made it back to COP Michigan in less than an hour. Inside the COP everyone was taking knees and taking their helmets off, trying to catch their breath. My squad leader and I went straight to our hooch, dropped our gear off, and went to the TOC. When we got into the TOC, we headed straight to the phone. But before we made our call, the Navy liaison officer in charge of relations with the Afghanistan locals in the Kunar province already knew the outcome. He walked over and looked us straight in the eye and said, "He didn't make it." My gut dropped. Chris Wright was dead. My brother whom I had trained with and lived with year round around the clock was dead. I was speechless. He couldn't be dead; there is no way. I didn't know what to do. My squad leader was also speechless. We both just stood there. I needed fresh air so I walked out of the TOC, and as I stepped outside I saw Escobar and Gronbeck walking up to the TOC door through the tunnels of sandbags and HESCO barriers. I looked at them and shook my head. Escobar and Gronbeck dropped to a knee and wept. Once again,

I did not know what to say. All I could do was try and comfort them, so I walked up and touched their shoulders. The three of us in the middle of COP Michigan mourned the loss of our brother, Christopher Shane Wright.

As I had my hand on Gronbeck's shoulder, he looked up at me and told me he was wounded. Gronbeck walked all the way back to COP Michigan with shrapnel in his knee and a minor bleed in his internal organs. However, he would not learn of his internal bleed until he passed out in an AT&T store seven months later. I went back inside the TOC and told my squad leader that Gronbeck has shrapnel in his leg and I was going to take him to the medics. Escobar and I walked Gronbeck to medic station in COP Michigan and then went back to the TOC to write our piece in preparation for the AAR of Operation Wolverine.

While we were in the TOC, we found out that a fellow Ranger and brother named Sergeant Martin Lugo from first platoon, Charlie Company, and a Navy SEAL named Collin Thomas were also killed in action last night on a raid mission to invade a group of Taliban fighters that had been setting up ambushes on a route near their FOB. This only amplified our already life-altering pain. It was unbelievable to hear and with everything that we were doing and going through, I was not able to process the impact that this night had had on the special operations community, especially Charlie Company, 1st Ranger Battalion. In this separate battle, though, first platoon and the SEALs took it to the Taliban group, killing all combatants on the battlefield.

In order to get Wright home and Gronbeck to a hospital,

Rooster, Gronbeck, and the Navy SEALs loaded up into MRAPs with the 101st and went to the casevac to pick up Wright. That was the last time I saw Gronbeck until I got home from deployment in October. En route to the casevac they took contact on MSR Rhode Island, but luckily no one was hurt. Once they finally got to the casevac, Rooster told Plagge and Wyatt that Wright and Lugo from 1st Platoon were dead and that they were there to escort Wright to Bagram Airfield. The nurses did not have the couth or intestinal fortitude to tell them that their Ranger buddy died in surgery. Once Rooster and the guys got to Bagram Airfield, they were rushed by soldiers that they did not know. As the soldiers tried to help, one of the SEALs barked at them and said we got it; Rooster, Gronbeck, and the Navy SEAL (name unknown) carried Wright's body off of the helicopter. Wright is a special operations soldier, an Army Ranger, and we will take care of our own brethren.

Meanwhile back at COP Michigan, I was getting all of Wright's equipment gathered up to take back to Jalalabad, Afghanistan. While I was checking to make sure I had everything, I picked up his kit to check it over and shrapnel fell out and rolled onto the ground. As I continued to look over Wright's body armor, plate carriers, and kit, I noticed that he had been shot two more times and the 7.62 rounds grazed the right side ballistic plate, passing through his 40-mm HEDP rounds that were still in the 203 pouches attached to his right side ballistic plate. The additional two rounds did not wound him, but as I pulled the two HEDP rounds that the 7.62 bullets passed through, they fell apart in my hand. It was just another testament to the barrage of fire that our squad had been in the midst of.

As I continued to work on getting everything packed up to fly back to Jalalabad that night, Escobar came into my hooch, and when he shut the door behind him mortars started to go off. We were still so jumpy from last night that Escobar flinched as if the overpressure was a round headed for us in the hooch. What happened last night was still so real and fresh in our minds that we both did not have a grip on reality. It was life-altering and to see Escobar jump like that made me realize that it could have been any of us that took those rounds. We wept, talked, and asked questions that we could not answer. We both just sat there thinking and digesting what had just happened. We were not able to stomach it; we did not understand how that could happen to us. We were too good; we were invincible. Or, at least, we thought we were invincible.

Night fell and our Chinook was inbound for COP Michigan. We were headed back to Jalalabad and were staged in the same tunnel that we met Cameron Boe in when we arrived. After the Chinook landed inside the gates of COP Michigan, Escobar and I ran out carrying a rigid litter with all of Wright's, Gronbeck's, and our squad leader's equipment. Once we sat down in the Chinook, it started to lift off into the night. As the Chinook picked up altitude, it turned and headed west, flying over the Pech River. Before we even flew over the Shamun Village, an RPG was shot at us from the Tantil Village mountainside. The pilot steered away, barely dodging it, and the crew members started scanning the mountainside and making radio calls with a sense of urgency. I didn't even flinch and was not the least surprised that we were almost shot down on our way out of the Pech Valley. After last night it would take a lot more to get my blood pressure up, and to be honest, I didn't even care. Once we were directly over Shamun Village, the helicopter crew chief and crew members shot flares off the back of the helicopter to illuminate the rooftops to see if there were any targets of opportunity to engage with the mini- guns and 240B medium-weight machine guns at the tail of the aircraft. As the flares slowly burned out, I gazed out the back of the Chinook and watched the Pech Valley disappear into the night.

As soon as we landed in Jalalabad, we were informed by the Navy liaison of all operations in the Kunar province. He confirmed that we had killed three Salafist fighters, to include Sayed Shah and his two armed PSD. When Escobar, Blaise, and I heard this we didn't even say anything, we just headed for our hooch. As we walked in, there was an empty feeling knowing that two beds that were once used by our Ranger buddies were no longer going to be filled. In addition to them not being there, Rooster and Private First Class Sesh, the newest Ranger in our squad, were not in the hooch.

Sesh and third squad flew out to Bagram Airfield to link up with our squad leader to attend the memorial service in Bagram and to watch the C-17 Angel flight take off and fly Christopher Shane Wright, Martin Lugo, and Collin Thomas home to America. Without saying a whole lot, we all did our own thing. I took a shower to clean up in an attempt to try and get my mind right and boost my morale. On the way back to the hooch, I noticed the "Sign Out" board hanging on the hooch door. Wright's nickname, Stophemon, was written in magic marker on the board. This sight made me stop and just think about the impact of what was taking place.

After a few minutes of reflection, I got dressed and headed to
the TOC for the Operation Wolverine AAR. Being that my
squad leader was not there for the AAR, I just listened to our
platoon leader and platoon sergeant talk about the big picture. I
sat down and started thinking about what actions needed to be
talked about and which ones did not need to be talked about.
I looked around the room and saw Escobar sitting in the back
staring at the PL and PSG with a blank and scary stare. When
we were asked about what had happened on the rooftop with
second squad, I answered with a few basic responses because
the entire assault force was not even there to conduct a proper
AAR. Before it was over, I did make one thing clear: there was
an elevated fortified fighting position and we walked into an
ambush. There was no way for us to defend ourselves from that
even if we knew it was there. As for the PL and PSG, there was
no word mentioned as to why we did not have ISR.

After thinking about the countless measures that were not taken
by our PL, there was one significant, positive fact that came out
of the AAR. Sergeant Baumeister positively identified that the
Salafist fighter he killed was the Salafist commander Sayed Shah.
It was a bitter pill to swallow because of the losses we took to
accomplish the mission, but it was at least something that we
could take away to help us cope with those losses. We killed
Sayed Shah and freed up the Pech Valley to allow the 101st
to get back to operating. We also potentially saved the lives of
many soldiers living and working in the Kunar province.

After the AAR Escobar and I started to clean each article of

Wright's and Gronbeck's military issued equipment. We also
began to pack and secure their personal belongings and effects
to send home. This was a solemn and quiet task. Our hooch
seemed so quiet without him anyway. I felt almost as if I were
having an out-of-body experience; it was so new and fresh. Once
I was done cleaning Wright's gear and equipment to send home,
I lay down on my cot and got some rack. I fell into the deep
sleep that my body demanded, which was going to happen no
matter where I was. After all, I had not really slept in about three
days.

I was awoken about six hours later by the return of my squad
leader, Staff Sergeant Rooster, and Private First Class Sesh
barging through the hooch door. They were tired and hungry
and were accompanied by the chaplain's assistant. The chaplain's
assistant sat down on one of our couches and started asking
some rhetorical questions. Wiping the sleep out of my eyes, I
just stared back at him. Not knowing what to say, I just listened.
He explained that he will be here with us for a few weeks and
was going to help assist with our upcoming memorial.

After listening to what the chaplain's assistant had to say about
the upcoming week, I decided to start working on Gronbeck's
SAW. I examined the compressed gas tube that pinched the
operating rod from the 7.62 round that shot his gun, but I
could not figure out how to charge the bolt. Like Gronbeck, I
couldn't pull the charging handle back to save my life, but unlike
Gronbeck, I was not being shot at and had the time to stabilize
the gun and get all of my strength behind it. I walked it up to
the ready room and showed it to Staff Sergeant Cousins, who

was known for having the biggest biceps in the platoon. He also tried to charge the SAW and could not get it to budge either. After trying a few more times, Cousins went and grabbed a rubber mallet and hit the charging handle as hard as he could, finally getting the operating rod out of the gas tube. We then took the SAW apart and looked at it in amazement and just talked about the odds of this happening. As other Rangers started to gather around, we held the SAW as Gronbeck had been holding it that night and discussed the trajectory of the 7.62 round that struck his gun. For that round to have hit his SAW where it did it—missing Gronbeck's head by centimeters— was nothing shy of a miracle.

ONE FOR THE AIRBORNE RANGER IN THE SKY

*"A hero is someone who has given his or her
life to something bigger than oneself."*

- Joseph Campbell

We started planning and preparing for the task force memorial in Jalalabad during the period of darkness that evening. The memorial was in honor of three fallen brothers who paid the ultimate sacrifice on the night of August 18th and the morning of August 19th and the intent was to remember the lives of each. Two Charlie always endeavors to uphold the prestige, honor, and high "esprit de corps" of the Ranger Regiment, and at a moment like this, we were not about to fall short of anything but our best. The memorial was conducted on the morning of August 22, 2010, in honor of Army Ranger Specialist Christopher Shane Wright, Army Ranger Sergeant Martin Anthony Lugo, and Navy SEAL Chief Collin Trent Thomas. The preparation of the memorial was heart-wrenching, and as I practiced what I was going to say in the memorial in honor of Wright, I cried for the first time. I walked off to the side and away from the memorial formation … a rush of emotions that I could not control overwhelmed me. I began to cry so hard that I doubted I would be able to get up in front of anyone, let alone talk in front of a crowd. To my surprise, Ranger buddy Troy Jenkins grabbed my shoulder, and without a word, he was able to help me control my emotions by providing a sense of comfort.

I spoke after the chaplain's assistant and the platoon leader, and just as I had planned and rehearsed, everything went smoothly. There was hardly a dry eye in the Two Charlie formation. After I finished my speech on behalf of Wright, a Navy SEAL who was friends with Collin Thomas spoke on his behalf, and lastly a Ranger buddy from Two Charlie, who had once served as Martin Lugo's squad leader in One Charlie, spoke on behalf of Lugo. To conclude the memorial, we all took turns walking past three wooden crosses. In the center stood the boots Wright wore that night sitting in front of his M4, which was propped up in front of the cross with his ID tags hanging from the pistol grip of his M4. On top of the buttstock of his M4 was Wright's mitch (helmet), and in true spec ops fashion, his night vision goggles were left down like a true green-eyed ghost would want so that he could still see at night while he walks the halls of Valhalla, drinking and telling war stories with the best of them. As I took a knee and looked at the blood stain on Wright's M4, I swore to live every day to the fullest and not take one breath for granted. I slowly stood up and came to the position of attention. I saluted Christopher Shane Wright and came to a sharp left-face and marched off.

After the memorial concluded, I went back to the ready room by myself to have a moment of silence, and as I looked over at Wright's gear, I made another promise. This one was to take the fight to the enemy and to kill as many jihad Muslim terrorists as I could. After making the promise, I took Wright's nine fully loaded magazines of 5.56 that were still on his kit and swapped them out with the mags on my kit. My promise to Wright and to myself was to shoot every one of Wright's bullets before I went home and to kill as many terrorists as I could. This is what he would have done and I can say without a doubt that this is what he wanted me to do.

After spending a few more minutes looking over my weapons and gear and making sure that I was ready for the next mission, I went back to my hooch to lay down and read Leadership and Training for the Fight by Master Sergeant Paul Howe. Rooster just finished reading the book and suggested I read it as well. He said that it would help get my mind right and keep me focused on the mission and task at hand. It was in this book that I read the quote by Heraclitus, "Of every one hundred men, ten shouldn't even be there, eighty are nothing but targets, nine are real fighters, and we are lucky to have them, for they the battle make. Ah, but the one, one of them is a warrior and he will bring the others back."

When I first read this quote I thought it sounded hardcore so I wrote it down and hung it up above my bed to read before I went out on a mission. The words in the quote made me feel invincible and I imagined myself as "the One." Years later, I now read this quote with a new perspective, and it is clear as day when I say, I was not the one. Christopher Shane Wright was the *One*, he was the Warrior that made sure we Rangers of Two Charlie went home. *He* was the *One*!

FINAL HOUR AS AN
AIRBORNE RANGER

"But I served in a Company of Heroes."

- Major Richard D. "Dick" Winters,
Easy Company, 2nd Battalion, 506th Parachute
Infantry Regiment, 101st Airborne Division

Due to the circumstances and the joint investigation taking
place with the SEAL platoon for actions while attempting
to rescue Linda Norgrove, there were no missions. We were
ordered to stand down until the investigation was complete.
We immediately took full advantage of the downtime and got
some rack (sleep). Not having any missions toward the end of
the deployment wasn't bad news nor good news, but it sure was
nice to relax. As most Rangers would say, it is what it is. Over
the next few days if I wasn't sleeping to kill time, I was working
out, playing the board game "Risk," or joining in on the "Call
of Duty" video game competitions usually led by Plagge and
Rooster. It was a huge morale boost when we got word that
despite the option to stay in the U.S. and let his wounds heal
Plagge insisted on coming back and joining the platoon for the
rest of the deployment. It was an even bigger morale boost when
his cocky attitude returned and was back in the mix; it kind of
made things feel right again. Everyone had a lot of questions for
him and most of it had to do with what happened to him and
Wyatt as well as questions about Wright's funeral, which he was
able to attend.

The re-deployment window to return to the U.S. was
approaching fast. We only had about two weeks to go. In
addition to our rotation coming to an end and redeploying back
to the states, my enlistment was coming to an end. My four
year, twenty-week enlistment contract with the United States
Army was only a few months away. The looming discharge date
brought on one of the toughest decisions I have had to make
to date. I spent countless waking hours thinking about my next
move. One day I wanted to re-enlist and the next day I wanted

to get out of the army. I couldn't make up my mind. I even talked with my closest friend Rooster about what I should do. Then one day I woke up and it was clear as day. I wanted to get out of the army and did not want to re-enlist. The gut feeling that supported the decision to get out of the Army was very similar to the feeling that supported my decision to enlist.

Prior to heading home I had one last stop before hanging it up. After all I still had one of Wright's magazines of thirty rounds that needed to be used. I was headed to the Logar province on orders from my chain of command. I would work with a joint task force of Rangers and SEALs. The Ranger platoon that I would fall in with as a team leader was One Charlie. I would be working with the same joint task force that operated on the night of August 18th and 19th, the days we lost Chris, Army Ranger Sergeant Martin Lugo, and Navy SEAL Chief Collin Thomas. Being that we were not actioning missions and One Charlie was still in the fight, they could use another gun in the fight and I was happy to have the opportunity to be the one to bring the gun.

Escobar and a few other young Rangers loaded up with me on a C-130 at the Jalalabad Airfield and headed to the Logar province, which is also located in the eastern portion of Afghanistan. It was a quick flight and when we landed we were greeted by a Ranger from One Charlie who showed us to our room. We had recently visited One Charlie about a month ago and were put back in the same hooch. We stayed in Martin Lugo's squad hooch again, and being that we were recently here, we did not need a whole lot of help finding our way. After grabbing a top bunk bed, I downloaded my gear in the ready room and went to the TOC to link up with the platoon and get an idea of what things were looking like for the upcoming period of darkness.

In the TOC everyone was going about a routine I had seen a thousand times. Squad leaders were working diligently on mission planning and PowerPoint presentations for the operations order. Team leaders were quietly gathered around waiting for the poop (information and intel) from their squad leader to go disseminate to the guys. The platoon sergeant and PL were going over their respective tasks prior to the operations order and waiting for the phone to ring from higher. One Charlie was expecting me so no one was surprised to turn and see me walk in their AO. The welcoming was a simple few head nods, and as I made my way I stopped and talked to a few guys that I knew from the COF hanging out with in Savannah.

The platoon sergeant quickly turned around and gave me a quick grin from his seat, greeted me, and went straight into the mission that they were getting ready to action. He told me who to link up with and that I would be on the manifest tonight. He wanted me to get out on target with them and get a feel for how they operate. I was all about it and understood it would be best for me to get a feel with One Charlie before the rest of the guys with me from Two Charlie went out to. After the very quick brief I reassured my new PSG that I was good to go and then went and found my squad leader. He and I knew each other pretty well so it did not take long to hash out the details. The acting alpha team leader, who I did not know on a first name basis, was a prior service guy from the 101st Airborne. He recently made it through RASP as a sergeant and was on his first deployment with One Charlie and wanted to step up to the plate and lead out. Being that I was here to support as another fighter I had no issue. I was ready to help facilitate their operations in any capacity that they needed me to.

Shortly thereafter we all went to our hooch and changed into our mission gear and headed to the joint operating center to link up with the SEALs that they had been working with. I walked in and noticed that everyone was joking about a river crossing on a mission from the other night and saw that Rangers and SEALs were chatting it up and small talking together. These SEALs seemed a lot less egotistical than the yahoos in Jalalabad. I immediately noticed that this task force had a way better working relationship than we had and I was a little jealous of the comradery that am sure made for an easier working experience. In Jalalabad we hardly even acknowledge each other's existence let alone speak to one another.

After everyone had a good belly laugh, it was time to get started and everyone sat down and shut up. One Charlie's leadership introduced me to the SEAL platoon letting them know my call sign and that I would be accompanying them tonight. Escobar and the rest of the guys were in the brief as well and were also introduced. The squad that I was assisting tonight was a security element for the assault squads. There was a natural egress in a defiladed position behind the house/target building that lead straight to a wood line. Adjacent to the defilade and wood line was a ridge that provided a great position for us to have eyes on the village and its surroundings. This is where we planned to set up security. Going with us was the line squad plus a medium weight, fully automatic machine gun team.

Loading up on the Chinook was no different than how Two Charlie went about operations. As I sat down in a seat that lined the aircraft like a bench I went over everything in my head. We were conducting an offset infiltration that would be followed up by a four kilometer walk through the Afghanistan mountainous terrain. I made sure prior to loading up that my Camelbak was full of water and I threw a few licky's, chewy's to snack on and a can of Copenhagen was always in my shoulder pocket if need be.

One thing that was different from Jalalabad was the air package. We were being flown by a National Guard Aviation unit, not the 160th Special Operations Aviation Regiment, which made for a different ride. It wasn't a bad ride, just the landing was a little slower because the equipment wasn't as high speed, and the National Guard pilots do not have near the amount of flight hours as the 160th pilots. The 160th pilots make flying helicopters look like a walk in the park so I was a little spoiled if you will. Once we finally touched down we were reassured when we were all accompanied by a jolt from the impact of the war horse landing on mother Earth. After unhooking my snap link, I slowly stood up and waited my turn to run out the back of the helicopter like a football player does on Sunday afternoon when sprinting through the tunnel onto the field of battle.

I stayed close by to the guys in the squad that I was working with as I was still trying to get accustomed to who was who and how they looked under night vision goggles. I am used to knowing who guys are just by how their kits and helmets are arranged. I could tell who was who in Two Charlie just by how they walked. Being that I did not have this same cohesiveness and familiarity with the guys in One Charlie, I made sure to pay extra close attention. After all I did not want to make a mistake and make myself and Two Charlie look bad.

The walk was long and as we moved out through the rocky terrain I listened to radio calls and continued to scan the mountainous terrain, keeping an eye out for anything suspicious. After walking about two kilometers, we came to a village. It was very quiet and not a light was on in the entire village. It was a similar sight that I had seen over a hundred times. We were like ghosts in the shadows and not a soul knew we were there. Prior to walking through the narrow streets, we took a knee, grabbed a sip of water, and I took the opportunity to throw in a dip. It was always refreshing to have a little pinch while on a mission. The sensation became a bit of a habit over the years.

The walk seemed like it was taking forever. Moving over rugged terrain, covering long distances, and arriving on target to be lethal was always the goal. I wasn't upset that we were taking our time under the cover of darkness but was itching to get to the target. Once we made it to the target area, our squad split off from the assault force to go set in security. The new team leader leading out took the lead and after about one hundred meters took a quick left turn and started going the wrong way into the defilade rather than the easiest route to the ridgeline. The squad leader knew so we stopped to give him a chance to get his bearing. He must have been a little nervous, because if he would have just opened his eyes he would see the obvious.

After watching him walk off in the wrong direction I was given the go ahead to lead us up to the ridgeline where we would set up a hasty security position for the task force. Quickly I made it up to the front and continued to lead out at a brisk pace moving toward the military crest of the ridgeline with my weapon at the low ready. As I crept over the blind spot of the ridgeline, I could hear the rocks each time I set a foot down on the rocky terrain. We were spread out and as we crested the ridgeline we quickly cleared the area to make sure there were no insurgents. Once the area was clear we all took a knee and set up security, interlocking our sectors of fire, and got eyes on the surrounding area of the target building and the village. At about that same moment there were a few gun shots fired in the vicinity of the target compound. Not knowing what was going on my senses were heightened and I intently scanned the area looking for anything that moved.

Then I saw a squirter run out of the village area headed toward the defilade leading to the wood line directly behind the village to our three o'clock. My squad leader for the op was a few feet away so I looked over at him and said, "I got a squirter." I quickly lased him so that he could see him. It was obvious that he was a bad guy or he would not be running from the target building. Unfortunately, he was not armed. As I watched him run with his arms flailing and legs going as fast as they could go, I asked if I could shoot him. My request was quickly denied by higher. However, we were given the okay to send rounds over his head as containment fires to stop him in his tracks. I took a knee on the ridgeline, double pressed the pressure pad with my left thumb turning the laser on permanently, and aimed a few feet over the squirter's head, who was starting to gain some ground. I then immediately opened up at a rapid rate of fire sending round after round as close to his head as possible. The containment fires worked and he tripped and fell all over the place. He stayed put and didn't move. As I continued to shoot containment fires over his head he crawled behind a rock in the fetal position. He was obviously scared out of his gores and rightfully so, because those rounds were raining over him like a wall. Even though he wasn't running anywhere I didn't let up. I kept sending rounds down range a foot or so over his head, pinning him to the ground like a wrestler would do in a wrestling match.

Simultaneously the secondary assault squad was maneuvering on his position. The assault squad leader had his team leaders turn their infrared strobes on so we could identify them as they ran to the squirter. Once they got within hand grenade range, we lifted fires and they set up an L-shape ambush and called him out to put his hands up and stand up. He was not responding so they quickly threw a flash bang at him, and as the continuous concussion noises erupted near him he finally stood up and put his hands up. From our vantage point I watched two Rangers quickly snatch him up, throw cuffs on him, and detain him before he even knew what was going on; he was headed off to be interrogated. We continued to pull security from our position, and as I sat on the hill I rearranged my magazines and it hit me that I had just used the last of Wright's mags. It was a somber and sad feeling accompanied by a feeling of accomplishment.

A few weeks later I was en route back to Jalalabad to get the rest of my gear and equipment and to link up with the guys from Two Charlie who were headed home. As I was boarding the C-130 that was to take me from Logar to Jalalabad, I noticed my Ranger buddy from RIP Ben Will. He and I caught up for a few minutes until the rotors of the C-130 turned on. Trying to talk over the noise of a C-130 is like trying to communicate to someone on the front row at a rock and roll concert. I gave a quick wave to Will, grabbed my bags, and linked in with Escobar and the rest of the guys. It was a quick ride back to Jalalabad, and once we arrived we quickly ran off the back of the bird and loaded up on a bus headed to our hooch.

Everything was back to normal in Jalalabad. The investigation was over and we were back at it with missions being sent down the pipeline. While we conducted a few more missions the platoon, minus a few guys who were staying back, packed all our non-mission essential gear, including Play Stations, Xboxs, DVD players, and footballs and palletized it to be loaded onto a C-17 headed for the United States of America. Rooster and Plagge were some of the guys staying back for an additional month to work with One Charlie and Three Charlie. Rangers aren't the type to have long, drawn out goodbyes so I quickly gave each of them a bro hug, wished Rooster and Plagge the best, and said, "Look forward to having a beer with you in a few weeks." Rooster went on to do great things for another month but Escobar, myself, and the rest of the guys from Two Charlie loaded up on a bus headed to the flight line. It was daylight out so the same feeling of heading to the flight line prior to a mission was nonexistent. However, I took a moment to look around through the dusty sky at the mountains in the distance and took a deep breath of the dust-filled Afghanistan air one last time.

UPHOLD THE STANDARD

"Before joining the Army Chris's mom asked him, 'Why do you want to join the Army?'

Chris said, 'So that I can keep my brothers safe.'"

- Michele Cochran

The 75th Ranger Regiment has had sixty-four Rangers make the ultimate sacrifice in the Global War on Terrorism. Since 9/11 Rangers from the 75th Ranger Regiment have been awarded a Medal of Honor, a Distinguished Service Cross, Silver Stars, Bronze Star medals for Valor and over six hundred Purple Hearts. There is no task or obstacle that the Ranger Regiment can't overcome and accomplish. The Ranger Regiment will adapt and defeat any enemy put in front of them. Putting all bias aside, the Ranger Regiment was the backbone and main effort of the Global War on Terrorism.

Awards - Operation Wolverine

AWARDS - OPERATION WOLVERINE

Silver Star Medal
Staff Sergeant Rooster

Bronze Star Medal with "Valor"
Sergeant First Class Bill (aka platoon sergeant)
Sergeant Grant McGarry

Army Commendation Medal with "Valor"
Corporal Dan Escobar
Corporal Troy Jenkins
Specialist Chris Wright
Specialist Ethan Gronbeck

Purple Heart
Staff Sergeant Wyatt
Sergeant Jacob Plagge
Specialist Chris Wright
Specialist Ethan Gronbeck

Charlie Barry before we got lost in Steamboat Colorado on December 31, 2006

On leave for Christmas in 2006 after Airborne school prior to attending RIP (Ranger Indoctrination Program)

RIP (Ranger Indoctrination Program) graduation class 03-07, February 2, 2007

My family and I at Ranger School graduation on September 28, 2007 after my dad pinned my Ranger Tab on my shoulder

SGT. Kurtis Frasier, Balad Iraq, December 26, 2007

2nd Platoon, Balad Iraq 2008

Post mission of 3rd Squad, Iraq, December 6, 2008

SGT. McGarry, Afghanistan 2009

2nd Squad, Salerno Afghanistan, November 30, 2009

2nd Squad, Salerno Afghanistan, Shooting Range

Vaughan, Plagge and McGarry, Ranger Ball March 20, 2009

CPL Jenkins holding an alligator we brought back from the demolitions range. Jason Kendall in the backround at his locker. RIP Jason, May 1, 1999 - February 14, 2015. Picture taken July 29, 2009.

Chinook making what is called the Kopp halo effect. Named in honor of CPL. Benjamin S. Kopp, Killed in Action on July 18, 2009.

SSG. Jim Ross, October 21, 2009

2nd Squad, Salerno Afghanistan, November 30, 2009

2nd Squad, post mission behind Chinook

Jalalabad Afghanistan Memorial, August 22, 2010. From left to right, Chief Collin Thomas, SPC. Christopher Wright, and SGT. Martin Lugo. All three were KIA on the night of August 18th - 19th

Rangers from 2nd platoon paying their respects to the fallen at the memorial on August 22, 2010

2nd Squad, Jalalabad Afghanistan Memorial, August 22, 2010

SSG. Kevin M. Pape, Killed in Action,
November 16, 2010, Operation Enduring Freedom

SGT. Alessandro Plutino, Killed in Action,
August 8, 2011, Operation Enduring Freedom

SPC. Christopher S. Wright, Tollesboro Kentucky

SPC. Christopher S. Wright Memorial Highway, Tollesboro Kentucky

Jim and Michele Cochran, Chris' parents, July 27, 2014

Zach Pope, Chris's younger brother teaching me how to work the kitchen at T-City Pizza. April 9, 2015

Grant and Karin McGarry, November 8, 2014

EPILOGUE

Even though I physically left the mountains of Afghanistan, I have found over the years that I will never leave them mentally. At night I still walk the mountains in my dreams, and on a daily basis while doing ordinary activities, I think on the events that took place while I served. Without a doubt my time in Ranger Regiment was the best four years of my life. It molded me into the man I am today.

Almost five years had passed after that night in the Pech Valley and I finally headed to Tollesboro, Kentucky, Chris's hometown, to see Jim and Michele Cochran on April 7, 2015. The last time I saw Jim and Michele was January 21, 2011 at the 1st Ranger Battalion memorial ceremony in Savannah, Georgia. The ceremony was also when I met Chris's parents. Some people say time heals all wounds, but I do not think this theory applies to something of this magnitude.

As I pulled into town I called Jim to let him know I made it and as the phone rang I couldn't help but acknowledge a nervous feeling in the pit of my stomach. That nervous feeling didn't last long because Jim was quick to pick up the phone. We hit it off immediately—as if we were hanging out the day prior, and after catching up for a few minutes he told me to meet him at the Road Ranger gas station off of Kentucky Highway 57.

As I sat in the Road Ranger parking lot it started to rain and then I saw a Chevy 2500 pull in on two wheels with a 1st Ranger Battalion sticker on the side. I knew exactly who it was, so I sat up straight. As Jim pulled up next to me he rolled down his window smiling ear to ear and said, "Follow me. We are going to drive down Chris's highway and stop in at T-City Pizza, and see Michele and Zach, Chris's younger brother."

As we crossed over a four-way intersection, I saw the sign titled "Specialist Christopher S. Wright Memorial Highway," which runs from the intersection of Kentucky 9 to the intersection of Kentucky 10 in Tollesboro. As I followed Jim down Chris's highway into downtown Tollesboro, I couldn't help but let everything sink in. After going down memory lane we pulled into T-City and just like that we were hanging out over a pizza. For the next couple days we shot guns, fished, and worked on the farm and in the T-City Pizza kitchen. At night we hung out in Jim's barn, drank cold beer, and told stories. Some of the stories made us laugh and some made us cry. Overall, it was therapeutic for all of us.

As I left Kentucky a few days later and headed home I thought about how I was getting ready to start a new chapter in life. Two weeks later, on April 25, 2015, I married my best friend and the love of my life, Karin. It has been almost a year since that trip and my wedding, and I am excited to soon be a Dad. My boy,

Gunnar Andrew McGarry, is due on February 24, 2016. My wish is to be an amazing dad like my father, Michael Andrew McGarry. With all of these blessings I remind myself to earn each day, to never forget where I came from, and to always do the hard right over the easy wrong.

I have spent so many waking hours on this manuscript and venture that I do not know where or how I could begin to count the hours dedicated. I am honored to have had the opportunity to write this book and now I hand it over to God and the warriors in Valhalla, because it is only in heaven that the truth is revealed. Until it is my day to be judged and to stand in front of the Father Almighty at the pearly white gates I will continue to serve the Lord, be happy, and not let anger consume me.

ACKNOWLEDGEMENTS

First, I would like to thank everyone that believed in me and this project. Second, I would like to thank my Ranger buddies. This would not be possible if it were not for their sacrifices to this great nation. I would also like to thank my wife, Karin. I love her dearly. And my parents, Andy and Lynn McGarry. I would like to thank them for teaching me how to enjoy life, and to occasionally stop and smell the roses. Last, I would like to thank everyone that has contributed to this book. God bless America and God bless the Army Rangers.

ACRONYMS

AAR	after action report/review
AO	area of operations
AQ	Al-Qaeda
CAS	close air support
casevac	casualty evacuation
CCP	casualty collection point
CLP	cleaning lubricant protectant
COF	Company Operating Facility
COP	command outpost
CQ	control of quarters
DUI	distinctive unit insignia
EKIA	enemy killed in action
EMS	Emergency Medical Services
EMT-I	Emergency Medical Technician-Intermediate
FAM	familiarization training
FO	forward observer
FOB	forward operating base
FOM	follow-on missions
FRAGO	fragmentary order (mission brief)
GRG	ground reference graphic
HEDP	high-explosive, dual-purpose (grenades)
HLZ	helicopter landing zone

HVT	high value target
IED	improvised explosive device
ISR	intelligence, surveillance, and reconnaissance (platform)
JDAM	Joint Direct Action Munition
JDQ	Jamaat ul Dawa al Quran (Taliban subgroup)
JP8	jet propellant 8 (gas)
KIA	killed in action
K-G Pass	Khost-Gardez mountain pass
KP	kitchen patrol
LAW	light anti-tank weapon
MAM	military-aged male
MBITR	multiband internal team radio
MEPS	Military Entrance Processing Station
MRAP	Mine-Resistant Ambush Protected vehicle
MRE	meal ready-to-eat
MSR	main supply route
NCO	non-commissioned officer
NCOIC	non-commissioned officer-in-charge
NLT	no later than (time)
NOD/NVG	night optical devices/night-vision googles
NPA	nasopharyngeal airway
Op-For	opposing force
ORP	objective rally point
PA	physician assistant
PCI	pre-combat inspection

PL	platoon leader
PMCS	preventive maintenance checks and services
PSD	personal security detachment
PSG	platoon sergeant
PT	physical training
QRF	quick reaction force
RASP	Ranger Assessment and Selection Program
RFS	released for standards
RI	Ranger Instructor
RIP	Ranger Indoctrination Program
RPG	rocket-propelled grenade
RTO	radio telephone operator
RWS	remote weapons system
S-1	personnel (staff/office)
SAF	small arms fire
SAW	squad automatic weapon
SBF	support by fire
SCAR-L	Special Operations Forces Combat Assault Rifle, light
SF	Special Forces
SITREP	situational report
SOAR	Special Operations Aviation Regiment
SOP	standard operating procedure
SP	start point
SSE	sensitive site exploitation
TB	Taliban

TC   tactical commander
TOC   tactical operating center
TOT   time on target
TTP   tactics, techniques, and procedures
VC   vehicle commander
WIA   wounded in action

THE RANGER CREED

Recognizing that I volunteered as a Ranger, fully knowing the hazards of my chosen profession, I will always endeavor to uphold the prestige, honor, and high esprit de corps of my Ranger Regiment.

Acknowledging the fact that a Ranger is a more elite soldier who arrives at the cutting edge of battle by land, sea, or air, I accept the fact that as a Ranger my country expects me to move further, faster, and fight harder than any other soldier.

Never shall I fail my comrades. I will always keep myself mentally alert, physically strong, and morally straight, and I will shoulder more than my share of the task whatever it may be, one hundred percent and then some.

Gallantly will I show the world that I am a specially selected and well-trained soldier. My courtesy to superior officers, neatness of dress, and care of equipment shall set the example for others to follow.

Energetically will I meet the enemies of my country. I shall defeat them on the field of battle for I am better trained and will fight with all of my might. Surrender is not a Ranger word. I will never leave a fallen comrade to fall into the hands of the enemy and under no circumstances will I ever embarrass my country.

Readily will I display the intestinal fortitude required to fight on to the Ranger objective and complete the mission, though I be the lone survivor.

RANGERS LEAD THE WAY!!!

The first Rangers were formed in Europe during the middle ages to protect the land, under the direction of their king. Their mission was to search for bandits and criminals.

ROGERS' RANGERS STANDING ORDERS

1. Don't forget nothing.

2. Have your musket clean as a whistle, hatchet scoured, sixty rounds powder and ball, and be ready to march at a minute's warning.

3. When you are on the march, act the way you would if you were sneaking up on a deer. See the enemy first.

4. Tell the truth about what you see and what you do. There is an army depending on us for correct information. You can lie all you please when you tell other folks about the rangers, but don't never lie to a ranger or officer.

5. Don't never take a chance you don't have to.

6. When we're on march we march single file, far enough apart so no one shot can go through two men.

7. If we strike swamps, or soft ground, we spread out abreast, so it's hard to track us.

8. When we march, we keep moving till dark, so as to give the enemy the least possible chance at us.

9. When we camp, half the party stays awake while the other half sleeps.

10. If we take prisoners, we keep 'em separate till we have time to examine them, so they can't cook up a story between 'em.

11. Don't ever march home the same way. Take a different route so you won't be ambushed.

12. No matter whether we travel in big parties or little ones, each party has to keep a scout 20 yards ahead, 20 yards on each flank, and 20 yards in the rear, so the main body can't be surprised and wiped out.

13. Every night you'll be told where to meet if surrounded by a superior force.

14. Don't sit down to eat without posting sentries.

15. Don't sleep beyond dawn. Dawn's when the French and Indians attack.

16. Don't cross a river at a regular ford.

17. If somebody's trailing you, make a circle, come back onto your own tracks, and ambush the folks that aim to ambush you.

18. Don't stand up when the enemy's coming against you. Kneel down, lie down, hide behind a tree.

19. Let the enemy come till he's almost close enough to touch. Then let him have it and jump out and finish him up with your hatchet.

-MAJOR ROBERT ROGERS, 1759

ABOUT THE AUTHOR

Grant McGarry, a U.S. Army Ranger, is a combat veteran
with five deployments to Iraq and Afghanistan in the War on
Terrorism. Upon graduation in 2006 from the University of
Alabama with a degree in finance, Grant McGarry reported
to Fort Benning with an enlistment contract "for the hardest
thing the Army has to offer." Following his graduation from
the Ranger Indoctrination Program he was assigned to the 1st
Ranger Battalion, 75th Ranger Regiment. While assigned to
1st Battalion, Grant held a number of positions and leadership
assignments, from rifleman to machine gun team leader, as
well as both squad alpha and bravo team leader. Between
deployments, Sergeant McGarry graduated from the U.S. Army
Ranger School and was awarded the coveted Ranger Tab. On
his fifth and final deployment to Afghanistan, while searching
for a high value target, Sergeant McGarry and   his squad were
involved in a vicious firefight with enemy forces in the Pech
Valley. As a consequence of his heroic actions during the battle,
Sergeant McGarry was awarded the Bronze Star Medal with
"Valor" Device. Following the completion of his enlistment he

moved to his home town of Roswell GA. and founded his own company, Live the Ranger Creed, LLC. Grant is also the director and co-founder of The Darby Project (501-C-3). While working full time McGarry is a candidate at Emory University in the Goizueta Business School, Executive MBA program, with an expected graduation date of May 8, 2017. He is happily married to his wife, Karin, and enjoys spending time with his dog Elvis.

51289318R00205

Made in the USA
Lexington, KY
18 April 2016